SHAKESPEARE'S
GLOBE PLAYHOUSE

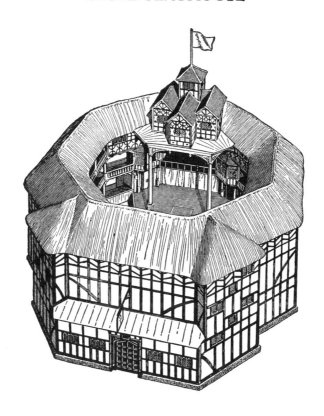

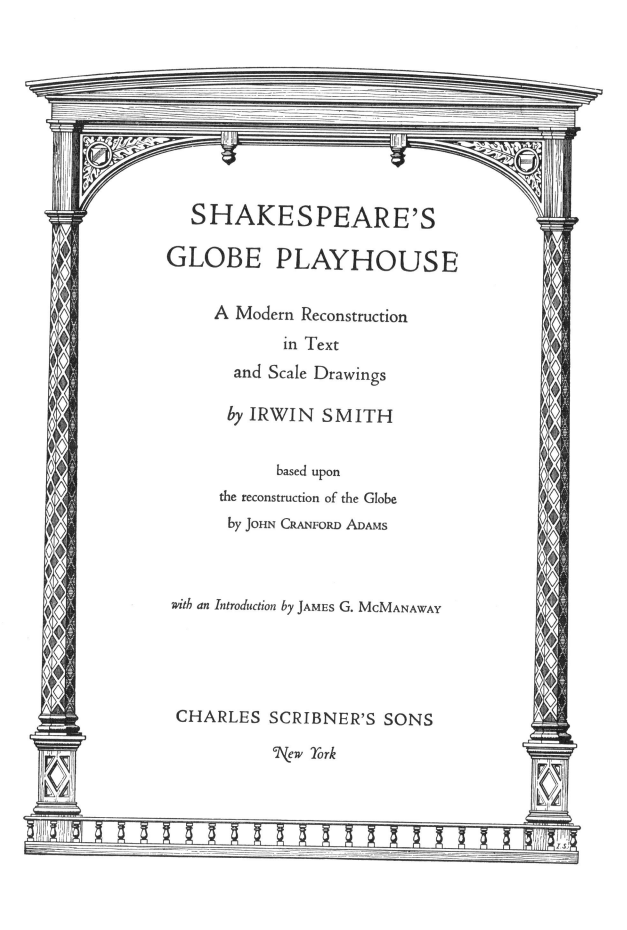

SHAKESPEARE'S GLOBE PLAYHOUSE

A Modern Reconstruction
in Text
and Scale Drawings

by IRWIN SMITH

based upon
the reconstruction of the Globe
by JOHN CRANFORD ADAMS

with an Introduction by JAMES G. McMANAWAY

CHARLES SCRIBNER'S SONS

New York

PRINTED IN THE UNITED STATES OF AMERICA

1 3 5 7 9 11 13 15 17 19 H/P 20 18 16 14 12 10 8 6 4 2

ISBN: 684-15972-4

Library of Congress Catalog Card Number 56-6150

TO
JOHN CRANFORD ADAMS
WITH GRATITUDE

INTRODUCTION

THE middle decades of the twentieth century are witnessing a remarkable burgeoning of Shakespeare festivals. In England, the Memorial Theatre at Stratford-upon-Avon has a home company performing before capacity audiences and a touring company that plays in London, the provinces, and on the Continent, and occasionally ventures as far as the Antipodes. In America, the spectacular success of the Shakespearean Festival at Stratford, Ontario, is being emulated by the American Shakespeare Festival Theatre and Academy at Stratford, Connecticut, while the older Shakespeare festivals at San Diego, California; Ashland, Oregon; and Antioch College, Yellow Springs, Ohio, flourish as never before. Every year, it seems, the number of college productions of Shakespeare increases, and several institutions have made Shakespeare's birthday the occasion for conferences of scholars in conjunction with the production of one or more plays and the performance of Elizabethan music.

One explanation of this outburst of interest in Shakespeare is perhaps the unparalleled success of Sir Laurence Olivier's motion picture of *Henry V*, which encouraged producers and prepared audiences. Thousands of people who had only text-book memories of Shakespeare discovered that he is exciting entertainment.

More important, certainly, has been the attempt to stage the plays as they were first acted at the Globe. This has brought release from the tyranny of naturalistic, historically accurate costumes and stage settings, with all the expense they entailed, which for the producer frequently has spelled the difference between financial failure and success. It has also eliminated tedious delays for scene shifting and given audiences the thrill of uninterrupted performances, sometimes almost breathless in their pace and breath-taking in their passionate intensity.

After long neglect, the much despised Elizabethan platform stage is coming into its own. Scholars and producers alike, who once found it easy to take Shakespeare's artfully deprecatory references to his stage ("this unworthy scaffold," "this cockpit," "this wooden O") as proof of its inadequacy, have of late given much thought to the shape and size of the Theater, the Globe, and the Fortune, and to their appointments. In their heyday, these playhouses were among the chief glories of London, "floure of cities all." But no one troubled to sketch them or even to describe them. So the research has been laborious, with many matters determined only by conjecture and others still hotly in dispute.

The platform stage, for which Shakespeare wrote his plays, is proving in use to be astonishingly flexible and enormously effective. And its employment, in pure or modified form, in several of the festivals and most of the off-Broadway productions, is one of the great factors in their success. It not only contributes to the enjoyment of the audiences but also discloses unnoted aspects of Shakespeare's mastery of stagecraft.

Several years ago, I visited the workshop of John Cranford Adams, President of Hofstra College, to see for the first time his nearly finished scale model of the Globe. He had begun it to test and exemplify the theories published in his book, *The Globe Playhouse*. And he was completing it with the expert assistance of his friend and neighbor, Irwin Smith. The model was so beautiful that I coveted it for exhibition at the Folger Shakespeare Library, where Dr. Adams had done part of his research—and to my joy it was upon completion offered to and accepted by the Folger on long-term loan.

As I was admiring the model, my better angel prompted me to challenge the builders to produce and publish a little book with a description of the Globe and scale drawings of the model that could be used by any high school boy to make a model for himself. Academic responsibilities barred Dr. Adams from participation in such a project, and at first Mr. Smith modestly protested his incompetence. But inquiries received at the Folger Shakespeare Library during its first fifteen years indicated to me that there was a widespread interest in the Elizabethan playhouse and an ever-increasing demand for guidance in building trustworthy models of the Globe. People were beginning to realize that a model of the Globe was an extremely valuable tool in the teaching of Shakespeare—at whatever level—and scholars and producers were discovering the utility of a good model in the solution of problems of stagecraft. And so I insisted that a heavy responsibility rested upon Adams and Smith (or one of them) to share their knowledge. A book was needed to which, for the first time, inquirers could be referred not only for specific information about the structure of the Globe but also for scale drawings that could be adapted to the requirements of a model builder.

Mr. Smith tested his wings in a trial flight that took the form of an illustrated account of Elizabethan carpenters' marks and their significance for historians of the Globe—a fascinating essay—and, encouraged by its reception, plunged into the writing of his book. His approach to the subject was empirical. What materials and tools did an Elizabethan builder have to work with, and how did he use them? What would an Elizabethan company of actors require of their stage, and how did they utilize what the builders could supply on a marshy site such as the Bankside? What can be gleaned about the physical conditions of the stage from the Elizabethan plays, and how did Shakespeare exploit their potentialities? In the basic Shakespearean texts, Mr. Smith sought independent answers to these questions, for he was not content to accept anything on authority, not even the explanations of his erstwhile collaborator, Dr. J. C. Adams. About controversial matters, he states his own opinions fearlessly, but he presents all the evidence so that his readers may decide for themselves.

A man who designs a scale model of the Globe cannot take refuge behind a pair of alternate conjectures. He must make a positive decision about every controversial detail and translate his opinion into wood and stone (or a model builder's equivalent). Those who read this book or use the scale drawings may not concur with the author at every point, but they will soon discover that Mr. Smith is not easy to confute; for there are very few who combine equal knowledge of Elizabethan craftsmanship with his intimate familiarity with the plays and his persuasiveness in presenting his interpretations of the evidence. This is a book which the specialists will have to take account of. Better yet, it is a book which any instructor with imagination and a little skill in carpentry can use in his classroom to transform the teaching of Shakespeare.

James G. McManaway

The Folger Shakespeare Library

PREFACE

WHEN, in 1907, Dr. Horace Howard Furness issued his New Variorum Edition of *Antony and Cleopatra,* he disclaimed any interest in the stratagem by which Caesar's soldiers captured the Queen, and by implication any interest in the play's original staging:

> For my own part, I see no need of any stage-direction at all. It is, at least for me, quite sufficient to see that the Romans rush in and seize the Queen. In these thrilling moments, how they got in, I neither know nor care.

In the intervening years there has been a change in the academic attitude toward the presentation of Shakespeare's plays on Shakespeare's stage. When *Henry IV, Part II,* was issued in 1940 in the same Variorum Edition whose first editor had neither known nor cared, it devoted one and a half pages of small foot-note type to the opinions of eleven scholars on the original staging of the Jerusalem Chamber sequence; and the very incident which held no interest for Dr. Furness has, largely through scholarly curiosity as to the stage business involved in Antony's hoisting and Cleopatra's capture, become one of the most controversial episodes in the entire Shakespearean canon. The new emphasis upon the physical stage as a factor in our understanding of the Elizabethan drama was thus summed up by Professor Allardyce Nicoll in the first paragraph of the first article in the first *Shakespeare Survey* (1948):

> Of one thing in particular Shakespearian scholarship during the past fifty years may justly be proud: only within the present century have we approached within measurable distance of an understanding of the methods employed in the original production of Elizabethan plays or endeavoured to set these plays, in our imagination, firmly against the background of their theatrical environment. No other field of investigation more characteristically belongs to our own age than this.[1]

A knowledge of Shakespeare's playhouse is ultimately of importance only as it illuminates the plays of Shakespeare and of his contemporary

[1] This and other quotations from *Shakespeare Survey* are printed by courtesy of the Cambridge University Press.

dramatists; but in this respect it is indispensable. A thousand passages acquire a new meaning when the resources and limitations of the Elizabethan stage, and the conventions to which they gave rise, are understood. Shakespeare's stage was flexible: it gave him freedom to present a rapid succession of scenes long or short, indoors or out, upstairs or down, or nowhere in particular. It was large enough to permit vigorous movement, crowds, spectacles, ceremonies; it was intimate enough to make it natural for an actor to pour out his soul in soliloquy or aside. It enabled the dramatist to place the action in the center of the auditorium, within arm's reach of many spectators and within fifty feet of all two thousand, or, if he chose, to put it in an inner stage thirty feet from the nearest spectator and eighty-five from the farthest. It allowed an unbroken continuity of action in spite of shifts of location, a deliberate ebb and flow of dramatic tension, and sharply-felt contrasts of mood between one scene and the next. On the other hand, it gave him no front curtain, a lack which has left its impress upon the content and construction of scores of scenes. It gave him no representational scenery, and so led him to write some of his loveliest poetry to persuade his auditors that they saw what his stage could not show. All these things are woven into the very texture of Shakespeare's plays. A reconstruction of the plays' original staging reveals many a graceful and ingenious resource, many a taut dramatic situation, which pass unsuspected in the reading of today's texts, conformed as they are to the conditions of a theatre born anew one full century later than the playhouse for which Shakespeare wrote. They are lost even more completely on the modern proscenium stage, with its restricted playing area and its concomitant of intermissions and abridgements.

Knowledge of the design and equipment of Shakespeare's playhouse has been slow in coming. The earlier editors thought of the Elizabethan period as barbarous, and believed it their first duty to Shakespeare to bring him up to date; complacently viewing the form and contrivances of their own stage, they thought Shakespeare's stage unworthy. The first researches were made by Edmund Malone and published toward the end of the 18th century: a scholarly and reasonably full account of the form and usages of the Elizabethan theatre, but still at fault in many important details. Additions to the store of knowledge were made by Collier, Cunningham, Fleay, Halliwell-Phillips, Tieck, and others, but it could yet be said, a century after Malone, that less was known of Shakespeare's playhouse than of the theatres of ancient Greece; it was still thought of as a bare and crude affair, with nothing to compensate for its want of scenery. In the present century the study has been pressed forward by English, American, French and German scholars. J. Q. Adams, Albright, Archer, Baker, Baldwin, Bentley, Bradbrook, Tucker Brooke, Creizenach, Feuillerat, Hodges, Kernodle, Lawrence, Ordish, Reynolds, Rhodes, Thorndike, Wallace, Wegener, and above all Chambers—these and others have made important contributions to our understanding of the physical stage and of its use.

The Globe Playhouse: Its Design and Equipment, by John Cranford Adams, was published by the Harvard University Press in 1942. Into its preparation had gone years of study of contemporary documents bearing even remotely upon the subject—plays and other dramatic entertainments by the hundred, playhouse records, legal papers, letters, maps, pamphlets, poems, and so on. From these Dr. Adams had extracted fragmentary and isolated facts, perhaps inconclusive in themselves, but significant when evaluated and related to other data; and out of his studies there emerged the first attempt at a complete and unified reconstruction of the playhouse for which Shakespeare wrote his greatest plays. As is inevitable in any inquiry where direct evidence is meagre and conclusions can for the most part be based upon nothing more substantial than informed conjecture, some details of his reconstruction have been questioned. For instance, some scholars have contended, both before and after the publication of Dr. Adams's book, that the Globe was round rather than polygonal; contemporary evidence supports both views, but not enough exists on either side to settle the issue conclusively. But if it should be settled, and in favor of the round Globe, what then? The question still does not affect the really important matters, the design of the multiple stage and the relationship of actor to audience. In spite of legitimate divergences of opinion on this and other points, Dr. Adams's book is generally recognized today as the most complete and integrated statement that Shakespearean scholarship has yet produced respecting the playhouse with which Shakespeare was associated during the period of his mature genius.

After the publication of his book Dr. Adams and I joined in the construction of a scale model of the Globe, so that his conclusions might be stated not merely in text, but also in tangible three-dimensional form. The model was finished early in 1950, and since then has been on exhibition at the

Folger Shakespeare Library in Washington. Book and model supplement one another. The book gives not only the conclusions, but the evidence and documentation upon which they are based. The model brings them home, in quickly apprehended form, to eye as well as to mind.

The scale drawings and photographs printed in the present volume were taken from the model. While it was under construction, hundreds of free-hand sketches and measurements were jotted down, and upon its completion dozens of photographs were taken to furnish supplementary details. These supplied the data from which the scale drawings were made.

This present book merely summarizes or cites illustratively the evidence upon which Dr. Adams based his reconstruction, and refers the reader to *The Globe Playhouse* for the complete documentation. On the other hand, its scale drawings (and, of course, the model upon which they are based) go beyond Dr. Adams's book in assigning definite forms and dimensions and positions to every individual piece of timber, every baluster, every brick. This has necessarily involved occasional excursions from the realm of fact or reasoned conjecture into that of mere assumption; but such excursions must be made when one attempts to visualize the Globe fully and concretely. Any reconstruction of the playhouse in all its details must forever remain in some degree a matter of conjecture; for even if important new evidence should be discovered, it would probably relate to the larger aspects only, and would still leave unanswered innumerable questions about details of construction and design. It may confidently be assumed, however, that the Globe was built in accordance with the principles of Tudor building construction and that it reflected the conventions of Tudor architectural design; and therefore some pages in this book have been devoted to those principles and conventions as explaining the particularized forms of the model and the scale drawings.

Dr. McManaway has spoken in his Introduction of the numberless requests that have poured into the Folger Shakespeare Library for graphic materials from which models of the Globe Playhouse might be built, and of the Library's regret at having to reply that no such materials existed. It was partly to meet this need that the task of making the scale drawings was undertaken. But it is to be hoped that they will serve also a larger purpose, for they constitute perhaps the most ambitious attempt yet made to state in graphic form the findings of modern scholarship with respect to Shakespeare's playhouse. They show, as not even a model can do, the Globe's interior arrangements, the interrelationship of its stages, its avenues of passage between level and level, between stage and tiring-house, and between one unit and another of the multiple stage. Unlike the Adams model, they can be studied at home by persons who, with a Shakespearean text in one hand and this book in the other, may wish to ponder the original staging of one of Shakespeare's plays. I hope that they will convey to the reader an impression of the beauty of the Globe, its essentially English character, its adaptation and adaptability to the needs of the Elizabethan drama. Perhaps, too, they may serve as aids to the construction of full-scale Shakespearean stages, upon which the dramatist's plays can be presented as he intended that they should be.

The statements made in this book with respect to the design and equipment of the Globe Playhouse are, in the great majority of instances, based upon the work of Dr. Adams. It could not be otherwise, for no one else has probed the subject as deeply and broadly as he. My study of his book, and the intimate awareness of structural details and relationships gained during the years of working on the model, have convinced me that his reconstruction of the Globe is as nearly complete and accurate as present-day scholarship is likely to produce; and my own inquiries into the original staging of Shakespeare's plays have led me to feel that the plays can do with no less than he proposes, and that they need no more. On questions of design, all the basic ideas are his, and nearly all the references. In the fourteen years that have elapsed since *The Globe Playhouse* was published, however, one or two new discoveries have been made. The researches of other scholars since 1942, many of them prompted by his book, have made it advisable that certain alternative opinions should be reviewed; and my own studies have in a few instances led me to adopt theories at variance with his, less in respect to the design of the Globe's stages than in respect to their use.

When Dr. Adams wrote *The Globe Playhouse,* his immediate concern was with the physical structure of the Globe. He therefore discussed the original staging of Elizabethan scenes only when they served to throw light upon some question of construction, equipment, or decoration—scenes, for instance, which by making unusual demands upon the resources of the stage, tended to show what those resources must be. In the present book I have however tried to combine structure with function, to survey the ordinary everyday use of the various units of the multiple stage, to suggest the stage placement of representative scenes, and to recognize the conventions forced upon the dramatist by the design of his stage. In doing so, I have chosen to relate the use of the stages to the plays of Shakespeare, and to draw my illustrations from his plays, in preference to those of other less known and less accessible dramatists.[2] I have gone farther afield only when Shakespeare provided no illustrations, or insufficient illustrations, of the point under discussion.

My indebtedness to Dr. John Cranford Adams cannot easily be expressed. I have to thank him not only for his generosity in permitting me to base portions of this book upon his researches, but also for my introduction to an aspect of Shakespearean study which for many years has been my preoccupation and delight. My grateful acknowledgments are due also to Dr. Raymond W. Short, who has guided me from the beginning of the present undertaking, and whose reading of the book in manuscript has given it and me the benefit of his wise and sympathetic criticism. I am indebted, furthermore, to Professor A. E. Richardson and Colonel E. H. Carkeet-James of London, to Frederick Sharpe, Esq., of Bicester, Oxon., and to Mr. Emery Nelson Leonard and Mr. Graydon Smith, respectively of Norwell and Concord in Massachusetts, for specialized information of great interest. Miss Barbara Damon, of the American Embassy in London, has given me invaluable help in securing prints of early maps of the Bankside, and Miss Virginia Wentworth, of Garden City, in preparing my manuscript for the printer.

I. S.

---

[2] Quotations from the Shakespearean text, and line numbers, are from *The Complete Works of Shakespeare*, ed. G. L. Kittredge (1936).

ACKNOWLEDGMENTS

THE AUTHOR gratefully acknowledges the courtesy of the following persons, institutions, and publishers, in permitting the reproduction of pictorial material included in this volume:

Dr. John Cranford Adams, for photographs of his model of the Globe Playhouse (Plates 26 to 29, and 31).

The Trustees of the British Museum, for the so-called Ryther map (Plate 11).

The Cambridge University Press, for the Hoefnagel map (Plate 1), the Hondius view (Plate 7), the Merian view (Plate 10), and the Hollar view (Plate 13), all of which had been printed in larger size in George Hubbard's *On the Site of the Globe Playhouse of Shakespeare*; and for Hollar's preliminary sketch (Plate 12), which had been printed in *Shakespeare Survey* 1.

The Clarendon Press, Oxford, for the Cockpit-in-Court plans (Plate 22) and the *Titus Andronicus* drawing (Plate 24). The former had been printed in Sir Edmund K. Chambers' *The Elizabethan Stage*, Vol. IV, and the latter in his *William Shakespeare*, Vol. I.

The Folger Shakespeare Library, for the Visscher engravings (Plates 8 and 9), the DeWitt sketch of the Swan (Plate 17), the *Roxana* and *Messallina* vignettes (Plates 18 and 19), the frontispiece to *The Wits* (Plate 20), and the drawing of the courtyard of the White Hart Inn (Plate 21).

The Shakespeare Quarterly, for the author's drawings of timber joints (Figures 1 and 2) and of carpenters' marks (Figures 3 and 4).

B. T. Batsford Ltd., for the drawing of an overhanging upper story (Figure 5), from *Old Cottages and Farm-Houses in Surrey*, by W. Galsworthy Davie and W. Curtis Green.

CONTENTS

LIST OF ILLUSTRATIONS

LINE DRAWINGS IN THE TEXT

SHAKESPEARE'S
GLOBE PLAYHOUSE

CHAPTER I

THE STORY

OF THE GLOBE PLAYHOUSE

THE story of the Globe must begin with the story of its predecessor, the Theater. Every Elizabethan public playhouse bore some kinship to the Theater, since it was the prototype of them all; but the bond between the Theater and the Globe was trebly close. The Theater had been the home of the Lord Chamberlain's Men, the company of which Shakespeare was a member; after it was torn down in 1598, the Globe became their home. The Theater had staged the first performances of most of Shakespeare's earlier plays; the Globe was to introduce most of his later ones. More than that, the very timbers which had been the Theater, salvaged at the time of its dismantling, became an integral part of the fabric of the new Globe.

The Theater was England's first building designed for the presentation of plays. Before it was built, troupes of travelling players had given their performances in any suitable place that proved to be available—in barns, town squares, in the mansions of nobles, in colleges and schools, and, most frequently of all, in the open rectangular yards of inns.

The inn-yard had served well as an impromptu playhouse. A platform for the actors could quickly be contrived out of planks laid across barrel-heads or trestles. A portion of the inn-yard gallery just above the scaffold could, if the play called for it, be used to represent the walls or towers of a fortified town, and nearby areas behind the stage could be made to serve as dressing- or tiring-rooms. The audience, attracted by a drum-and-trumpet parade through neighboring streets, entered through archways under the inn buildings. Payment of a penny apiece admitted spectators to standing room in the yard, and payment of an extra fee entitled those with nobler names or fatter purses to go up by the courtyard stairs into the surrounding galleries, and there to watch the play at their ease, with sack and bottle-ale ready at hand. It was a profitable arrangement, both for the players and for the inns; and eventually five great hostelries dedicated themselves wholly

3

to dramatic purposes, and built permanent stages equipped for theatrical performances.

But the inn-playhouses were subject to the constant hostility of the Puritans and the authorities of the City of London. The Puritans denounced the stage as contrary to Holy Writ, as destructive of religion and virtue, and as a menace to public morality. The Common Council attacked it as a breeding-ground for crimes and riots, and as a dangerous center of infection in time of plague. To escape the effects of this animosity, it became necessary for the drama to move out of the censorious jurisdiction of the City magistrates. This, and the expanding needs of an art which was constantly becoming more complex and of a business which was becoming more profitable, led to the erection of the first structure in England specifically designed for and devoted to the presentation of plays.

James Burbage was its designer and builder, and he was well equipped for his task. He had been an actor, and therefore knew what was required by plays and players in the design of the stage and its appurtenances. He had been the manager of one of the most important troupes in the country, and therefore knew what arrangements in the galleries would best serve the convenience of playgoers, and what at the doors would best serve that of the proprietors in the collection of admission fees. He was by early training a joiner or carpenter, and so knew how to create a structure that would meet these requirements. And in addition to his technical training, he had the ingenuity and audacity to tackle a job that no one had undertaken before him.

It was primarily the inn-yard that Burbage had in his mind's eye when he undertook the task of designing England's first playhouse. From it he borrowed the paved courtyard open to the sky, the platform jutting out deeply into the yard, the balcony above it to serve as an additional acting area, the tiring-rooms behind the stage, and the tiers of encircling galleries. True, he departed from his model to the extent of making the structure octagonal instead of quadrangular, and in this he was probably influenced by the amphitheatres used for the baiting of bulls and bears; but in the main his pattern was the inn-yard, and the building that he erected was "practically an inn-yard without the inn."[1]

He built his playhouse in 1576, in Shoreditch, a suburb to the north of London, and called it—with modest ostentation and a right conferred by

---

[1] William Archer and W. J. Lawrence, "The Playhouse," *Shakespeare's England*, II, 285.

priority—simply The Theater.[2] It was built on land for which Burbage had taken a twenty-one-year lease. The landlord, Giles Alleyn, had covenanted to give Burbage a new twenty-one-year lease at any time within the first ten years, and also to allow the tenant, "at any time or times before the end of the said term of one and twenty years, to have, take down and carry away to his own proper use" any structure that he might in the meantime have erected upon the land.[3]

From beginning to end Burbage was plagued by legal difficulties occasioned by a contentious financial partnership with his brother-in-law Brayne, by a mortgage which he and Brayne were unable to discharge, and above all by the failure of his efforts to secure the promised extension of his lease. For years he tried to induce his landlord, Alleyn, to give him the renewal which was stipulated as his right in the original contract; for years Alleyn met every request with evasions, half-promises, or counter-proposals based upon unacceptable conditions.

Just two months before the expiration of the lease, James Burbage died, and the Theater, tottering under a load of lawsuits and debts, passed to his son Cuthbert. Cuthbert, like his father, tried by every means in his power to have the lease renewed. Alleyn did not refuse; had he done so, Cuthbert would have known what steps to take: he would have torn down the building and carried away the timber to his own use, as the lease gave him the right to do. Alleyn knew that, and therefore did not refuse; instead, he promised to renew, but perpetually found excuses for putting it off; and Cuthbert Burbage, relying upon Alleyn's promises, "did forbear to pull downe and carry away the timber and stuff employed for the said Theater and playing-house at the end of the said first term of one and twenty years."

The lease expired in 1597. Late in 1598, after Cuthbert Burbage had

[2] For nearly all my statements of fact about the Theater, I am indebted to E. K. Chambers, *The Elizabethan Stage*, II, 383-400, and to Joseph Quincy Adams, *Shakespearean Playhouses*, Chapter III. For material on the history of the Globe I am indebted to the same works, pp. 414-423 and Chapter XII, respectively.

[3] A large majority of the playhouses built in London between the years 1576 and 1629 were built upon land which was leased, rather than owned, by the owner of the building itself. This is true of the Theater, the Rose, the Globe, the Fortune, the Red Bull, the Hope, the second Globe, the Phoenix or Cockpit, the second Fortune, the Salisbury Court, and probably the Curtain. The first Blackfriars, the Whitefriars, and Rossiter's Blackfriars were installed in leased buildings. On the other hand, the Swan and the second Blackfriars were erected on land owned by the builders. As to most of the playhouses, see the works previously mentioned, by J. Q. Adams and E. K. Chambers; as to the Phoenix or Cockpit, see Leslie Hotson, *The Commonwealth and Restoration Stage*, p. 88.

made a final futile effort to secure a renewal, Alleyn contended that since the building had not been removed before the expiration of the lease, "the right and interest of the said Theater was both in law and conscience absolutely vested" now in himself, and that accordingly he planned "to pull down the same and to convert the wood and timber thereof to some better use" for his own benefit.

But Cuthbert acted quickly. Whether or not the lease had expired and with it his legal right to remove the building, the only course now open to him, if he would save his property, was to tear down the structure immediately and to re-erect it on other ground. Unable himself to carry the whole financial burden of renting land and erecting a new playhouse, he and his younger brother Richard invited five of the leading actors of the Lord Chamberlain's Company to share with them, as a syndicate, in the cost and ownership of the projected building. The Burbages were to hold one-half of the stock and bear one-half of the expense (with credit for the value of the timber and other materials salvaged from the Theater), and the five actors were to bear the other half.

The members of the newly-formed syndicate were a distinguished company. There were Cuthbert Burbage and his brother Richard, the great tragedian, who was to create the leading roles in most of Shakespeare's later plays; William Shakespeare himself, a successful actor and a poet who already had made a reputation as a playwright; John Heminges, a fine actor and a trustworthy man with a good head for business, who until his death managed the financial affairs of the syndicate with extraordinary success, and who eventually became the dean of the English stage; Augustine Phillips and Thomas Pope, both of them excellent and well-known actors; and William Kempe, the greatest comedian of his time.

The syndicate's first problem was to find and lease a suitable site for the new playhouse. It must lie outside the authority of the City magistrates; and that meant that it must either be in the suburbs, to which their jurisdiction did not extend, or else within a "liberty," which, although geographically within the confines of the City, was yet exempt from the City's jurisdiction. Furthermore, it must be easily available to playgoers, near enough to the City, indeed, so that a flag run up on the playhouse flagpole could be seen and recognized as a signal that a play was about to be presented. Over on the far bank of the Thames they found such a place, in the Liberty of the Clink in Southwark, near the southern end of London Bridge and in a section which was rapidly becoming the amusement center of London. Already it held two other playhouses, the Rose and the Swan, and the notorious Bear Garden.

On Christmas day of 1598 the syndicate entered into a verbal agreement with Sir Nicholas Brend (confirmed by written contract in the February following) for the thirty-one-year lease of a tract of land abutting upon Maid Lane; and having found a location, the syndicate promptly engaged a builder, one Peter Streete, both to dismantle the old Theater and to erect a new playhouse which should incorporate as much as possible of the salvaged materials.

They wasted no time. On the night of December 28, 1598, just three days after the ground-lease had been arranged, they took advantage of Alleyn's absence from the City by starting to tear down the building. In the audacious party were the two Burbage brothers, a certain William Smith "of Waltham Cross, in the County of Hartford, gentleman," Peter Streete as "cheefe carpenter," and twelve others described as "laborers such as wrought for wages." Together they carried all the wood and timber across the Thames "unto the Banckside in the parishe of St. Marye Overyes, and there erected a newe playehowse with the sayd timber and woode." The new playhouse, of course, was the Globe.

It was by no accident that the job of dismantling the old building, as well as that of erecting the new, was given to a trained carpenter and builder. Any untrained crew of wreckers could have torn down the Theater, if a mere salvage of lumber were all that was required. Streete was one of the most skillful and sought-after contractors of his day; and the fact that he was employed for the antecedent dismembering as well as for the subsequent re-assembling suggests that something more than a mere wrecking job was required of him. This supposition is supported by what we know of the methods of construction followed by Tudor carpenters, as described on pages 37 to 39 of this book. They made use of elaborate jointings cut by hand in timbers which themselves were not of standard sizes. No two joints could be precisely alike in position or dimension, and it followed as a consequence that the timbers in which they were cut could not be interchanged. On original assembly or on re-assembly, the timbers must be used in the one relationship for which their joints were prepared; and to make this possible, each end of every timber had its own distinguishing carpenter's mark. It seems probable therefore that the basic octagonal frame of the Globe was piece-for-piece and timber-for-timber the same as the basic frame of the Theater, and that during the dismantling process, while his twelve men were engaged in the heavier tasks appropriate for "laborers such as wrought for wages," Peter Streete himself was making note of the carpenter's marks, so that when the timbers reached Bankside each would find its appointed place in the fabric of the Globe.

The Globe was not, however, merely the old Theater re-erected on new foundations. Except for the frame, perhaps some balustrades, and planks used in the flooring of galleries and stages, little can have been saved. The foundations had to be abandoned. Thatch and plaster had been reduced to rubbish under the crowbars of the wreckers. And even if it had been possible to salvage the minor fittings, it is probable that they were no longer suitable.

For in the twenty-three years that had elapsed since James Burbage built the Theater, unparalleled advances had been made in dramatic writing, in acting, and in stagecraft. An era of phenomenal development had intervened; the great traditions of the Elizabethan drama and stage had been established. The Theater, precisely because it had been the first building in England designed for the presentation of plays, had been necessarily experimental. In the interim others had been built—the Curtain, the Rose, the Swan, the first and second Blackfriars—and each had made some contribution, positive or negative, to the rapidly developing art of theatrical presentation. When the elder Burbage had designed the Theater, he had worked in a new field, and he had worked alone; but when his son Cuthbert designed the Globe, he was working in a field in which he and many others had had experience, and he had as his associates the greatest dramatist and five of the greatest actors of the age.

The most important single change was probably the enlargement of the inner stages—the rear stage on the first level, and the chamber on the second. Hitherto they had been small and cramped, and their visibility had been poor; in the Globe they were nearly doubled in size, with better light and improved sight-lines. Now there was room for more elaborate inner-stage settings, for realistic business involving interior wall-hangings, windows, and doors; now inner-stage scenes could compete in effectiveness with scenes on the outer stage. From 1599 onward, the drama shows a steady increase in the number of important scenes written for presentation on the inner stages, and of climactic scenes to be acted on the combined stages—the platform and the rear stage used together. As a matter of fact, the Globe's inner stages gave final form to the one unit of the Elizabethan stage destined to survive into modern times, and helped to point the way to the proscenium stage with its changeable settings.

The Globe was completed probably in the summer of 1599, and was immediately recognized as the handsomest and best-appointed playhouse in London. It was frankly used as a model by Philip Henslowe and Edward Alleyn when they built the new and splendid Fortune one year later: not only did they give the job of construction to the Globe's builder, Peter Streete, but their contract with him specified that the Fortune should be a replica of the Globe in every important respect except one; and that one exception they were afterwards to regret.[4] Ben Jonson later referred to the Globe as "this fair-fitted Globe," and as "the glory of the Banke."

The syndicate that had been created to finance the construction of the Globe was a new idea in theatrical management. Actors had previously had joint ownership of dramatic scripts, costumes, and properties, but never before had they participated in the ownership of a playhouse. All the expenses of leasing a site, erecting a building thereon, and subsequently operating the building as a theatre, were paid by the members of the syndicate in proportion to their respective holdings; and thereafter all the profits that accrued were distributed on the same basis. The members of the syndicate were thus the owners and proprietors of the Globe. They were known by the technical name of "housekeepers."

Wholly distinct from the housekeepers, as a legal entity, was the organization of actors, known as the "company." The company owned the play-scripts, properties, and costumes; the company produced the plays, and was responsible for their casting, costuming, and interpretation. Like the syndicate, it too was divided into shares for the purpose of allocating costs and distributing profits. But though the two organizations were distinct, they could and did overlap: at least six of the Globe's seven housekeepers were members of the company also, and thus shared twice in the profits of the

[4] The first Fortune was a square building; but Henslowe and Alleyn seem to have found the square floor-plan unsuitable for a public playhouse, for when the Fortune burnt down in 1621, it was replaced by a building more nearly conforming to the Globe's shape—"a large round brick building." See Chambers, II, 439, 443.

venture. In actual operation, the housekeepers in this period received one-half the income from the galleries; the company took the other half, plus the gatherings at the door. Ironically, it was Shakespeare's share in the ownership of the Globe, and later of the Blackfriars also, rather than his authorship of immortal plays, that made him a man of affluence and enabled him toward the close of his life to retire to Stratford as the most distinguished and perhaps the wealthiest citizen of the community.

This admirable plan of organization served its members well, not merely at the beginning, but for as long as the first and second Globes lasted. It provided both stability and stimulus. Since the leading members of the company had their own personal stakes in the success of the Globe (and later of the Blackfriars, which was owned by the same group), the company as a whole was deterred from shifting to another playhouse, and its individual members from deserting the Lord Chamberlain's Men to join another company. An ambitious young actor might always aspire to a share in the ownership of the playhouse if he achieved distinction in his profession; and so the arrangement served both as an incentive to members of the company and as a bait to lure exceptional actors from other troupes.

From the first the Globe and its company took and held the leadership in the drama. They had Richard Burbage, the foremost actor of the age, to whom year after year they entrusted the creation of the greatest roles that the language affords. They had Heminges, Condell, Phillips, Pope, Armin, Sly, and other good men, all of them excellent actors individually and capable of working together in harmony to give to each play as fine a production as could be contrived by great artists, conscientious workmen, and good friends. Above all, they had William Shakespeare, then at the peak of his powers. When James I came to the throne, he placed the seal of supremacy upon the Globe's players by taking them under his royal patronage: on May 19, 1603, he granted them a patent which authorized them thenceforth to play as the King's Men. Until the playhouses were closed under Cromwell in 1642, the preëminence of the Globe's company was never seriously challenged.

In an age of hot-tempered individualism, when any difference of opinion or interest might lead to litigation, the relationship of the Globe's original housekeepers was remarkably friendly and placid. As a matter of fact, this very lack of internal strife accounts in large part for the meagreness of the records that have come down to us about the Globe as a functioning playhouse. While the temperamental and restless trade of the theatre was breeding a multiplicity of lawsuits in other troupes, no single dispute between the original Globe housekeepers or company seems ever to have reached the crowded courts; and, the times being what they were, the absence of litigation implies an extraordinary story of mutual loyalty and comradeship. Heminges had the confidence of all his associates; his stewardship, so far as the records go, was never once called into question. Shakespeare was admired and revered. Three of his fellow-actors seem to have named their sons after him, and he himself left memorial rings as legacies to Heminges, Burbage, and Condell, the only three of the original seven who outlived him.

In 1608 or 1609 the King's Men began to act at the Blackfriars as well as at the Globe. Richard Burbage had owned the Blackfriars since 1597, but for a decade had leased it for performances by a company of boy actors, who for a time were serious competitors of the adult companies. It was what is known as a "private" theatre, which meant that it was roofed in, gave its plays by candle-light, and charged higher admission fees. It was situated north of the Thames in a fashionable district of London, and occupied a house which originally had been one of the priory buildings of the Blackfriars monastery and which therefore was still exempt from the jurisdiction of the Common Council. In 1608 Burbage secured a surrender of the lease, and formed a new syndicate, consisting of his brother and himself, Shakespeare, Heminges, Condell, Sly, and an outsider named Evans, to own and operate it. Thereafter the King's Men used the Globe as their summer home, and the Blackfriars in winter. Shakespeare's latest plays show an increased tendency toward the music and dances, the spectacles and masques, which had become traditional at the Blackfriars and were expected by its audiences.

Contemporary records of various sorts indicate that the Globe staged performances of *The Taming of the Shrew, Love's Labour's Lost, Romeo and Juliet, Richard II, Othello, Macbeth, Pericles, The Winter's Tale,* and *Henry VIII;* others, less explicit, imply Globe performances of *Julius Caesar, Troilus and Cressida, King Lear,* and *Cymbeline.* As to the other plays in the canon no direct evidence exists. Even so, however, there can be little doubt that all the plays written by Shakespeare during the great decade from 1599 (when the Globe was built) to 1609 (when the King's

Men began to act at the Blackfriars also) were first presented on the Globe's stage. In addition to some of the plays already mentioned, they included *As You Like It, Twelfth Night, Hamlet, The Merry Wives of Windsor, All's Well That Ends Well, Measure for Measure, Antony and Cleopatra,* and *Coriolanus.*

On the afternoon of June 29, 1613, the playhouse caught fire during the performance of a play, and was burned to the ground. The play was a new one called *All Is True,* or, as we now know it, *King Henry VIII,* "set forth with many extraordinary circumstances of pomp and majesty." On the entrance of the King in the fourth scene of the first act, two cannon were discharged in a royal salute, the unhappy result of which is thus set forth in two contemporary accounts, the first being by Howe, in his continuation of Stow's *Annals:*

> Upon S. Peters day last, the play-house or Theater, called the Globe, upon the Banck-side near London, by negligent discharging of a peal of ordinance, close to the south-side thereof, the thatch took fire, and the wind sodainly disperst the flame round about, and in a very short space the whole building was quite consumed, and no man hurt; the house being filled with people to behold the play, viz. of Henry the Eighth.

to which Sir Henry Wotton, in a letter to his nephew, adds the following details:

> Now, King Henry making a masque at the Cardinal Wolsey's house, and certain chambers being shot off at his entry, some of the paper, or other stuff, wherewith one of them was stopped, did light on the thatch, where being thought at first but an idle smoke, and their eyes more attentive to the show, it kindled inwardly, and ran round like a train, consuming within less than an hour the whole house to the very grounds. This was the fatal period of that virtuous fabric, wherein yet nothing did perish but wood and straw, and a few forsaken cloaks; only one man had his breeches set on fire, that would perhaps have broiled him, if he had not by the benefit of a provident wit put it out with bottle ale.

A new Globe was promptly erected on the same site; and this time, to prevent a repetition of the disaster, the building was prudently roofed with tiles. It was finished sometime in the summer of 1614. It stood until 1644, when it was pulled down and houses were erected on its site.

Over the years the membership of both syndicate and company had changed. William Kempe had withdrawn early, to be succeeded as chief comedian by Robert Armin. Pope and Phillips had died within a year of each other, not long after James came to the throne. Shakespeare, after spending the last years of his life in the Stratford he knew as a boy, had died in 1616, less than two years after the second Globe was opened. Richard Burbage had died in 1619, mourned by all London. Heminges and Condell lived on for a few years more, eventually to give Shakespeare his greatest monument in the First Folio of 1623.

CHAPTER II

THE SITE AND SHAPE

OF THE GLOBE

THERE are in existence several maps or views which purport to depict London from a time well before the first Globe was built until after the second Globe was demolished. They are not true maps as the term is understood today, two-dimensional plans drawn to a constant scale throughout as if from an imaginary point always directly overhead, plans on which distances can be measured and relative positions accurately determined; they are rather pictures drawn in greater or less perspective, as seen from a hypothetical tower or by the eye of a bird flying low. Fortunately for our purpose, the playhouses on the south bank of the Thames receive special prominence in the views, for the standpoint of the observer is always on the south, with the Bankside in the foreground and the City of London in the distance on the far side of the river. Unfortunately for our purpose, the real dates of the views—the years in which the pictorial data were compiled, as contrasted with the year of publication—are often obscure; their authorship is sometimes uncertain, and therefore their reliability; they are in some cases conventionalized, crudely drawn, even merely copied from earlier views; and worst of all, seem in some instances to be mutually contradictory. On the whole they are disappointing guides. They must nevertheless be taken into consideration in inquiring into either the site or the shape of the Globe.

The geographical area under present discussion was a rough rectangle about one-half mile long by 600 to 700 feet wide, running from Southwark on the east to Paris Garden on the west, and from the Thames on the north to Maid Lane on the south. Within or near this rectangle stood all or most of the Bankside amphitheatres. Its principal topographical features are clearly indicated on Norden's map of 1593 (Plate 3). Near the right edge of the plate, London Bridge crosses the Thames in a north-to-south direction from the City to Southwark. Just west of its southern end are the Church of St. Mary Overyes and Winchester House (indicated by the figure 20). The prison of the Clink stands a little north and west, on the river's edge;

southward from the Clink runs a road called Dead Man's Place, with a ditch in the middle of it spanned by bridges. Near the bottom of the plate, Maid Lane strikes out from Dead Man's Place and runs westward over the marshes, with ditches on either side of it, finally to make a junction with two divergent ways, Love Lane and Gravel Lane, near Paris Garden.

The exact site of the Globe has been the subject of some little controversy, in spite of the fact that a certified legal transcript of the original ground-lease is still in existence.[1] There can be no doubt that the playhouse stood in Surrey, on the Bankside, in the Liberty of the Clink, and in the parish of St. Mary Overyes (later St. Saviour's); the question which until recently has remained in doubt is whether it stood to the north or the south of Maid Lane. The ground-lease places it to the north, and so do some of the contemporary views; local tradition and the researches of Southwark antiquaries have however tended to place it to the south. In 1920-1924 W. W. Braines made an exhaustive study of all the available evidence on behalf of the London County Council, and arrived at the conclusion that the Globe stood on the south side of Maid Lane (now the east-to-west portion of Park Street) at or near the point where it is now crossed by Southwark Bridge Road; and scholars have generally accepted his opinion, even though it involved the admission that the ground-lease meant north when it said south, and east when it said west. The question seems to have been settled conclusively by the recent discovery of two maps, neither of them known to Braines: Norden's revised map of 1600 (Plate 4), and a map of Southwark, presumably drawn about 1620, found in the City Guildhall in London (Plate 16). Both unmistakably place the Globe to the south of Maid Lane.

On the basis of Braines's fully-documented and closely-reasoned study,[2] it seems clear that the Globe stood some 600 or 700 feet from the Thames, and about 1,500 feet west of the southern end of London Bridge. Another playhouse, the Rose, was on the north side of Maid Lane, in the corner formed by Maid Lane and Rose Alley, and was therefore to the north and west of the Globe. The Bear Garden was still farther to the north and west, and about 200 feet from the river; and the Swan was more than a quarter

---

[1] *Ostler v. Heminges, Coram Rege Roll 1454*, 13 Jac. I, Hilary Term, M. 692. The document was discovered by Dr. C. W. Wallace of Nebraska University in 1909.
[2] *The Site of the Globe Playhouse, Southwark* (1924).

of a mile to the west of the group of three, in Paris Garden. The Norden map of 1600 is thus approximately correct in its placement of the amphitheatres with reference to one another, with the Globe as the most southerly and easterly, the Bear Garden as the farthest north and west of the Bankside trio, and the Rose about midway between them. These relative positions will be found to have a bearing upon the consideration of the early representations of the Globe, in the pages that follow.[3]

The section of the Bankside in which the Globe stood had originally been a marsh, only recently drained and divided into plots. A general description of the immediate neighborhood is given in Strype's 1720 edition of Stow's earlier *Survey of London*:

> Maiden Lane, a long straggling place, with ditches on each side, the passage to the houses being over little bridges, with little garden plots before them, especially on the north side, which is best both for houses and inhabitants.

Norden's map of 1600 shows the Globe as being situated within the point of an angle formed by two drainage ditches, one of them running along the south side of Maid Lane and the other branching off from it in a southeasterly direction, with yet a third ditch splitting off from the second at a point just west of the playhouse and continuing due south along the dividing-line between the Globe's property and the Bishop of Winchester's park. On the evidence of the map, it would appear that Ben Jonson, when he spoke of the Globe as being "Flanck'd with a Ditch, and forc'd out of a Marish" in his poem *An Execration upon Vulcan*, intended a more literal description of its environment than was realized before the map was discovered. Three times at least (the documents are extant) the owners of the Globe received orders from the Surrey Sewers Commission regarding the care of their neighboring ditches.

The London County Council's *Survey of London* says that the Globe stood on land which was eventually absorbed into the grounds of the Anchor Brewery, later to become Thrale's and still later the Barclay and Perkins Brewery; and that Nos. 31, 29 and 27 Park Street, now occupied by employees of the brewery firm, stand on ground on which the Globe

---

[3] For a more extended discussion of the Globe's site, see Braines, op. cit.; the London County Council's *Survey of London*, Vol. XXII (Bankside), pp. 75, 79, 82, 133; *Globe Playhouse*, pp. 11-12; Chambers, II, 416-417 and 427-433; George Hubbard, *On the Site of the Globe Playhouse of Shakespeare* (1923).

originally stood. If this be the case, the commemorative tablet erected by the Shakespeare Reading Society on the wall of the Anchor Brewery next to 25 Park Street is somewhat too far to the east.

THE SHAPE OF THE GLOBE

The maps and views mentioned at the beginning of this chapter are neither clear nor consistent in indicating whether the Globe was polygonal or round in ground-plan. Twelve of them were produced between 1599, the year in which the first Globe was erected, and 1644, the year in which the second Globe was torn down, and in all of them the Bankside playhouses are pictured. Under such conditions one would expect a conclusive answer to a simple question. In not a few of the engravings, however, it is difficult to establish the identity of the playhouses represented, and, in all, to know how much weight to allow to their evidence as to the Globe's shape.

The first three maps reproduced in these pages do not show the Globe; all three were drawn before it came into existence. They are reprinted here largely because of the light which they throw upon the sources and accuracy of later views.

(a) Plate 1 reproduces a portion of the map published in Cologne by Braun and Hogenberg in their *Civitates Orbis Terrarum* of 1572. It is usually called the Hoefnagel map of London, on the assumption, which may or may not be justified, that its style shows it to be the work of Georg Hoefnagel; it was probably copied from an English original, now lost, dating from sometime between 1554 and 1572. As one's eye travels across the Bankside terrain from east to west, one sees first, just to the west of Dead Man's Place, an area divided into small plots, with a dead-end lane dividing the four northerly plots from the three to the south; beyond that, a larger plot with "The Beare bayting" ring and its kennels, and a square pond; still farther to the west, a long narrow strip with three ponds, and then another large plot with "The Bowll baytyng" ring and kennels. Beyond this comes a field with two small and two large ponds, and then a larger area divided into gardens in its northern half and with open meadows in its southern portion. These details are mentioned not as being necessarily correct, but merely to aid their recognition in later views; as a matter of fact, the Hoefnagel map is demonstrably unreliable in many respects, including its layout of Southwark roads.

(b) The so-called Agas map (Plate 2) was printed in 1633, but was probably drawn much earlier. As a comparison of the two maps instantly reveals, it was obviously based upon Hoefnagel in its delineation of the Bankside.

(c) Norden's map (Plate 3) was published in his *Speculum Britanniæ* in 1593, and is the first to show any of the Bankside playhouses. Correctly for its date, it shows two amphitheatres, of which the more northerly and westerly is labelled "The Beare howse," and the other "The play howse," which at that date can only have been Henslowe's Rose. Both of the amphitheatres are represented as circular. Norden, for the first time, shows Maid Lane as continuing easterly to make a junction with Dead Man's Place.

(d) In 1600 Norden issued a revision of his map of 1593. The later map (Plate 4) is inset in an engraved panorama of London as viewed from the south bank, published under the title of *Civitas Londini*. A copy of the engraving, preserved in the Royal Library at Stockholm, was brought to the attention of Shakespearean scholars by I. A. Shapiro no longer ago than 1948, too recently to have been mentioned by Dr. Adams in *The Globe Playhouse*. In its delineation of the larger topographical features of the Bankside, the 1600 map is substantially identical with the map of 1593. "The Beare howse" has however been renamed "Beargard[en]," and "The play howse" has become "The Stare": clearly an error, since no Star is known ever to have existed. The two structures occupy the same sites as the Bear House and the Rose in the earlier map. But now a third playhouse, labelled "The globe," has been added to the Bankside group, and a fourth, "The Swone," far to the west. The amphitheatres in the later engraving resemble those in the earlier in being cylindrical; they differ from them in having thatched roofs, "huts," and playhouse flags.

(e) In the accompanying *Civitas Londini* panorama (Plate 5) the same four amphitheatres are shown again, unlabelled but unmistakably placed with reference to each other precisely as in the inset map; in the panorama, however, all four are polygonal. The two elements of the same engraving are thus in direct disagreement the one with the other with respect to the Globe's shape; but since the panorama is more pictorial in treatment than the map, and since it gives some indication of having been drawn from new data, it is perhaps to be preferred as a representation of the playhouses. Regrettably, the Globe is concealed by trees up to its eaves-line, but its roof is unquestionably octagonal. However conventionalized the drawing of the Globe may be in the 1600 map, and however incomplete in the accompanying perspective view, the Norden map and panorama nevertheless provide the two earliest known pictures of the Globe.

(f and g) The Delaram and Hondius views (Plates 6 and 7) must be considered together. There is clearly some relationship between the two: some borrowing, perhaps by Delaram from Hondius, or by both from an earlier source now lost. Both show, at left, a polygonal structure generally accepted as representing the Bear Garden; and to the right and nearer to the observer, a strange round building, smaller above than below and windowed only in its upper part. Each building has a superstructure in Delaram, but none in Hondius; except for this one detail, the two engravings accord with one another closely in the drawing of the two amphitheatres.

The Delaram engraving uses a view of Southwark, the Thames, and the City, as background for an equestrian portrait of James I. It is undated, but must be later than 1603, when James came to the throne. Unlike Hondius, Delaram shows a third amphitheatre to the east of the other two, and it may therefore be assumed that he represents the Bankside as of some time between 1599 and 1605, for only during that period were there three amphitheatres in the area: in 1599 the Globe made a third in the Bankside group, and in 1605 the Rose was torn down. It is, however, impossible to identify the three structures with any degree of assurance. They lie at the three points of a triangle, not in the north-west to south-east line in which we know the Bear Garden, Rose and Globe to have been sited. It seems clear therefore that the drawing was not made from direct observation, and that its evidence is of doubtful value.[4]

[4] Chambers (II, 377) thinks it probable that the circular building in the middle of the Delaram group is the Globe, and the polygonal buildings at left and right the Bear Garden and the Rose respectively; but all available information indicates that (a) far from being sited at the river's edge, the Rose stood perhaps 300 feet from the Thames; (b) the Rose and the Bear Garden stood near each other; and (c) the Rose was west of the Globe, their relative positions being established beyond question not merely by the Norden map of 1600 but by street-names surviving for a century or more on the Bankside. I. A. Shapiro ("The Bankside Theatres: Early Engravings," *Shakespeare Survey 1,*

The Hondius view is a small picture set in a large map of "The Kingdome of Great Britain and Ireland," in John Speed's *Theatre of the Empire of Great Britaine*. It is dated 1610, and properly for that date shows only two amphitheatres, presumably the Bear Garden toward the north and the Globe toward the south, with the Globe pictured as a circular structure. Dr. Adams, however, believes that the 1610 date is misleading, and that the Hondius drawing shows, not the Bear Garden and the Globe (as of the period 1605-1613), but the Bear Garden and the Rose (as of the period 1587-1599).[5] In either case, the relationship of Hondius to Delaram, or of both to a common lost source, cannot be overlooked; and the considerations which discredit the Delaram view as evidence apply with equal force to Hondius. The views printed on the title-pages of Holland's *Herωologia Anglica* (1620)[6] and Baker's *Chronicle* (1643)[7] are derived from Hondius or his source, and have no independent authority.

(h) The two Visscher engravings are the most important of all the views as delineations of the first Globe. Each exists in a unique copy. The one in the Folger Shakespeare Library (Plate 8) bears the signature "Visscher excudit"; that in the British Museum (Plate 9) carries the signatures "J. C. Visscher delineavit" and "Ludovicus Hondius lusit," and the date 1616. In some areas the two engravings show obvious dissimilarities, but not in their representations of the Globe; at first glance the two Globes seem to be identical. On closer examination the Globe in the British Museum print is found to be slightly the larger building of the two, as scaled by the height of the man who peers into a peep-hole in the south-west wall: from ground to eaves, it is almost three times as tall as he, whereas the Folger Globe is only about two and a half times as high, and correspondingly narrower;

p. 32) also identifies the circular building with the Globe, as being the farthest south; he conjectures, however, that the other two are the Bear Garden and the Swan; but this is manifestly improbable, since the Globe lay east of the Bear Garden, and the Swan lay a quarter of a mile or more to the west, too far to be included in the Delaram view. J. C. Adams (*The Globe Playhouse*, p. 386) believes the octagonal structure toward the east to be the Globe, and the other two the Bear Garden and the Rose; but this ignores the fact that the Globe was the most southerly of the three buildings, and 600 feet or more from the Thames.
[5] *Globe Playhouse*, p. 387.
[6] Reproduced by Shapiro, op. cit., Plate IX.
[7] Reproduced in *Globe Playhouse*, p. 387, and J. Q. Adams, p. 147.

the windows in the former are generally smaller, too, and set higher in the walls. But the differences, such as they are, are doubtless unintentional and without significance. Both engravings show the Globe as octagonal in plan.

The conventional portrayal of the Globe as an octagonal structure stems ultimately from Visscher. It therefore becomes pertinent to ask how authoritative his representation may be supposed to be. Dr. Adams places a high estimate upon its credibility:

> In beauty, in completeness of detail, and in skillful execution this original [Folger] Visscher view easily surpasses any other seventeenth-century view of London. . . . It is clearly the most authoritative contemporary panorama of London in the first half of the seventeenth century, and as such its representation of the Globe . . . is more valuable and trustworthy than any other.[8]

It may be so; and yet there are considerations which raise doubt as to whether the Visscher engravings are in fact original eye-witness records of the London of their time. Some of those considerations had not yet come to light when Dr. Adams wrote; the existence of the *Civitas Londini* panorama was not yet known to students of the Elizabethan stage, and Visscher's borrowings from it were therefore not yet recognized. As to the borrowings there can be no dispute. The full extent of Visscher's dependence upon *Civitas* can be demonstrated only by a comparison of the Visscher and *Civitas* panoramas in their entireties, for most of the details which Visscher copied from the earlier engraving lie outside the areas of the partial views printed in these pages as Plates 5 and 8; more extensive views are needed to establish Visscher's copying from *Civitas* in, for instance, his drawing of London Bridge and of some buildings on the far side of the Thames, the twin vessels labelled "The Eell Schipes" at anchor in the river, and his spelling of some place names which he misinterpreted in his reading of *Civitas*. One conclusive instance of borrowing, however, falls within the area of our small views: the ship to which, following *Civitas*, Visscher has tagged the seemingly meaningless label of "The Gallÿ fuste."

Nor is this the full story of Visscher's dependence upon earlier engravers: in the topography of the Bankside, he followed the Agas map of perhaps fifty years earlier, which in turn was based upon the Hoefnagel map of yet earlier date. A study of the complete engravings makes the derivative nature

[8] *Globe Playhouse*, pp. 9, 10.

of Visscher's Bankside foreground abundantly clear; in innumerable details, some of them manifestly inaccurate, he followed Agas faithfully. Even the incomplete views printed as Plates 2 and 8 bear evidence of this; they show the same rows of trees (after allowance has been made for the difference in perspective), the same fields, the same ponds. Conspicuously, Visscher followed Agas in his placement of the two amphitheatres; he placed his Bear Garden and his Globe on the sites of the bull-baiting and bear-baiting rings in Hoefnagel and Agas, and in doing so mislocated his Globe certainly, and probably his Bear Garden as well. Further, he followed Agas in making Maid Lane a *cul-de-sac*, which, if it were extended to the west as it should be, would have the Globe on its north side rather than its south. Visscher's dependence upon Agas was noted as long ago as 1917 by Joseph Quincy Adams, who said that "in drawing the Bankside, Visscher rather slavishly copied the Agas map of 1560."[9]

None of these borrowings, however, has any necessary bearing upon the question of Visscher's accuracy in depicting the Globe and Bear Garden as octagonal structures. It is still possible to suppose that he had made preliminary sketches of the two buildings and knew their relative positions, and that while making the finished engraving in Amsterdam he fell into the error of putting them on the sites of the two rings in the Agas engraving. Shapiro, to be sure, suspects that in his representation of an octagonal Globe Visscher merely copied the Rose in the *Civitas* panorama[10]; but this supposition would seem to be refuted by the fact that Visscher's Globe is detailed far beyond the *Civitas* Rose. In drawing the Globe he could in fact have been little indebted to any known engraving, for none before his time had shown the building in comparable detail. True, he took an artist's license in representing his Globe as too narrow for its height, as had all the engravers before him. True also, he drew the building as if it were made of stone or brick rather than timber; but if his preparatory sketch was no more fully elaborated than that of Hollar at a later date (Plate 12), the error was one into which he might easily be led in making the final engraving perhaps three years later and far from London.

The case for and against the Visscher engravings may be summed up as follows: the engravings are clearly derivative in many details, but those

[9] *Shakespearean Playhouses*, p. 328.
[10] Op. cit., pp. 30-31.

details do not include the representation of the Globe and Bear Garden; and although the drawing of the Globe is probably erroneous in at least two respects, it still gives evidence of direct observation, and conveys a sense of reality as no earlier engraving had done.

(i) There are several derivatives of the Visscher engravings, the nearest in time and fidelity being the Merian view of 1638 (Plate 10). Merian follows Visscher closely in his drawing of London north of the Thames, but deepens his Bankside foreground slightly by adding new details. He labels both the Bear Garden and the Globe, but between them he introduces a third unnamed octagonal structure which had no known existence.

The undated *Londinum Urbs* view[11] and Howell's *Londinopolis* view of 1657[12] are indifferent copies of Merian and without authority of their own.

(j) The so-called Ryther map exists in two versions. The earlier, sometimes dated 1604 but probably published about 1636-45, leaves the Bankside largely unfinished and shows only one amphitheatre, which by its location may be identified as the Bear Garden or Hope. The later version (Plate 11) has the Bankside completed. In addition to the Hope, it shows a second amphitheatre, situated south of Maid Lane and near the point of an angle formed by drainage ditches, and therefore undoubtedly the Globe. In view of the precise agreement of the Ryther map with Norden's map of 1600 respecting the Globe's site, it is surprising to find that in drawing the Bankside Ryther followed, not Norden's 1600 map with its Globe, but Norden's Globe-less map of seven years earlier (Plate 3). Three out of the many indications of Ryther's dependence upon the map of 1593 are to be found in the shape and arrangement of the four ponds west of the Hope, the inexplicable line below them, broken by a bulge, and the vertical row of trees farther west. But since the 1593 map showed no Globe, Ryther was forced to look elsewhere for information as to its site and shape. Perhaps the second Norden map (Plate 4) was his authority for the site of the Globe, but if so he rejected its evidence as to the Globe's shape. Ryther's Globe is octagonal.

[11] Reproduced by Hubbard, Plate 8, and Hodges, p. 128.
[12] Reproduced by George Pierce Baker, *The Development of Shakespeare as a Dramatist*, p. 155.

(k)   The Hollar "Long View" of 1647 (Plate 13) pictures the Hope and the second Globe. Hollar can never have seen the first Globe; he did not arrive in England until 1637, twenty-four years after it had burned to the ground. He shows both buildings in considerable detail, and represents them both as round.

Hollar was a masterly draftsman; his hundreds of surviving drawings, many of which can be checked for accuracy by reference to existing buildings, give ample proof of his dependability. He engraved the "Long View" while he was living in Holland, a fugitive from England on account of his royalist sympathies, and published it three years after the second Globe had been demolished. This fact has sometimes been cited as a reason for discrediting his representation of the Globe; but the same objections might be urged against the credibility of Visscher's view, which also was engraved in Holland and published some three years after *his* Globe was destroyed. In the case of Hollar, as it happens, the disparagement on this score would seem to be even less justified than in the case of Visscher, for Hollar's preparatory sketch of the two amphitheatres is still in existence (Plate 12), and a comparison of the original sketch with the finished engraving shows how faithfully he followed his preliminary drawing.

There are good reasons for believing that Hollar inadvertently interchanged the names of his "Beere bayting h[ouse]" and "The Globe." For one thing, the former (which by now had become the Hope) lay to the north and west of the Globe, not, as in the engraving, to the south and east. For another, Hollar's "Globe" has only a strange peak in its roof, and lacks the "huts" which *deus ex machina* scenes made necessary and which most other views depict; and on the other hand, he has given his Hope massive huts extending over fully one-half of the inner yard, in spite of the fact that the Hope had a removable stage (to make way for animal-baiting sports) and less need of huts than any other playhouse. The mistake is one that could easily occur under the circumstances. The buildings were not labelled in his preliminary sketch, and while in Holland he perhaps followed Visscher in naming the left-hand building the bear-baiting arena and the right-hand building the Globe. His preparatory drawing of the building which he later misnamed the Bear-baiting House is in all probability an accurate representation of the second Globe; but whether or not the names have been interchanged, Hollar's Globe in any case remains round.

The F. de Wit engraving is obviously copied from Hollar in its portrayal of the two playhouses, and therefore carries no authority of its own.[13]

(l) In 1638 Inigo Jones made two hurried sketches as alternative designs for a theatrical backdrop for D'Avenant's play *Britannia Triumphans* (Plates 14 and 15). One of the sketches seems to show two playhouses; the other, one. None of the playhouses is labelled, but in 1638 only the Hope and the Globe remained on the Bankside. If the Globe is intended in either sketch, it must, by reason of date, be the second rather than the first. From their vague indications, all the playhouses are, or seem to be, round.

To review the evidence of the engravings, the *Civitas Londini*, Visscher, Merian, *Londinum Urbs, Londinopolis,* and Ryther maps show the first Globe as polygonal. The Norden map of 1600, and perhaps the Delaram and Hondius views and the latter's derivatives, picture it as round. The second Globe is pictured as round by Hollar, F. de Wit, and Inigo Jones. The weight of evidence, for whatever it is worth, seems therefore to support the octagonal-Globe theory as relating to the first Globe; other interpretations and other evaluations have however led some scholars to prefer the round-Globe theory.[14] Since the contemporary engravings cannot of themselves yield an answer everywhere accepted as final and conclusive with respect to the shape of the first Globe, the greatest possible weight must be allowed to Dr. Adams's analysis of the practical difficulties attending upon circular construction in wood:

> . . . A circular seating plan wholly or partially surrounding the platform stage is, of course, ideal; but a literally cylindrical wooden playhouse would be difficult to make and decidedly more expensive than a polygonal playhouse of equivalent size. Wood does not lend itself readily to curved lines. The heavy beams required in the main frame of so large a structure—unlike the relatively slender ribs of a boat—cannot be bent to a curve, however flat. Yet at every level of the playhouse, beginning with the sills and ending with the roof plates and ridgepole, all horizontal beams in the frame forming the inner and outer walls (the "breast-

[13] Reproduced by Hubbard, *On the Site of the Globe Playhouse of Shakespeare*, Plate 7. F. de Wit is not to be confused with the Johannes De Witt whose sketch of the interior of the Swan Playhouse is reproduced in Plate 17 of the present volume.
[14] Chambers, II, 434; Shapiro, pp. 32, 35. For a more extended discussion of the early engravings, see *Globe Playhouse*, pp. 5-11 and 385-389; Chambers, II, 353-355 and 376-379; Shapiro, pp. 25-35; Hodges, pp. 91-95; Braines, pp. 46-60; J. Q. Adams, *cursim.*

summers" of the contracts) would have to be cut by hand to the requisite curve out of bulks of timber far heavier than the finished members. If placed end to end, these curved beams in a playhouse the size of the Globe would approach a total length of 1900 feet, so that the labor involved in shaping them would add greatly to the cost.

Yet even when these specially hand-shaped beams were prepared, the difficulties of fabricating a circular playhouse would have only begun. In a polygonal playhouse all beams would, of course, be straight lengths of timber; each breastsummer could therefore carry up to the limit of its breaking strength all the weight placed upon it without twisting or moving from place, for the thrust of the load would descend in the plane of the posts which supported it at both ends. If, on the other hand, the structure were circular, each breastsummer would have to conform to the curve of the wall and would be incapable of carrying as much weight as a straight beam, for the thrust of the load would descend not in the plane of the supporting posts but at the mid-point of the curve (well outside that plane), thus tending to twist the breastsummer loose. Long before the breaking point of the timber was reached, its pegged joints would tend to give way, thereby endangering the spectators in that section of the playhouse. Needless to say, those concerned in theatrical affairs were eager to avoid a repetition of the Paris Garden accident of 1583 in which eight persons were killed and several others injured by the collapse of the galleries.

To offset the weakness caused by a load resting on a curved beam it would be necessary to reduce the length of the span, either by shoring up the breastsummer in the middle of every gallery bay or by constructing a frame with much narrower bays. Both plans would considerably increase the number of posts standing between the gallery spectators and the stage, thus nullifying the advantages possessed in theory by the circular design.

One could compromise, of course, and achieve the effect of a circle by setting up curved banks of seats and curved balustrades inside a polygonal frame, but such a plan would be structurally illogical and would materially reduce the capacity of the house.[15]

Some students of the problem, recognizing the contradictory evidence of the early engravings and the difficulties inherent in cylindrical construction in wood, have suggested that the Globe may in fact have been a twelve-sided or sixteen-sided affair, built of straight timbers and yet easily mistaken for a round building when seen at a distance or pictured at small scale.[16] Their conjecture receives some support from the twelve-sided Swan

[15] *Globe Playhouse*, pp. 24-26. This and other quotations from Dr. Adams's book are by generous permission of John Cranford Adams and of the Harvard University Press.
[16] Cf. G. Topham Forrest's reconstruction in Braines's *The Site of the Globe Playhouse, Southwark*, pp. 99-108, the scale model of the Globe in the Brander Matthews Museum at Columbia University, and Hodges, op. cit., p. 18.

in the Visscher engravings and the many-sided Hope Playhouse in the Ryther map. It offers a tempting compromise; one hesitates to accept it, however, for while there is contemporary evidence for either a round Globe or an octagonal, there is none for a Globe with more sides than eight.

Shakespeare's reference to "this wooden O" in the Prologue to *Henry V* is sometimes cited to support the thesis of a circular Globe. It seems unlikely, however, that Shakespeare had the Globe in mind when he penned the line; more probably he referred to the Curtain, which the Lord Chamberlain's Men occupied from the summer of 1597 until they moved into the Globe two years later. On the basis of dates alone, either the Curtain or the Globe seems to have been possible: *Henry V* was finished between March 27th and September 28th of 1599, during the early part of which period the company was undoubtedly still at the Curtain, and during the latter part probably at the Globe. Not date, but the deprecatory attitude of the dramatist, makes the Curtain seem more probable than the Globe for the role of "this wooden O." The Choruses of *Henry V* contain more than one apology for the limitations of "this unworthy scaffold"; and if the stage were that of the just-opened Globe, the new and handsome playhouse of which Shakespeare was part owner and which he had helped to design, one would expect him not to ask for indulgence, but rather to point with pride. In any case, whether applying to the Curtain or to the Globe, "this wooden O" may still have been intended as no more literal a description than our current "prize-ring."

Under all the circumstances, it is inevitable that there should be a difference of opinion as to the shape of the Globe's outer walls; there is however less reason for disagreement as to the shape of its inner frame. Circular construction, as Dr. Adams has pointed out, would necessitate the use of additional posts to support each curved breastsummer where it swings out of the plane of the posts which carry it at each end. In the outer wall, the extra posts would add to the expense in labor and materials, but nothing worse; along the inner frame, on the other hand, they would interpose an intolerable barrier between audience and stage. Whatever the shape of the Globe's outer shell, therefore, it may confidently be supposed that the inner frame was polygonal.·I. A. Shapiro, one of the most vehement of the round-Globe advocates, concedes the probability of a polygonal inner frame for "some theatres," not excluding the Globe:

> But it does not follow that because the outer walls were circular the inner walls were necessarily circular also. . . . It would be quite easy to build a theatre with outer wall circular, and inner wall polygonal. This plan would presumably be easier and cheaper to work to than one which used curved timbers and the more closely spaced vertical supports this would entail, and my own opinion is that it may have been adopted in some theatres.[17]

The question of outward shape thus involves fewer consequences than may at first have been supposed; it does not necessarily affect the shape of the inner frame, nor, therefore, the design of auditorium and stage.

On the basis of his evaluation of the early engravings, and in view of the impracticability of wooden construction in the round, it is assumed by Dr. Adams in *The Globe Playhouse*, and it is assumed in the present book, that the first Globe was octagonal both without and within. On the evidence of Hollar and Inigo Jones, however, and in spite of the structural difficulties involved, it seems necessary to entertain the idea that the second Globe may have been round. If so, the second Globe would have needed new foundations, and this assumption runs afoul of a reference to "The [second] Globe playhouse nere Maide lane built by the Company of Players with timber about 20 yeares past vppon an old foundacion."[18] But the word "foundacion" may easily have been used in the general sense of site rather than in the more limited sense of a masonry substructure, more especially since the allusion is to an event twenty years past; and the supposition that the first Globe's foundations may in fact have been rendered unusable by the fire receives some support from Ben Jonson's lament when the playhouse was destroyed: "nothing but the piles / Left." New piles, as well as new foundations, would of course be necessary if a round building followed an octagonal upon the same site.

---

[17] "An Original Drawing of the Globe Theatre," *Shakespeare Survey* 2 (1949), p. 22. Cf. also Hodges, op. cit., p. 18.
[18] An item in the revised "return" of buildings made to the Earl Marshal in 1637. It is preserved among the parish papers of St. Saviour's.

CHAPTER III

THE DIMENSIONS

OF THE GLOBE

NOTHING is known directly as to the dimensions of the Globe Playhouse. No specifications survive, no plan, no builder's contract. Fortunately, however, the builders' contracts for two other contemporary playhouses are extant. Neither gives complete dimensions or specifications, and each avoids the statement of many particulars that one would gladly know, by the frustrating device of referring to another playhouse already standing, and by saying that in this or that respect the projected building is to be like it or unlike it, as the case may be.

For our purposes the more important of the contracts is that for the Fortune, built one year after the Globe and by the same master-builder, Peter Streete. Streete was instructed by Philip Henslowe and Edward Alleyn to create in the Fortune a building which should be a replica of the Globe in every important respect except one: it was to be a square building instead of round or polygonal. Three times in the course of the contract strict adherence to the design of the Globe is insisted upon, as in the following clause:

> And the saide howse and other thinges beforemencioned to be made & doen To be in all other Contrivitions Conveyances fashions thinge and thinges effected finished and doen accordinge to the manner and fashion of the saide howse Called the Globe.

Only two minor divergences from the design of the Globe are specified: the timbers of the Fortune are to be stouter than the Globe's, and the principal posts of the frame and stage are to be square in cross-section, and topped with carved satyrs. The Fortune contract specifies the following dimensions:

> The frame of the said house to be set square and to contain four-score foot of lawful assize every way square without, and fifty-five foot of like assize square every way within [i.e., it was to be a hollow square 80 feet wide over-all, surrounding an inner yard 55 feet in width]; with a good

sure and strong foundation of piles, brick, lime and sand both without and within, to be wrought one foot of assize at the least above the ground;

And the said frame to contain three stories in height, the first or lower story to contain twelve foot of lawful assize in height, the second story eleven foot of lawful assize in height, and the third or upper story to contain nine foot of lawful assize in height;

All which stories shall contain twelve foot and a half of lawful assize in breadth throughout, besides a juttey forwards in either of the said two upper stories of ten inches of lawful assize; . . .

With a stage and tiring-house to be made, erected and set up within the said frame, . . . which stage shall contain in length forty and three foot of lawful assize and in breadth to extend to the middle of the yard of the said house . . .[1]

The second builder's contract is that for the Hope. It was entered into in 1613 between Henslowe and Meade on the one part and a carpenter named Katherens on the other, and it provided for the pulling down of the outmoded Bear Garden and the erecting of a new house, suitable both for plays and for animal-baiting, in its place. It is of less value to us than the Fortune contract because it is shorter, because it omits any reference to the larger proportions of the building, because it contemplates an unorthodox playhouse with a removable stage, and because it uses the Swan, rather than the Globe, as its basis of reference. It specifies dimensions only in the following particulars:

The inner principal posts of the first story to be twelve foots in height and ten inches square, the inner principal posts in the middle story to be eight inches square, the innermost posts in the upper story to be seven inches square;

The prick posts in the first story to be eight inches square, in the second story seven inches square, and in the uppermost story six inches square;

Also the breastsummers in the lowermost story to be nine inches deep and seven inches in thickness, and in the middle story to be eight inches deep and six inches in thickness;

The binding joists of the first story to be nine and eight inches in depth and thickness, and in the middle story to be viii and vii inches in depth and thickness.

Item, to make a good, sure, and sufficient foundation of bricks for the said playhouse or game place, and to make it xiii inches at the least above the ground.[2]

[1] The spelling has been modernized and the text divided into paragraphs for the reader's convenience. Other provisions of the Fortune contract will be quoted later in connection with corresponding elements of the Globe's design. The contract is reprinted in full, and in its original spelling, in Appendix A.

[2] The Hope contract is reprinted in full in Appendix B.

The two contracts agree that the height of the first story shall be twelve feet, and they agree within an inch as to the height of the foundation. But the Hope contract tells nothing about horizontal measurements or floor plan.

Still a third source of data—not a builder's contract this time, but an architect's design—merits consideration as having a possible bearing upon the size of the Globe: the plans, formerly attributed to Inigo Jones, for the Cockpit-in-Court (Plate 22). The plans were drawn in 1632; they thus followed the erection of the first Globe by 33 years, but were contemporary with the second. To be sure, the Cockpit-in-Court (if it was ever actually built) was not a public playhouse, but an intimate theatre for the use of Charles I and his courtiers; not a free-standing structure, but a part of Whitehall Palace. It had, however, the great advantage for our purpose of being octagonal in plan; and if the drawing be measured by the scale of feet marked off along its lower edge, the octagon is found to be 58 feet in breadth.

Dr. Adams bases his reconstruction of the Globe's dimensions upon the Fortune contract (*Globe Playhouse*, pp. 22-23). Since the Fortune's galleries were 12½ feet deep and constructed in the form of a hollow square, the corner bays would necessarily be square and would measure 12½ feet on a side. He assumes therefore that the vertical posts which formed the corner bays were spaced exactly 12 feet between centers in both directions; and since large wood-frame buildings are whenever possible constructed in modules or units of the same size, he suggests that the other structural bays also were square and of the same convenient 12-foot unit of measurement. On each side of the Fortune's square frame, then, there would be six such 12-foot-square bays, plus a half-bay 6 feet wide in the clear and therefore 7 feet between the centers of the neighboring posts; and if to the 79 feet thus arrived at be added two 6-inch allowances to cover the distances from the centers to the outer surfaces of the two outermost posts, the total is precisely 80 feet, the given dimension of the Fortune exterior.

Having thus verified his tentative conjecture of a 12-foot module in the Fortune, Dr. Adams applies the same module to the Globe. In an octagonal frame the bays could not, of course, be square; but assuming the same 12-foot spacing between the centers of the posts which surrounded the inner yard, and further assuming two bays on each side of the yard, one arrives at an octagon with 24-foot sides and with a breadth of 58 feet—and this again is precisely the same as another given dimension, the width of the octagonal auditorium of the Cockpit-in-Court.

On each side of the Globe's 58-foot-wide inner yard Dr. Adams places galleries 12½ feet deep in the clear, plus a 6-inch outer wall of studs, lath, and plaster, and so arrives at 84 feet as the over-all width of the playhouse frame. He points out that these figures—58 feet and 84 feet respectively— are remarkably close to the Fortune's corresponding dimensions of 55 and 80 feet, and that the differences are what one might expect in shifting from an octagonal to a square plan; i.e., that the octagon would be the wider of the two forms, to compensate for its lack of deep corners.[3]

The dimensions of the Cockpit-in-Court deserve some further comment, for they are perhaps significant. The side of an octagon is to its breadth as 1 is to 1 plus the square-root of 2, or as 1 is to 2.414 . . . . Now, in this relationship of side to breadth, there are only three pairs of numbers, within the range worth consideration as applying to the dimensions of Cockpit or Globe, that are substantially whole numbers in both instances: (1) 17-foot sides, with a breadth of 41 feet plus a fraction of an inch; (2) 24-foot sides, with a breadth of a fraction of an inch less than 58 feet (the Cockpit dimensions); and (3) 29-foot sides, with a breadth of almost precisely 70 feet. The importance of whole numbers becomes immediately apparent when one realizes that the Elizabethan designer, as often as not, omitted measurements on his drawings; as with the Cockpit drawings (Plate 22), he left it to the builder to arrive at the dimensions by "scaling" the plans. Such a process made the reading of fractional numbers difficult and precarious, and the prudent designer might well go out of his way to keep to simple whole numbers for major dimensions. And of the three pairs of whole numbers listed above, the designer of the Cockpit-in-Court chose the one

[3] In adding 6 inches for an outer wall to the gallery depth of 12½ feet, Dr. Adams departs from the Fortune contract, in which the thickness of the outer wall was included in, not added to, the 12½-foot depth of the gallery (12½ plus 12½ plus 55 equals 80). Two other points in Dr. Adams's analysis seem to invite question: first, his assumption that there was a half-bay on each side of the Fortune, which nothing in the contract seems clearly to require; and second, his assumption that one-foot-square posts framing a 12½-foot bay would be 12 feet between centers, rather than 11½ feet. The latter point would be negligible were it not for the fact that he bases his 12-foot module upon the supposition that the posts were centered at 12 feet.

Actually, the Folger model and the scale drawings printed in this book show a yard 58 feet wide, with lower galleries 12½ feet in the clear and walls 9 inches thick, to give a total width of 84½ feet across the outer walls.

pair in which both whole numbers were themselves divisible into whole numbers. These considerations may conceivably have influenced the designs of both the Cockpit-in-Court and the Globe.

The Globe unquestionably had three stories. In this respect all the public playhouses seem to have been alike from the beginning, as evidenced by the DeWitt sketch of the Swan's interior (Plate 17), the three levels of windows in the Visscher and derivative views, and descriptions by visitors, as for instance Samuel Kiechel's reference to three galleries in the Theater and Curtain in 1585. The heights of the three stories are specified in the Fortune contract as 12 feet for the lowest story, 11 for the second, and 9 for the third. The Hope contract specifies the same 12 feet as the height of the first; and although it fails to give the heights of the upper stories, the fact that their posts and beams were to be made progressively lighter in scantling implies a corresponding reduction in their heights. Under the terms of the Fortune contract, each of the two upper stories was to overhang the story below it by 10 inches. There is no reason to suppose that the three galleries in the Globe had other heights or overhangs than those specified for the Fortune.

Unfortunately, reconstruction of the dimensions of the Globe cannot be a process of starting with clearly applicable data and proceeding thence through close reasoning to an inescapable conclusion. The data are few, and their applicability doubtful. The fact remains, however, that Dr. Adams's dimensions for the Globe are perhaps as nearly accurate as one may hope to make them, and certainly as accurate as present-day information permits. They have never, to my knowledge, been challenged. Most importantly, they tend to prove themselves and each other by their ability to accommodate, conveniently and logically, all the manifold details of construction and equipment to be discussed in the pages that follow.

CHAPTER IV

THE FABRIC OF THE GLOBE

THE Globe is known to have been built of timber. This fact is established by the repeated references to timber—"timber and stuff," "wood and timber," "timber and woode," etc.—in the long-drawn-out controversy between Giles Alleyn and the Burbages over the dismantling of the Theater. And if it was built of timber, then it was built of oak. Whether for frame or for embellishment, oak almost exclusively was used in Tudor timber construction. The buildings that have come down to us from Tudor days prove this fact beyond dispute; and to their tacit evidence we may add the testimony of William Harrison, whose *Description of England* was published in 1577 as a companion-piece to Holinshed's *Chronicles*. Harrison wrote:

> In times past men were contented to dwell in houses buylded of sallow, willow, plum-tree, hardbeame, and elme, so that the use of oke was in a manner dedicated whollie unto churches, religious houses, princes' palaces, noblemen's lodgings, and navigation; but now all these are rejected, and nothing but oke anie whit regarded.

The use of "oken tymber" is twice specified in the contract for the building of the Hope Playhouse, and once in the contract for the Fortune. In the latter "deale bourdes" are specified for the flooring.[1]

THE FRAME

Timber building in Tudor England was what we now know as half-timber, or black-and-white, construction. It was a natural expression of the resources, the limitations, and the skills, of mediaeval England. Oak was still plentiful, and there were axes and broad-axes and adzes, and men whose skill in the handling of them had come down from grandfather to father, and from father to son, for generation after generation. They squared the timber with

---

[1] *The Shorter Oxford English Dictionary* defines "deal" as "1. A slice sawn from a log of timber, in Great Britain 9 inches wide, not more than 3 thick, and at least 6 feet long. . . . 2. The wood of fir or pine, such as deals (sense 1) are made of." There is good reason to believe that in Elizabethan times the word "deal" sometimes referred to dimension only, and not necessarily to any specific wood. The floors in the Fortune's galleries were intended to be trodden by thousands of feet, and it may therefore be supposed that they were of oak, not of soft woods such as fir or pine.

34

axe and adze, and left it large, partly because massive timbers gave strength and the appearance of strength, and partly because it was easier to use heavy balks and beams than to cut them down into smaller scantlings. During the 17th century the woodlands were to be progressively depleted under the expanding needs of the ship-building yards and of the iron-smelting works, which burned oak for fuel before the advent of coal; but in Elizabeth's time oak was still abundant enough to be used lavishly.

The sizes of the balks, and the resultant consumption of timber, were extravagant by today's standards. For their corner posts the builders often used pieces 12″ x 12″ or 15″ x 15″ in cross-section, or even larger,[2] where today we might use two or three two-by-fours in pine. For their joists they used timbers 9″ x 7″ or 8″ x 6″, as in the Hope contract, where today a 2″ x 8″ would serve. But the fact that thousands of old half-timber buildings still stand in England today, still serviceable after the passage of three or four centuries, is the best proof of the soundness of their construction. Whatever excess of strength they may have had in the first instance has been more than justified by the years that they have lasted.

The axe was the mediaeval carpenter's tool-of-all-work. With it he felled his trees, and with it he squared them where they lay, to reduce the weight to be transported. With it he dressed them as with a plane, but to a rippled surface texture more interesting and beautiful than any plane work. Saws of several kinds, including the great two-man pit-saw, had been in use from the Middle Ages; but the evidence afforded by the timbers themselves, which seldom show saw-marks even on faces that were entirely concealed, indicates that saws were little used, and that the timbers were usually shaped by axe alone.[3] If saws had been more generally used, it is likely that construction with timbers of lighter scantling would have followed as a result, since with a pit-saw a large tree could without great difficulty be cut into several spars.

---

[2] A mere door-post in the Brewer Street Farmhouse in Surrey measures 16½ by 13 inches, and the post supporting the dragon-beam is out of timber about 36 by 16, set root-end uppermost. The richly-carved corner post of the Abbot's House in Shrewsbury approximates two feet on each side, with a huge spread at the upper end. Perhaps the largest logs of English oak on record are the eight vertical members of the octagonal lantern of Ely Cathedral, collected by Alan de Walsingham in 1322 "after many tedious personal journeys." They measure 3′4″ by 2′8″ in cross-section, by 63 feet long. They are still in place; but now, after 630 years, they are threatened with destruction by the ravages of the death-watch beetle.

[3] Cf. Nathaniel Lloyd, *A History of the English House*, p. 27.

But axe-men in Tudor England despised the saw as "a contemptible innovation fit only for those unskillful in the handling of the nobler instrument,"[4] so the carpenter tended to choose logs that needed merely to be squared, and to use sawn planks only when nothing else would serve.

To fill the spaces between the posts and beams that framed his outside walls, he had something that would meet his needs just as well as planks and was far easier to make: he used plaster or "daub," applied over a trellis of stakes and twigs which served as lath. This then is the essence of half-timber construction: a firm skeleton of squared oak timbers placed vertically and horizontally, framing and supporting the panels of lath and plaster that filled the spaces between. Today's pseudo-Tudor black-and-white exteriors are black-and-white only superficially, and are not true half-timber at all: both the exposed wooden slabs and the plaster infilling are mere veneers imposed upon the structural members. It was not so in Tudor construction. The exposed timbers then were structural working members, as thick as the wall was thick and passing quite through it from outer surface to inner. The plaster was equally functional, filling, to a thickness of six or eight or even ten inches, the areas between the oak balks.

There was a delightful irregularity and home-spun quality in Tudor design and construction. To begin with, the oak faces themselves, squared and dressed with axe and adze rather than with machine-saw and planer, showed the honest marks of the tools that shaped them. The timbers varied in width and straightness, and were used just so. The struts were the slightly curved boughs of trees, selected for their size and shape and used without much trimming, perhaps no more than a flattening on the side to be exposed; the crookeder branches were used for curved braces or decorative elements. Commenting upon this economical use of material, Harrison remarked:

> And such is their husbandrie in dealing with their timber, that the same stuffe which in time past was rejected as crooked, unprofitable, and to no use but the fire, dooth now come in the fronts and best part of the worke. Whereby the common saieng is likewise in these daies verified in our mansion-houses, which earst was said onelie of the timber for ships, 'that no oke can grow so crooked but it falleth out to some use.'

The irregularities inherent in the materials compelled irregularity and

[4] Alex. Beazeley, *Transactions of the Royal Institute of British Architects*, 1882-83, quoted by C. F. Innocent, *The Development of English Building Construction*, p. 97.

improvisation in their use. The varying widths of timber faces and the deviousness of their lines, combined with a certain unconcern in spacing and an engaging casualness and spontaneity on the part of Tudor artisans in all that they did, gave to their work a soft, informal, and gracious presence. Not merely the strength and vigor of the age, but also its unrest and waywardness, are mirrored in the buildings of the Elizabethan era.

Partly because nails were scarce and expensive, they were little used; but even if they had been cheap and plentiful, no amount of simple nailing, with spikes however heavy, would have served to join the bulky timbers together to form a rigid frame. In order to bring his thick balks together in firm joints capable of bearing the thrusts and strains put upon them, the Tudor carpenter employed fitted jointings of a variety and complexity unapproached in today's construction: scarfings, notchings, coggings, dovetailings, housings, halvings, mortises and tenons, joggles, bridles, wedgings, and so on. The carpenter of today may take a short step in the same direction by staggering the ends of the separate pieces that make up his composite timbers; but the Tudor carpenter, working with far heavier single-piece balks, was forced to cut his joinery out of solid oak; and at the corners of the building especially, where three or four or more timbers might come together in a compound joint, he imposed mortises and notchings and dovetailings upon one another with unbelievable complexity.[5]

After the pieces had been snugly fitted together, auger-holes were bored through the assembly to receive round oaken pegs in lieu of nails: pegs which carried no part of the weight or strain, but which merely served to prevent dislodging. The pegs were not driven all the way in, but were left slightly projecting, perhaps as much as an inch or so. This permitted their being driven in still farther if the joints should loosen and need to be drawn more closely together; it also permitted their being withdrawn altogether if the need should arise to dismantle the building and re-use the timbers elsewhere. That need might arise as a result of the declining supply and increasing cost of new lumber, or (as in the case of the Theater) through the expiration of a ground-lease. Re-use of old timber was a practicable possibility because English oak possesses extreme durability; indeed, it im-

[5] The sketches of timber joints on pages 38 and 39 were drawn by the author. They show actual jointings found either in English houses or in early New England houses built in the English tradition. In all instances they are believed to be representative of normal Tudor building construction.

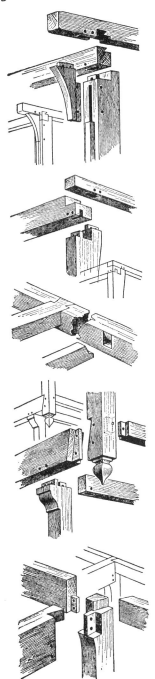

proves and hardens with age. It was not unusual in Tudor times for the same timber to be used over and over again;[6] and this practice increased as the growing shortage of new lumber began to make itself felt.

It is obvious from what has already been said of the irregularities of the timbers themselves and the intricacies of their jointings, that the pieces used in a frame could not be interchangeable. The timbers varied in width, in thickness, in straightness; their jointings varied as any hand-cut joints must do. No two balks, no two joints, can have been precisely alike, and therefore no two could fit equally well into any given position in the frame. Whether on initial assembly or on subsequent re-assembly, it was thus necessary for each piece to be returned to the one relative position which it, and it alone, was shaped to fill; and to make this possible the Tudor builder devised a system of marks which would guide him when the frame came to be assembled, or, as in the case of the Globe, re-assembled.

The marks were incised in one or both of a pair of timbers at their point of juncture. They consisted characteristically of two elements: a Roman numeral, and an arbitrary device grafted onto one of the numeral strokes. Roman numerals were employed because straight lines are easier to incise in wood than the curved lines of Arabic digits; but the system was by no means orthodox. For one thing, the character I coming before a V or an X was not subtracted from it to make 4 or 9, but added to it to make 6 or 11; when the carpenter wrote IIIIXX, for instance, it was precisely as though he were saying "four-and-twenty" instead of

[6] Cf. C. F. Innocent, op. cit., pp. 102, 103.

PLATE 1. The so-called Hoefnagel map, published in Braun and Hogenberg's *Civitates Orbis Terrarum*, Cologne, 1572. In Plates 1 through 13, only a part of the original engraving is reproduced in each instance.

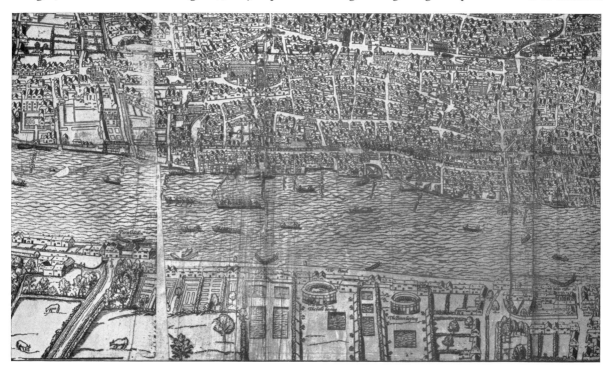

PLATE 2. The so-called Agas map, drawn between 1569 and 1590, and published in 1633.
By permission of the Master and Fellows of Magdalene College, Cambridge.

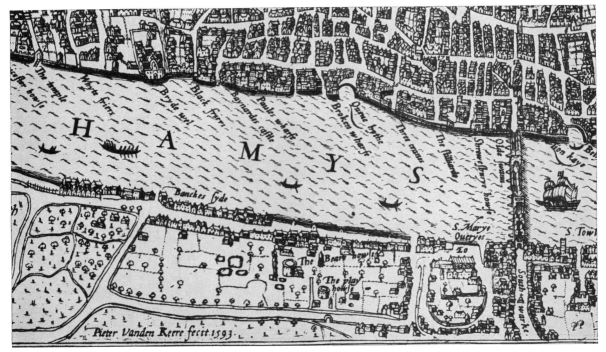

PLATE 3. The first Norden map, published in *Speculum Britanniae*, 1593.

By courtesy of the Birmingham Reference Library.

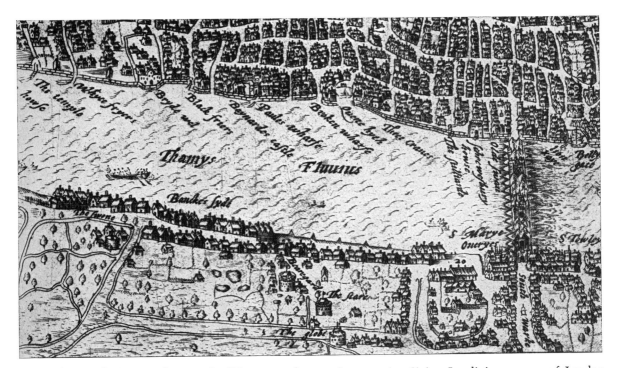

PLATE 4. Norden's revised map of 1600, engraved as an inset to the *Civitas Londini* panorama of London.

By courtesy of the Royal Library, Stockholm.

Swan   *Bear Garden*   *Rose*   *Globe*

PLATE 5. The *Civitas Londini* panorama of 1600, by an unknown engraver.

By courtesy of the Royal Library, Stockholm.

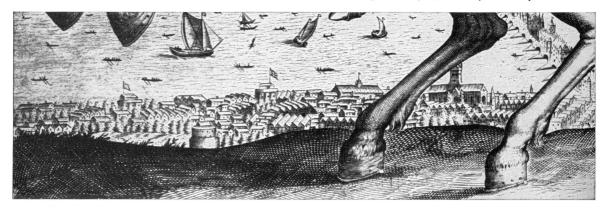

PLATE 6. The Delaram view, engraved as background to an equestrian portrait of James I.

By courtesy of the Royal Library, Windsor Castle.

PLATE 7. A small view by Hondius, engraved as an inset to the map of Britain in John Speed's *Theatre of the Empire of Great Britaine*, 1611.

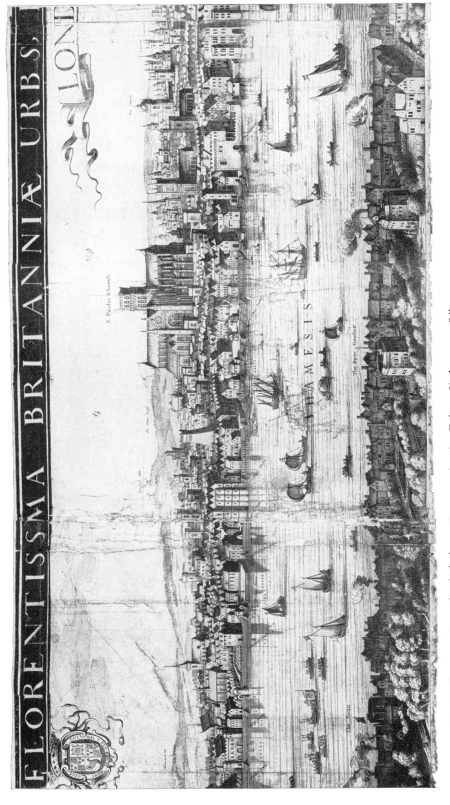

PLATE 8. Visscher's engraving of 1616, from the copy in the Folger Shakespeare Library.

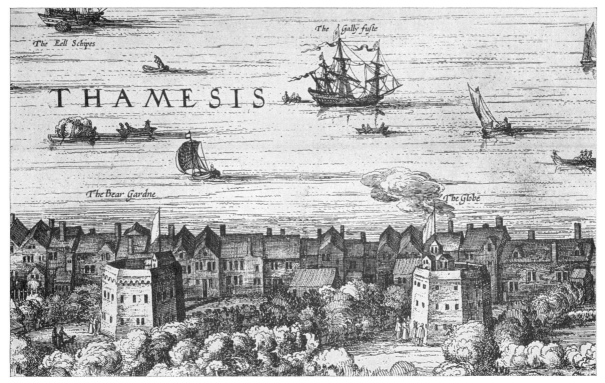

PLATE 9. Visscher's Bear Garden and Globe, from the copy in the British Museum.

PLATE 10. The Merian view, published in Gottfried's *Neuwe Archontologia Cosmica,* Frankfort, 1638.

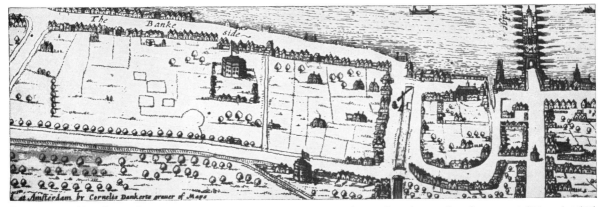

PLATE 11. The finished version of the so-called Ryther map, published in Amsterdam between 1631 and 1656.

PLATE 12. Hollar's sketch of the "West part o[f] Southwarke." The original is in pencil, partly inked over. The portion printed here is reproduced at full scale. *By courtesy of Iolo A. Williams, Esq.*

PLATE 13. Hollar's "Long View," published in Amsterdam in 1647.

PLATES 14 AND 15. Two sketches by Inigo Jones, drawn as alternative designs for a scene in D'Avenant's *Britannia Triumphans*, produced in 1638.

From the Devonshire Collection, Chatsworth; courtesy, the Trustees of the Chatsworth Settlement

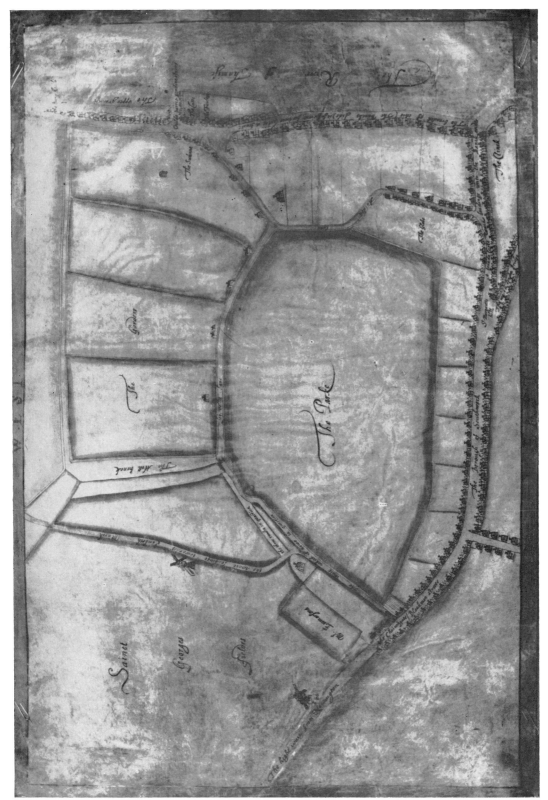

PLATE 16. A map of Southwark, recently discovered in the City Comptroller's Office at Guildhall, and presumed to have been drawn about 1620. North, and the River Thames, are toward the right-hand side of the map.

By courtesy of the Corporation of London.

"twenty-four"; and very likely he was doing just that. For another thing, as a labor-saving device, he often permitted a single stroke to do double duty as a part of two separate numbers; he might write his XV as X/, his XX as X, and his XXX as XX. And to the numeral he usually attached an arbitrary symbol to indicate the surface or section of the building, the wall or part of a wall, to which the numerical sequence applied. The symbol might be a semicircle, a trident or crow's-foot, a spur, a branched twig, a pair of opposed semicircles, or any one of several other devices. Figure 4, on page 41, presents a number of carpenter's marks sketched directly from the timbers themselves, in London, Buckden, Lavenham, Salisbury, Stratford-on-Avon, Shrewsbury, Ludlow, and Chester.[7]

Tudor methods of joinery thus made it necessary, and Tudor carpenter's marks made it possible, for framework timbers, if re-used, to be re-used in their original relationship with one another. It may therefore be assumed that the basic frame of the Globe was piece-for-piece the frame of the Theater, and consequently that their size and shape were the same. If our knowledge of the design of the Theater exceeded our knowledge of the Globe, the point would be an important one; but that is not the case. Little information about the Theater has survived. Its cost (£700, as compared with £360 for the rebuilt Hope and £520 for the great Fortune, handsomest of the later playhouses) proves that it was a large building. During its last years, when other playhouses were available

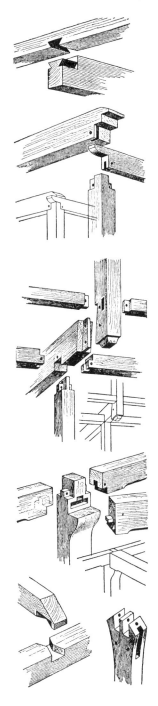

[7] For a more extended discussion of Tudor joinery and carpenter's marks, see my article entitled "Theater into Globe," *Shakespeare Quarterly*, Vol. III No. 2 (April 1952), pp. 113-120.

to serve as a basis for comparison, writers still described it as "vast" or spoke of it as "the great house called the Theater."[8]

The salvaging of the Theater's heavy oak framework undoubtedly enabled the Burbages to effect a saving both in time and in money in the construction of the Globe. The total cost of the Globe is not known; it has been estimated at from £400 to £600. But if the Theater of twenty-two years earlier

Door frame, Ireland's
Mansion, Shrewsbury
(c. 1566)

FIGURE 3.   CARPENTER'S MARKS ON A DOOR-
WAY IN SHREWSBURY

cost £700, the Fortune (which also was built partly from old timber) £520 and the second Globe £1,400, the saving must have been considerable. It was largely to effect these economies that the Burbages dismantled the Theater, in spite of the expiration of the recovery clause which gave them the legal right to do so, and risked the wrath and litigation of the infuriated Giles Alleyn.

Let us suppose that the framework timbers of what used to be the Theater have been brought across the Thames to Bankside. Peter Streete's first task must be to build a foundation. Since, like the Fortune and the Hope, the Globe would stand upon marshy ground, the foundation must rest upon piles; and the use of piles in the Globe's foundation is in fact attested by Ben Jonson's line already quoted: "nothing but the piles / Left." Two concentric octagonal "rings" of brick foundation were needed, the one to support the outer wall, and the other the inner edges of the three galleries (see Scale Drawing X); and it may be supposed that the foundations

[8] Cf. J. Q. Adams, p. 46; *Globe Playhouse*, p. 20.

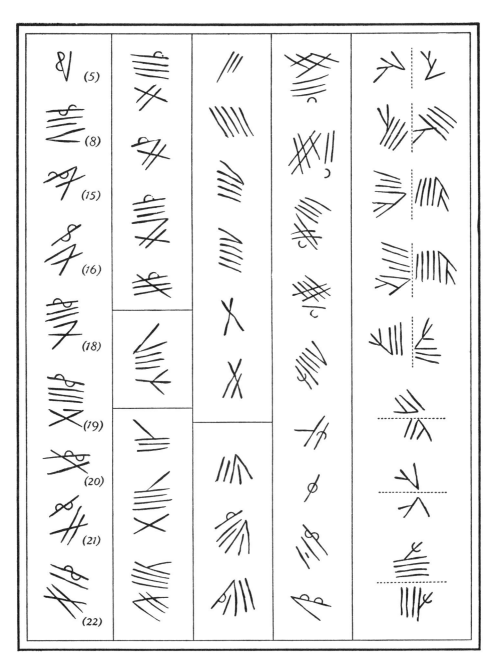

FIGURE 4. TUDOR CARPENTERS' MARKS

All marks are shown in their present relationship to the vertical, as incised in timbers imbedded in the wall. The marks in the right-hand column are paired marks, incised in two timbers at their point of junction, with the crack between them indicated by a dotted line.

were "wrought one foot of assize at the least above the ground" as in the Fortune contract, or "xiii inches" as in the Hope.

Horizontal sills were laid upon the foundation walls, and into them were tenoned the upright posts. The posts at the external corners were perhaps 15″ x 15″ in cross-section at first-story level, and ran up the whole height of the building in one piece.[9] Lighter posts, perhaps 12″ x 12″, were set at the midpoint of each section of the outer frame; and between them and the corner posts were yet smaller ones, referred to as "prick-posts" in the Hope contract, and then still others, each tenoned at its foot to lock into the sill, and at its head to engage the mortises in the wall-plate of the second level of galleries 12 feet above the first. Some indication of the size of the beams used as "breastsummers" and "binding-joists" spanning the gallery bays is given by the specifications for corresponding beams in the Hope; but since the Globe was probably the larger and certainly the more expensive building of the two, the presumption is that its timbers were heavier in scantling throughout.

Almost universally among the timber buildings of the Tudor period, each upper story projected beyond the story below it, the overhanging portion being supported by brackets and by prolongations of the upper-story floor-joists, upon whose projecting ends the sill was laid. In the earlier construction the overhang had often jutted out on all four sides of the building, in which case stout diagonal beams (corrupted to "dragon beams" in common parlance) cut through the floor-joists at an angle and extended beyond the corners, to provide a still securer footing for the upper-story corner posts. In later Tudor building the upper floors were apt to project only at the front. Usually the overhang was as much as eighteen inches or two feet, or sometimes even three, but the Fortune contract provides good reason for believing that in the Globe it did not exceed ten inches. The Globe's builders did wisely in holding it to a minimum, because every additional inch of overhang would demonstrably have tended to impair the view of the stage for playgoers in the rear of the galleries; indeed, the sight-lines to the stage would have been the better for the reverse of an overhang—a set-back—as in today's theatres and stadia. Therefore the builders, while they availed themselves of the structural advantages which the overhang offered, minimized its disadvantages by carrying the upper floors forward as little as possible.

[9] Cf. Joseph Moxon, *Mechanick Exercises, or the Doctrine of Handy-Works* (1678).

Overhangs served more than one useful purpose. They protected the sills and walls from wet, by causing rainwater to drip free of foundations and frame, and so kept it from seeping into joints and rotting them. They reduced the strain on the joists, since the upper wall's weight on their pro-

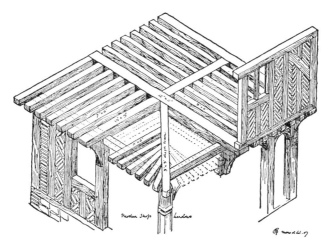

FIGURE 5.   CONSTRUCTION OF AN OVERHANG
Reprinted, by permission, from *Old Cottages and Farm-Houses in Surrey,* by W. Galsworthy Davie and W. Curtis Green.

jecting ends caused them to become internal as well as external brackets. They gained for the frame a certain amount of stiffness in yet another way, by throwing forward the sills into which the uprights of the upper story were tenoned, so that the joints were not weakened too much at any one point by mortises. Further, they reduced the need for long upright timbers.[10]

THE OUTER WALLS

The Tudor artisan fashioned a lattice of interwoven stakes and twigs between the timbers of the external frame, to support the panels of white plaster. The stakes were usually oak poles or riven oak laths, perhaps as thick as a boy's wrist, and set vertically at distances of 12 or 15 or 18 inches apart, with their ends wedged into grooves cut in the upper and lower

[10] Cf. Garner and Stratton, *The Domestic Architecture of England during the Tudor Period,* II, 191; Fred H. Crossley, *Timber Building in England,* p. 117.

horizontal members of the frame.[11] Unpeeled hazel wands were interlaced through and about the stakes in basket fashion. Two daubers, one working on each side of the wall, laid over this lattice a plaster of clay or loam into which chopped straw or hair had been mixed, and over the clay a final skin of lime plaster to give whiteness and to resist weather.

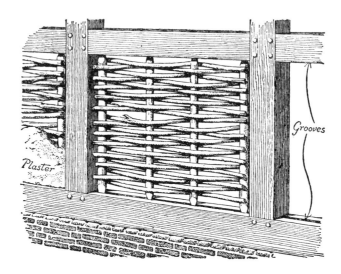

FIGURE 6. WATTLE-AND-DAUB CONSTRUCTION

Originally the surface of the plaster was set well back, half an inch or so, from the faces of the surrounding timbers. Then, in later work, the plaster was laid flush with the timber faces. Finally, either to cover cracks that had developed in shrunken or decayed joints, or merely because it had become fashionable to do so, the timbers themselves were plastered over, with the plaster flush over panel and framing alike. This development, however, did not come until the mid-17th century and later; before then the timbers were always exposed.[12] It is therefore the more remarkable that the Globe should be shown without exposed timbering in all the early engravings. As has

[11] In Shakespeare's Birthplace at Stratford-on-Avon, a certain interior wall has been removed to give better lighting; and on the upper surface of the horizontal beam which still spans the room, the groove is plainly to be seen.
[12] The transitions from recessed panel to flush panel, and finally to the all-over plaster surface, have been mentioned by the late C. F. Innocent and others, who have not, however, given the approximate dates at which the transitions took place. I am therefore

already been mentioned, Visscher pictures his Globe—and all his other build-ings, too, for that matter, whether church or dwelling, palace or hut—as if made of masonry. But every one of the contemporary engravings is, like Visscher's, unreliable in its representation of wall surfaces. Certainly the black-and-white exterior wall was the one most often to be seen in London during Shakespeare's lifetime, and until the Great Fire of 1666; and yet not a single building, out of all the thousands within the range of the several pictorial views, is shown with exposed timbering. For reasons that may readily be understood, the engravers simply elected to ignore all timber patterns: their thousands of houses are for the most part tiny box-like affairs, and black-and-white patterns would merely have confused their outlines; or perhaps the treatment of wall surfaces reflects the fact that many of the views were executed in Holland, where brick and stone, rather than wood, were the usual building materials. Whatever the cause, the timbering has been omitted on all of the buildings within the area of any of the views. Its omission in the case of the Globe therefore ceases to have any significance.

We of today find pleasure in the soft silvery patina of weathered oak and the off-white of plaster mellowed by exposure to sun and rain. But not so the householder of Elizabethan times: he preferred an exterior with magpie contrasts of black and white. Sir Thomas Kytson's clerk entered the follow-ing item in his household accounts for August–September, 1574:

> For plastering and whitening the fore front of my Mr. his house in Coleman Street and the courte, with the blackening of the timber work, xlijs. vjd.[13]

ROOFS

The first Globe had a roof of thatch—an economy which, it will be remembered, led to its total loss by fire on the afternoon of June 29, 1613. Neither the Fortune nor the Hope contract gives any indication of the shape of a playhouse roof, and the early engravings show only the outer slopes.

---

fortunate in being able to quote A. E. Richardson, Professor of Architecture in the Royal Academy and a member of H. M. Historical Monuments Commission, who, in response to an inquiry, wrote to me as follows:

> . . . The faces of the timber work were exposed in Elizabethan times. The practice of covering them came in the 17th Century and later. . . . The Shakesperian Globe Playhouse was finished with plasterwork flushed to the framing.

[13] Quoted by Nathaniel Lloyd, *A History of the English House*, p. 80.

The safest assumption is that the roof of the Globe followed the design usual for its period, in having a centered ridge from which slopes descended on each side to the eaves. Only the galleries, of course, were roofed; the line of the ridge presumably ran continuously over the eight sections of the octagon, centered over and parallel to each of them in turn. A roof of thatch needed to be a steep roof: it was pitched at an angle of about 48 degrees in the days of Elizabeth, and as steeply as 60 degrees in houses of earlier date.[14] Rye straw was used by preference in thatching, as being the longest and strongest of the grasses. It was sewn to the rafters with staples made of bent hazel wands, which for the most part were concealed by overlying layers of straw; at the eaves, the verges, and the ridges, however, where the thatch was most likely to be torn away by wind, the wands or "ledgers" were fastened on top of the thatch, usually in diamond-fashion or some other decorative pattern. The thatch was laid a foot or more thick; at the eaves it projected about 18 inches, and was trimmed clean at a right-angle to the surface of the wall.

The smaller secondary roofs of the Globe—those which covered the huts, the bay windows, and the rear stairwell—were perhaps tiled. Their relatively small roof areas, and particularly the many gables and valleys of the huts, called for tiles rather than thatching. The flat roofs over the stage-cover and the entrance door would need yet a third type of roof covering, sheet lead. Lead was used on very steep surfaces, such as spires, and on very flat surfaces, such as those just mentioned, on which thatch and tiles would have been equally unserviceable. The conjectural use of lead on the stage-cover receives some slight confirmation from the terms of the Fortune and Hope contracts, both of which specify rain-water gutters. A lead roof over the stage would need a gutter, but none would be needed by a roof of thatch, for thatch absorbs much of the rain that falls on it during a light shower; and on really wet days, of course, no performances would have been given. The Fortune contract calls for "a sufficient gutter of lead to carry and convey the water from the covering of the said stage to fall backwards." Similar gutters were specified for the Hope, and may be presumed to have been provided at the Globe as well. They are indicated in Scale Drawings IX and XIII as carrying the rain-water from the stage-cover to the rear of the building.

[14] The roofs on the model and in the scale drawings are pitched at 50 degrees.

CHAPTER V

THE AUDITORIUM

THERE are in existence four contemporary drawings of 16th- and 17th-century English stages. Like the maps or views discussed in Chapter II, they are baffling witnesses. They contradict each other on important details; their dates, authorship, and reliability are doubtful; and with respect to three out of the four drawings, there is question not merely as to the specific playing-place, but even the type of playing-place, which the drawings purport to represent. They are nevertheless indispensable as being the only pictorial representations that survive. They are reproduced in this book as Plates 17 to 20 inclusive.

THE DE WITT SKETCH OF THE SWAN

The so-called DeWitt sketch of the Swan Playhouse is by all odds the most important of the four drawings. It is not merely the most comprehensive and the most fully elaborated of the four, but it is the only contemporary drawing which is known to be intended as a representation of the interior of an Elizabethan public playhouse.

The sketch was made not by Johannes DeWitt himself, but by his friend Arend van Buchell. DeWitt was a Dutchman, a priest of St. Mary's in Utrecht, who visited England, probably in 1596, and saw a play at the Swan. It is generally assumed that he wrote an account of his visit and to it attached a sketch of the Swan's interior, and that van Buchell copied the drawing and transcribed DeWitt's comments upon it, in his own common-place book. The documents that survive are van Buchell's copies, rather than DeWitt's originals. They were discovered in 1888 in the University Library at Utrecht, by the German critic Karl Gaedertz.

Some details of the sketch immediately challenge credulity. For one thing, the platform is supported by formless bulks which resemble nothing that any carpenter ever built in any period or place. For another, the forward corners of the platform lack any support whatsoever; and for a third, the stage posts rising from the platform seem needlessly massive for the weight they carry. Other details of the drawing are open to suspicion, as for instance the absence of any curtained aperture between the stage doors, and of any forward-reaching stage-cover from which celestial descents could be made. Except for the three items specified, however, no details of the DeWitt drawing are inherently improbable.

Students of the Elizabethan theatre are in doubt and disagreement as to the degree of credence that should be granted to the DeWitt sketch. All agree that it is crude and inexact. Professor John Dover Wilson calls it "one Dutchman's copy of another Dutchman's sketch of what he remembered about the interior of the Swan Theatre after a single visit."[1] Dr. Adams says that "it abounds in so many contradictions, omissions, and obvious errors that no reliance can be placed upon any detail unless that detail is sustained by evidence from other sources."[2] Sir Edmund K. Chambers, on the other hand, while warning against "the hazardous interpretation of bad draughtsmanship," nevertheless regards the sketch as "the inevitable basis of any comprehensive account of the main structural features of a playhouse";[3] and Mr. Hodges says that "if evidence is to have any value at all we are not at liberty to differ from it [the drawing] very widely."[4]

The superstructure shown in the DeWitt sketch tallies closely with the Swan's hut as shown in the Visscher engraving; and since the history of the DeWitt drawing makes it extremely improbable that Visscher can ever have seen it and been influenced by it, it may be supposed that in this detail both drawings are correct.

THE *Roxana* AND *Messallina* VIGNETTES

The *Roxana* and *Messallina* vignettes are small elements in two elaborate title-page designs. Each occupies a compartment at the foot of the page, in the center, and each covers an area only a trifle larger than an ordinary postage-stamp: one and one-quarter inches high by seven-eighths of an inch wide in the case of *Roxana*, and one and three-sixteenths inches high by one inch wide in the case of *Messallina*. The *Roxana* title-page is the earlier of the two by eight years, and in all of its elements is superior in design and draftsmanship to the unskilled *Messallina* engraving.

[1] *Shakespeare Survey* 1 (1948), p. 21.
[2] *Globe Playhouse*, p. 49.
[3] *The Elizabethan Stage*, II, 540, 527.
[4] *The Globe Restored*, p. 26.

The tragedy of *Roxana* was written in Latin by William Alabaster. It was performed at Trinity College, Cambridge, in 1592 or thereabouts, and was published in 1632. It was never performed in a London public playhouse. The presumption would be, therefore, that the *Roxana* vignette pictures an academic stage rather than a public, but one cannot be sure that the publisher, when he printed the play forty years after its production, was so scrupulous as to insist that the engraver should picture a university stage in his decorative vignette. The artist may have drawn a more accessible stage nearer home.

The Tragedy of Messallina was written in 1637 by Nathanael Richards, acted by the Revels Company at Salisbury Court, and published in 1640. The little engraving might therefore be accepted as representing the Salisbury Court stage, were it not for the fact that it follows the *Roxana* drawing so closely, in its delineation of the platform, as to exclude any supposition other than that the engraver merely copied the *Roxana* vignette. In both engravings the degree of taper on the stage is substantially the same; in both the sides of the platform are cropped at the same points by the side borders; in both, plain posts take the place of turned balusters at the stage's forward corners. The supposition that the *Messallina* engraver copied the *Roxana* title-page is strengthened by a comparison of the two title-pages in their entireties, for in both the arrangement of elements is suspiciously similar. In neither case, therefore, do we know what sort of stage—whether public, private, or academic—the engravings represent; but in both cases the lack of any lighting apparatus, if it be granted full importance, seems to point to an outdoor stage.

The Wits ENGRAVING

The frontispiece to *The Wits, or Sport upon Sport*, first published in 1672, shows an improvised stage of the sort used in the performance of Drolls during the period when the public playhouses were closed and plays forbidden by the Puritans. Drolls were humorous one-act episodes, sometimes abstracted from longer plays (witness "Sᵣ I Falstafe" and "Hostes" in *The Wits* drawing), and acted by strolling players on makeshift stages. In publishing his collection of Drolls under the title of *The Wits*, Francis Kirkman said that the scenes had been played "in London at Bartholomew Faire, in the Country at other Faires. In Halls and Taverns. On several

Mountebancks Stages, at Charing-Cross, Lincoln-Inn-Fields, and other places. By several Stroleing Players, Fools, and Fidlers, and the Mounte-bancks Zanies."[5] The stage pictured in Kirkman's frontispiece therefore is intended to bear no relationship to the stage of a public playhouse. The presence of chandeliers and footlights suggests a stage in some sort of room.

FIGURE 7.   A SIGN-BOARD FOR THE GLOBE

The design is, of course, wholly conjectural. The figure of Hercules was copied from a Flemish tapestry of about 1550, and the Winds from contemporary maps.

For lack of any other pictorial material, the four drawings must inevitably be cited in connection with many details of the Globe's interior design. With the foregoing paragraphs as an aid to the evaluation of the evidence which they present, we turn now to a consideration of the auditorium at the Globe.

THE ENTRANCE DOOR

Londoners who were inclined toward playgoing could look across the Thames to see whether a flag were fluttering at the top of the Globe's flagpole; if so, they knew that a play would be presented that afternoon. They crossed the river by foot or by horse over London Bridge, or by boat to the Bankside water-stairs, and approached the playhouse by way of Maid Lane. A little bridge over the drainage-ditch admitted them to the Globe property. The main entrance doorway faced them as they approached from the north.

Probably a sign-board was suspended over the entrance door. No contemporary allusion clearly points to a sign hanging before the door of the Globe, but the Rose, the Swan, and the rebuilt Fortune are known to have had signs prominently displayed before them, and the Globe may be supposed to have followed the custom that was usual both for the playhouses and for the shops of the time. On the basis of notes made by William

[5] From the title-page of Part II of *The Wits*, published in 1673, as quoted by Victor E. Albright, *The Shakesperian Stage*, p. 40.

Oldys (1696-1761), Malone said that the Globe's sign bore "a figure of Hercules supporting the Globe, under which was written *Totus mundus agit histrionem.*"

As each playgoer passed through the entrance door, he dropped a penny (or two pennies if the day's play happened to be a new one) into a box held by an attendant called the doorkeeper or gatherer. To make the door-keeper's task the easier, the doorway was probably narrow enough to force the playgoers to enter in single file; and in fact its narrowness is attested by John Chamberlain, in a letter to Sir Ralph Winwood describing the burning of the Globe, when he wrote that "it was a great marvaile and fair grace of God, that the people had so little harm, having but two narrow doors to get out." (The second door, presumably, was the rear door which gave access to the tiring-house.) But no single-file entrance door would take care of the home-going crowds at the play's end, for although playgoers might arrive in ones or twos before the play began, they would depart in a crowd when it was over; and in fact we know that the Globe's main doorway, narrow though Chamberlain said it was, was capable of discharging perhaps two thousand persons under what must have been near-panic conditions. Perhaps the explanation is that the playhouse had a fairly wide door which could be thrown open when the play was over, but which was kept closed before the play began, and that through it was cut a small wicket-door, as was done so often in Tudor times, to which the passage of playgoers was restricted upon their entering. Such a main entrance door is shown in Plate 29 and Scale Drawing V.

THE YARD

Once the playgoer had paid his general-admission fee of one penny at the door, he could, if he chose, go straight forward through the corridor leading to the benchless and roofless playhouse yard. There he would have to pay no additional fee, but he would of course have to stand, along with some 600 other "groundlings," throughout the performance. As he entered the yard the platform stage lay before him, backed by the ornate façade of the tiring-house. Behind him and on both sides rose the sturdy carved oak columns and beams of the spectator galleries which occupied three-quarters of the octagonal frame. All was as splendid as Tudor artisanship and ingenuity could make it: of that we may be sure, for the playhouses of the time were praised or excoriated (depending upon the critic's point of view) for their gorgeousness. Contemporary documents speak of "the sumptuous theatre houses," "the beauty of the houses and the stages," "our stately stage," and so on. DeWitt described the wooden columns of the Swan in 1595 as being "painted in such excellent imitation of marble that it is able to deceive even the most cunning," and William Harrison judged it to be "an evident token of a wicked time when players wax so rich that they can build such houses." The interior of the Globe, "the glory of the Bank," was undoubtedly enriched with wood-carving and color and curtains of tapestry.

Virtually nothing has been told by contemporary writers about the yard itself. No known document says how high the platform stood above the yard's floor; none says whether the floor was level, or whether it sloped downward from its edges toward its center; none says whether it had a hard pavement of brick or stone or merely a surface of beaten earth. All the questions can however be answered with some degree of confidence. Evidence has already been cited to indicate that the yard was octagonal in shape and that it measured 58 feet across, with each of its sides 24 feet long. There is good reason to believe further that it was excavated so that its floor sloped gently downward from rear and sides toward the platform's edge; for while the floors of the platform and of the first gallery were almost certainly on the same level, and while the surface of the yard was probably only some two and a half feet lower than the gallery floor at the yard's outer edges, it seems to have been four or five feet lower than the platform floor at the yard's center. The demonstration lies in these facts:

The floor of the first gallery, and therefore of the platform also, can hardly have been much more than 30 inches high with relation to the outside ground level. This figure is based upon the assumption that the Globe's foundation walls were (as in the Fortune and Hope contracts) 12 or 13 inches high above the ground, that the sills laid upon them were perhaps 15 inches in cross-section, and that upon the sills were laid floor-boards three inches thick.[6]

At its forward edge, however, the floor of the platform seems to have been at least four feet, and perhaps five, above the surface of the yard. This

[6] Cf. footnote 1, page 34. The Fortune contract specifies flooring of "good and sufficient new deal boards of the whole thickness where need shall be," and therefore the full three-inch thickness may be supposed to have been intended.

is evidenced by the early drawings of English stages, three of which show human figures and thus convey a hint of dimensions. The height of the stage in the Swan drawing (Plate 17) seems to be about two-thirds the height of the striding actor. In the *Roxana* drawing (Plate 18) it would appear (making allowance for the high point of view) that the low wooden railing is about on a level with the spectators' eyes. In the somewhat later *Wits* drawing (Plate 20) the stage would seem to be about shoulder height; and in the Carolinian Cockpit-in-Court (Plate 22) the architect seems, if one may judge by scale, to have prescribed a stage four and a half feet above the floor of the pit. If, therefore, the Globe conformed to the usual practice in having its platform even as little as four feet above the level of the yard, it follows that the yard itself must have been excavated eighteen inches or more at the platform's edge.

But from center the surface seems to have sloped upward as it approached the surrounding galleries, and to have reached the normal ground level at its outer edges. This is indicated by a further specification in the Fortune contract, which provided not only for "the lower story of the said frame withinside" to be "paled in below with good strong and sufficient new oaken boards," but "to be also laid over and fenced with strong iron pikes." The pikes were presumably necessary to keep groundlings from climbing from the pit into the more expensive and desirable gallery accommodations, and the implication is that without them the paling would have afforded an insufficient barrier. But if the yard had been excavated everywhere to a depth of eighteen inches or more, at gallery-edge as well as at platform-edge, the total height of the palings from yard floor to cap-rail would have exceeded six and a half feet, which of itself would have sufficed to keep the groundlings in their place without the need for pikes. The addition of the pikes therefore suggests that the palings were actually only five or five and a half feet high—30 inches from yard surface to gallery-floor level, and 32 or 36 more from gallery floor to cap-rail—and thus that the outer edges of the yard were level with the ground outside the playhouse.

A slope of a mere 18 or 19 inches in 29 feet would hardly be perceptible underfoot. It would however materially improve the view of the stage for spectators in the more distant parts of the yard.[7]

[7] The yard in the model and in the scale drawings has been excavated to a depth of 18 inches at center. See Scale Drawings X-XIII, XV.

The surface of the Globe's yard was doubtless paved, for otherwise the ground would in wet weather have been churned into an ankle-deep mud by the feet of the groundlings. Whether the pavement was of brick or stone one cannot be sure, but in the absence of any direct evidence some preference must be given to brick, merely because there is reason to believe that brick was used in paving the yard of the Fortune. Henslowe bought 9,000 bricks for the Fortune on May 30, 1600, by which time the Fortune's foundation walls must already have been completed; and since it is unlikely that bricks were needed for chimneys or other structures above ground level, it may be supposed that they were used for the paving of the yard.[8]

GALLERY ENTRANCES AND STAIRS

The general-admission fee of one penny, as has already been said, entitled the playgoer to nothing more than standing room in the yard; a further fee or fees must be paid by the more wealthy or prodigal patron who sought a seat or a standing in one of the galleries. From him a second penny was collected by a gatherer stationed in the vestibule, at the foot of the stairs which led up to all the gallery sections of the auditorium. Having paid it, the playgoer had the choice of mounting without additional charge to the relatively undesirable third gallery, or of finding a place in one of the two lower galleries upon payment of yet a third fee. The pennies gathered at the main door went to the company of actors; those collected for admission to the galleries were divided equally between the actors and the housekeepers who owned the building.

There is reason to believe that the gallery stairs were placed at the back of the auditorium near the main entrance, so that playgoers could find their way easily and so that the disturbance caused by latecomers would be held to a minimum. Further, they were constructed outside the frame of the building, as was a common practice in those days. Both the Fortune contract

[8] A brick pavement for the Globe is indicated in Scale Drawing I. The pattern is, of course, purely conjectural, but based upon the supposition that the Tudor artisan, with his restless inventiveness, would not have been content to lay his bricks in a simple and obvious pattern if he could find an intricate and subtle one. The pattern used in the model and shown in Scale Drawing I has gores radiating from center to each of the eight points of the octagon, with a barely-perceptible eight-pointed star worked into it as a subsidiary pattern. Within each gore the general pattern is the herring-bone, a pattern as familiar in Elizabethan times as it is today. The prescribed size of the Elizabethan brick was 9 x 4½ x 2¼ inches.

and the Hope provide for external staircases. The Fortune contract is the less explicit of the two, but its specification of a roofing material for the stairways clearly indicates that they needed roofs of their own and therefore that they stood outside the frame. With respect to the staircases the Fortune contract reads:

> With suchlike stairs, conveyances, and divisions, without and within, as are made and contrived in and to the late erected playhouse . . . called the Globe . . . and the said . . . staircases to be covered with tile . . . and . . . to be sufficiently enclosed without with lime, lath and hair.

The Hope contract is explicit both with respect to the number of the stairways and their placement outside the building:

> Build two staircases without and adjoining to the said playhouse in such convenient places as shall be most fit and convenient for the same to stand upon, and of such largeness and height as the staircases of . . . the Swan now are or be.

Both economy of space and the convenience of playgoers demanded that the entrance door, the vestibule, the passageways to the stairs, and the entrances to the first gallery, should be one closely related unit. If, as seems probable, the entrance door and vestibule of the Globe were centered on the north side, there would be room enough left on each side of the door for the four or five steps up to first-gallery floor-level and for a doorway leading from stair-landing to gallery, but not enough room in addition to those elements for a flight of stairs leading to the second gallery twelve feet above. In an octagonal building, therefore, the nearest "fit and convenient" place for the outside stairs would be just beyond the first corner of the frame, against the flat wall beginning at that point (Scale Drawings I and V). Stairs so placed on the north-west and north-east exposures would naturally not be shown in the Visscher or any other of the earlier engravings of the Bankside, since in all such engravings the playhouses were viewed from the south; precisely such roofed and enclosed external staircases are however pictured in Hollar's "Long View" of 1647 and even more clearly in his preliminary sketch (Plates 12 and 13), jutting out from the wall of each building toward the north-east, and, from the wall of the building misnamed the Bear-baiting House, toward the north-west also. Hollar's staircases exactly bear out the terms of the building contracts; for the second Globe at least, they also confirm the conjectured location of the external stairs with relation to the front entrance.

We may further assume that the stairs were designed in two straight flights, one above the other, each extending from one level to the next. Any other type of staircase, whether a spiral stair or a single long flight from the lowest gallery to the highest, would clearly be less advantageous. The spiral stair would be more costly, more difficult to build, and treacherous for departing crowds; the single straight flight would be weaker and would need twice as wide a stairwell. But if, as we assume, the Globe's gallery stairs were designed in two one-story flights, then an enclosed passageway inside the frame would be required on the second level to connect one flight with the next, so that spectators bound for the third gallery could continue on their upward way without having to pass the second-gallery gatherers, and so that they could at the same time be prevented from invading the second gallery without paying the supplementary fee. Such a passageway is shown in Scale Drawing II.

On this assumption, entrance to the first gallery would be by either of two doors, both of them in the northern section of the frame; to the second and third galleries, by two doors each, in the north-east and north-west sections.

But the supposition that the galleries were entered from the rear has not been accepted by all students of the Elizabethan theatre. Some hold that entrance to the galleries was by way of the yard. They base their theory primarily upon the DeWitt sketch of the Swan's interior, which on each side of the yard shows a flight of steps (labelled "ingressus" on the left-hand side) apparently leading up from yard to first-gallery level; and to the evidence of the DeWitt drawing they add that of a passage from Stephen Gosson's *Plays Confuted in five Actions,* 1582:

> In the playhouses at London, it is the fashion of youthes to go first into the yarde, and to carry their eye through every gallery, then like unto ravens where they spye carion thither they flye, and presse as nere to ye fairest as they can.

As for Gosson, it should perhaps be noted that his sentence can be interpreted as making prior entrance to the yard a matter of fashion rather than of necessity, and that it does not in any case exclude the idea that flight to the galleries was made by way of stairs at the rear of the auditorium. But that leaves us still with the "ingressus" stairs in the Swan sketch.

The more one studies the problem—even without reference to evidence pointing toward other means of access, such as the clear indications of external staircases in the Fortune and Hope contracts and the Hollar view— the more probable it seems that the DeWitt stairs did not as a matter of fact provide a means of entrance to the galleries. Let us suppose for a moment that they did; what then must be the result? All playgoers, instead of being separated into divergent streams as soon as they entered the building, must together flock to the yard. The gallery patron must elbow his way through the unruly groundlings, to their discomfort and his own. If he sought one of the coveted gallery positions near the stage and therefore near the stairs, he and his fellows would block the entrance of galleryites who arrived later. If on the other hand he wished a seat in the rear of the auditorium so that he could view the stage from the front, he must double back through one of the galleries toward the point at which he entered the building. And always the stairs would offer a standing invitation to groundlings to invade the galleries. Dr. Adams summarizes the arguments thus:

> In short, with gallery entrances placed as DeWitt indicates, the groundlings either would have been forced to wait until the last gallery patron had passed through the yard before taking their final places—a supposition which, to one who knows something of the temper of the groundlings, is little short of fantastic; or the gallery patrons would have been put to no little trouble and delay in reaching their places. Such a system, the reverse of all that a modicum of experience and common sense prescribes in planning the entrances and exits of any auditorium, would at all times operate clumsily. When the yard was filled with groundlings coming early to a popular play, it would not work at all.[9]

Professor R. C. Bald has a different explanation for the DeWitt steps. He interprets them, not as leading up into the lowest gallery, but as leading under it to a passageway; not as giving access to the upper levels, but as being entrances to the yard, as the label "ingressus" would seem to imply. He relates the two DeWitt stairs to the two external staircases in the contracts and in the Hollar engraving, and associates one internal stair and one external staircase with each of two main entrance doors. As he sees it, two doors, rather than merely one, gave admittance to the playhouse, each of

[9] *Globe Playhouse*, p. 50.

them in or near the foot of an outside stairwell, and each with its pay-box. At one side of each door, stairs rose to the galleries; at the other side, a passageway led straight forward, under the lowest gallery, to the "ingressus," and then down a few steps to the excavated floor of the yard.[10] Professor Bald's attractive theory avoids all the difficulties which discredit the alternative conjecture. In providing two entrance doorways instead of one, however, he runs counter to Chamberlain's statement that the Globe had "but two narrow doors to get out" (for it must still be supposed that there was a door at the tiring-house end of the playhouse), and other references cited by Dr. Adams (*Globe Playhouse,* p. 34), which imply a single entrance door and doorkeeper.

Still a third possibility remains: that the DeWitt stairs, if indeed they were normal features of Elizabethan playhouses, were intended for the use of actors and playhouse attendants rather than of spectators, and could be barred off during the hours of a performance. Such a point of entrance, it would seem, would be a great convenience to the theatre staff in getting to the yard and entrance door, and would also be of use to actors in returning from yard to tiring-house after those rare scenes in which the yard was used as an area of dramatic action.

SEATS AND STANDING ROOM

From the early days of Burbage's Theater, benches were provided in the galleries of Elizabethan playhouses for some part of the audience; but then and for many years thereafter, probably more gallery patrons stood than sat as they watched the play. The proportion of seated spectators undoubtedly increased from year to year, but at the end of the century standing was still not unusual. Thomas Platter mentions standing at the Globe in the autumn of 1599. "There are," he writes, "separate galleries, and there one stands more comfortably and moreover can sit . . . ." It may be assumed that the benches were arranged in tiers near the forward edges of the galleries. Spectators who came early took the benches as long as any were available; later arrivals stood at the rear and peered over the heads of those in front.

Both the Fortune and the Hope contracts mention seats, but in both instances the references are vague. At the Fortune there were to be

---

[10] "The Entrance to the Elizabethan Theater," *Shakespeare Quarterly,* Vol. III No. 1 (January, 1952), pp. 17-20.

necessary seats to be placed and set as well in those rooms [i.e., the gentlemen's rooms and the two-penny rooms] as throughout all the rest of the
galleries of the said house.

The Hope contract merely alludes to benches and seats without necessarily
implying their use in the playhouse. No known contemporary document
gives the number of rows of seats in the gallery of any Elizabethan public
playhouse, but it can perhaps be estimated with some confidence. In modern
theatres and outdoor grandstands, the minimum front-to-back allowance
for a row of seats is 30 inches; three rows then occupy a depth of $7\frac{1}{2}$ feet,
and four rows a depth of 10. If we assume that the same allowances applied
in Shakespeare's time, and further assume that the depth of the lowest
gallery in the Globe was $12\frac{1}{2}$ feet, then three rows of benches would leave
a space 5 feet deep for standing room, whereas four rows would leave only
$2\frac{1}{2}$ feet between the rear bench and the outer wall. It therefore seems
probable that the Globe had three rows of benches, and no more, in each
of its galleries; and this supposition receives some confirmation from the
Swan sketch, which seems to show a like number of rows. Necessarily, the
benches were placed upon rising tiers or "degrees" in the gallery flooring.

There were no reserved seats in the modern meaning of the term; by and
large, it was a case of first come first served, as in today's motion-picture
theatres. Even so, it was probably possible for a gentleman to reserve seats
for himself and his guests by sending servants to the playhouse early, to hold
the seats until their masters arrived.

THE GALLERY SUBDIVISIONS

The Fortune contract presumably reflects the Globe in its specifications
of the types of accommodation to be provided in the galleries, and of the
interior finish to be given to the rooms of higher price. Its specifications
call for

> four convenient divisions for gentlemen's rooms and other sufficient and
> convenient divisions for two-penny rooms with necessary seats to be
> placed and set as well in those rooms as throughout all the rest of the
> galleries of the said house . . . the gentlemen's rooms and two-penny
> rooms to be ceiled with lath, lime, and hair . . . the said Peter Streete shall
> not be charged with any manner of painting in or about the said frame
> house or stage or any part thereof nor rendering [i.e., plastering] the
> walls within nor ceiling any more or other rooms than the gentlemen's
> rooms, two-penny rooms and stage before remembered.

With respect to gallery accommodations the Hope contract provides merely that the builder

> shall also make two boxes in the lowermost story fit and decent for gentle-men to sit in, and shall make the partitions between the rooms as they are at the said playhouse called the Swan.

On the evidence of these and other contemporary documents, it seems clear that Elizabethan playhouses made available three types of accommodations in their galleries:

(1) For the wealthy or titled few, the more desirable accommodations variously known as gentlemen's rooms, lords' rooms, orchestra, boxes, and twelve-penny rooms;

(2) For theatre-goers of average means, the two-penny rooms of the Fortune contract;

(3) For the poorer patrons, the less desirable accommodations sometimes called penny galleries, sometimes two-penny galleries, or, as in the Fortune con-tract, merely "the rest of the galleries."

Each of the three types will be considered separately.

THE GENTLEMEN'S ROOMS

At the Fortune there were to be "four convenient divisions for gentlemen's rooms." The contract's very silence as to their size and their location perhaps implies that in these respects, as in so many others, the Fortune was closely modeled upon the Globe. The Hope contract throws a little light upon the subject of location by stipulating that Katherens shall make "two boxes in the lowermost story . . . and shall make the partitions between the rooms as they are at the said playhouse called the Swan." The reference to the Swan is in this instance especially fortunate, for the DeWitt sketch (Plate 17) shows precisely where "in the lowermost story" of the Swan the two boxes were situated. The key to the answer is the word "orchestra," written across the low wall of palings just to the left of the tiring-house, and implying a similar designation to the right; for "orchestra" in the then current terminology meant a place near the stage reserved for the nobility,[11] just

---

[11] Thomas Heywood defined "orchestra" in 1624 as "a place in the Theatre onely for the Nobilitie"; and Cotgrave's *Dictionary* of 1611 defined "orchestre" as "the senators' or noblemen's places in a theatre, between the stage and the common seats." Both definitions are cited by Dr. Adams, *Globe Playhouse*, p. 71.

such a place as Dekker had in mind when, in his *Gull's Hornbook*, he mentioned the presence of lords in "the twelve-penny room next the stage."

The Hope, smaller than the Globe and the Fortune and frequented by fewer well-to-do patrons, needed only two boxes; the Fortune, however, needed four, and so presumably did the Globe. It may confidently be assumed that two of the Globe's four gentlemen's rooms were situated, like the two in the Hope and the Swan, in the bays immediately adjoining the tiring-house in the lowermost story (Scale Drawing I). The probability is that the second pair occupied the corresponding bays in the middle gallery (Scale Drawing II). This second-level placement seems to be indicated by the antecedents which led up to the provision of special rooms for the gentry and nobility.

In the early days of the Theater and the Curtain, a few spectators of superior wealth or rank were permitted to enter by the stage door and to view the performance from the second level of the tiring-house. In spite of the fact that they were to the rear of the stage, they could still see well enough, for the acting was "in the round" rather than addressed forward as in modern theatres; besides, they could come and go as they liked, and could avoid all contact with the commonalty. By 1590, however, the rising popularity of the historical play increasingly demanded that actors should appear on the walls of fortified castles or towns, and therefore increasingly demanded that the second level of the tiring-house be reserved for that use; and the house-keepers were faced with the alternatives of providing new accommodations for the gallants or foregoing a source of profit. By 1596 (as the DeWitt sketch suggests) lower boxes had already been created; and when more boxes were needed, it was entirely natural that they should be placed on the second level, where the nobility had sat from the beginning.

From the point of view of the Elizabethan gallant, the gentlemen's rooms had one great advantage in addition to their proximity to the stage: they were accessible from the tiring-house. There was no need for him to elbow his way through groundlings and commoners in vestibule and gallery. Instead, he entered the playhouse by the stage door at the rear, hobnobbed with the players, and proceeded through the tiring-house to the front of the outer stage, to show off his finery and to search for acquaintances either there or in the boxes. In some playhouses he could, if he chose, remain on the stage, seated on a stool or bench or on rushes strewn on the floor; but if his survey led him to prefer a seat in one of the gentlemen's rooms, he turned back into the tiring-house and found his way to a box on lower or middle level.

Evidence as to the cost of a seat in a gentlemen's room is neither clear nor consistent; but the probability is, as intimated by Dekker in his reference to a twelve-penny room, that it was a shilling except on the occasion of a new play.

TWO-PENNY ROOMS AND THE TWO-PENNY GALLERY

The contemporary references to the gallery subdivisions are confused and confusing. The Fortune contract, it will be remembered, distinguished between three types, and only three, of gallery accommodations: the gentlemen's rooms, the two-penny rooms, and "the rest of the galleries." Other writings of the period speak of the gentlemen's rooms under various names, and of two-penny rooms (in the plural), the two-penny room (in the singular), the two-penny gallery, and the penny gallery. Nothing exists which says precisely what the several terms meant, where the rooms and galleries were located, nor how large they were. It is nevertheless possible to reconstruct the gallery subdivisions with some degree of confidence.

In the first place, the Elizabethan word "room," as applying to a section of a playhouse gallery, seems to have carried no connotation of size or enclosure; it denoted merely a gallery subdivision, large or small. Further, a "room" seems to have been differentiated from a "gallery" by the fact that entrance to a room entailed payment of a room fee in addition to the fees previously paid at the entrance door and at the foot of the gallery stairs, whereas entrance to a gallery involved no supplementary payment. Even so, however, some of the contemporary writers must be taxed with inconsistency; for in using the phrase "two-penny room" they must be supposed to have recognized the room supplement alone, ignoring the previous payments which brought the total cost of admission to fourpence, while on the contrary in using the phrase "two-penny gallery," they had in mind the whole cost, there being no gallery supplement.

The Fortune contract makes it clear that, next after the gentlemen's rooms, the two-penny rooms were the best accommodations in the playhouse. Like the gentlemen's rooms, they had an interior finish of plaster; the rest of the galleries could go unceiled. They were designed for playgoers of average means, those who could not afford a seat in a box but who yet could pay for something better than standing room in the yard or a place in the topmost gallery; and since at the Globe such playgoers undoubtedly comprised a large part of the audience, it may be assumed that two full galleries, excepting only the bays partitioned off as gentlemen's rooms, were assigned to their use. The two galleries were, of course, the first and second, as being the most desirable; and the supposition that two galleries were involved receives some slight confirmation from the wording of the Fortune contract, which twice uses the plural noun in referring to the two-penny rooms.

The term "penny gallery" seems to have meant the same thing as "two-penny gallery," with the inconsistency arising from the fact that some writers had in mind only the general gallery supplement, and others the total cost of admission. The two-penny gallery was very different from the two-penny rooms; it was the cheapest of the accommodations that the galleries offered, and, in accordance with the theatrical rule of "the higher the cheaper," was undoubtedly the gallery on the third level. References cited on pages 62 and 63 of *The Globe Playhouse* seem to confirm the supposition that it was at the top of the house, and that it occupied only one gallery.

On these assumptions there would be, except for the boxes, no price distinctions within any of the galleries, and therefore no valid reason for subdividing any of them with partitions. The lowermost gallery was, of course, broken in the middle by the corridor giving access to the yard (Scale Drawing I). Each half was entered by a door leading in from the vestibule, guarded by a gatherer charged with the duty of collecting the two-penny room supplement. On the second level the two-penny room extended without a break around five-eighths of the octagonal frame, from the gentlemen's room on one side to the gentlemen's room on the other, again with gatherers stationed at the doors to collect the supplementary fees. It was ten inches deeper than the gallery below, and the degrees in its floor were necessarily steeper.

The top gallery was again ten inches deeper than the gallery below, and therefore twenty inches deeper than the first, with yet steeper degrees in its flooring. It lacked the plastered ceilings of the lower galleries; overhead the underside of the thatch was probably visible. It needed no gatherers at its doors.

THE AUDIENCE AT THE GLOBE

DeWitt reported in 1596 that the Swan could accommodate 3,000 persons. Fynes Moryson asserted in 1617 that the London theatres were together "capable of many thousands"; and in 1614, in his petition to the King on behalf of the Thames watermen, John Taylor stated that the opening of the Fortune and Red Bull theatres in Middlesex had diverted "three or four thousand people, that were used [daily] to spend their monies by water" in crossing by boat to the Bankside playhouses. No known contemporary document relates specifically to the capacity of the Globe.

Modern estimates are concerned primarily with the Fortune, the one Elizabethan playhouse whose over-all dimensions are known beyond cavil. On the basis of a conjectural seating plan and an allowance of so many square inches for each seated patron and so many for each one standing, C. W. Wallace estimated the capacity of the Fortune at 1,320, John Corbin at 2,138, and Alfred Harbage at 2,344. On the basis of quite different data, the records of gallery receipts as recorded in Henslowe's Diary, W. W. Greg estimated that the Fortune's capacity may have approximated 3,000.

Dr. Adams estimates the capacity of the Globe at 2,028. He allows three rows of benches in each of the three galleries, a width of 22 inches for each seated spectator, 4 square feet of room for each spectator standing in the galleries, and 3 square feet of standing room for every spectator in the yard. His estimate of the Globe's capacity is made up as follows:

			Seated	Standing	Total
GALLERY	I	{ Gentlemen's rooms (two)	40	20	60
		Two-penny rooms (two)	208	170	378
GALLERY	II	{ Gentlemen's rooms (two)	40	20	60
		Two-penny room	220	186	406
GALLERY	III	Two-penny gallery	270	254	524
THE YARD				600	600
		Totals	778	1,250	2,028

In view of our modern distaste for open-air spectacles in the bleak temperatures and under the gray skies of mid-winter, it is surprising to find that the Elizabethans flocked to the unroofed playhouses almost as much in winter as they did in summer. Henslowe's Diary records an average of 25 performances in January in the years 1592-3, 1594, and 1596, as compared with an average of 27 performances in May. It shows too an average receipt of £37/11/0 for January, as compared with an average of £44/19/0 for May.

CHAPTER VI

THE PLATFORM

A S we have seen, each side of the Globe's inner frame was a full 24 feet long; and, as a consequence, a post was needed at the midpoint of each side to aid in supporting the heavy upper galleries. At the tiring-house end of the frame, the midpoint posts on the south-east and south-west sides would seem to have been the logical termini for the sides of the platform; and since, in an octagon with 24-foot sides, the distance between the midpoint of one side and the midpoint of the next-side-but-one is almost precisely 41 feet, this dimension may be accepted as the width of the Globe's platform at its rear, where it met the tiring-house wall. The 41-foot width compares agreeably with the 43 feet specified for the stage of the Fortune, for the converging lines of the Globe's octagonal frame would naturally suggest a lesser width, at the point of junction with the tiring-house wall, than the parallel lines of a square. The front-to-back depth of the Globe's platform is nowhere specifically mentioned. Like that in the Fortune, however, the stage may be supposed to have extended to "the middle of the yard," and if so it was 29 feet deep. Its front edge was unquestionably a straight line; all stages are so depicted in every contemporary view.

The question of the sides of the platform—whether they paralleled each other to form a rectangle 41 feet wide by 29 feet deep, or whether they tapered as they approached the front—has been and remains in dispute. The contemporary evidence is conflicting. The drawing of the Swan interior and the frontispiece to *The Wits* show stages with parallel sides. The *Roxana* and *Messallina* vignettes, on the other hand, show tapering stages. The phraseology of the Fortune contract—"which stage shall contain in length [i.e., width] forty and three foot of lawful assize and in breadth [i.e., depth] to extend to the middle of the yard"—is inconclusive.

To the majority of scholars[1] the indications for a rectangular platform have seemed convincing. They base their opinions upon their reading of the Fortune contract, upon the Swan and *Wits* drawings, upon conjectures as to the amount of space required by stage-sitting gallants, and upon certain

[1] J. Q. Adams, Archer, Baker, Tucker Brooke, Chambers, Lawrence, Thorndike.

Jacobean stage-directions which call for traps in all four "corners" of the platform. Mr. C. Walter Hodges adds the further argument that the typical Elizabethan stage derived from a long tradition of rectangular platforms originating in the street theatres. He therefore supports the theory of a rectangular stage, while granting that the tapering form would make for better general design, allow better movement, and give more room for spectators in the yard.[2]

To Dr. Adams the weight of evidence favors the tapering stage. The Fortune contract perhaps suggests the rectangular form, but does not exclude the possibility of its tapering, more especially since the contract needed an accompanying diagram or "plott" (now unfortunately lost) to show how the platform, the tiring-house, and the staircases were to be "placed and set." The Swan sketch is pre-Globe and unreliable in many details, and the *Wits* drawing is post-Globe by nearly a generation and unrelated to the professional stage. Of the four early drawings, only the *Roxana* and *Messallina* vignettes were contemporary with either the first Globe or the second, and they are for that reason slightly to be preferred. As for the evidence of traps in the four "corners" of the stage, all the plays concerned are of Jacobean date, and there would in any case be four corners in a tapering stage, not less than in a rectangular.

The argument that a considerable space would be needed to accommodate gallants seated on the platform is of doubtful validity. True, there is some evidence that fashionable gentlemen sat on the Globe's stage, as for instance in the Induction to Marston's *The Malcontent,* and in Ben Jonson's *Every Man Out of his Humour* (Q1), in the line "Sit o' the stage and flout; provided, you have a good suit"; but how much toleration was given to the custom at the Globe cannot be known. At the Blackfriars, where stage-sitting probably originated, the platform extended from one side wall of the hall to the other, with the audience in front of its forward edge; and on a stage so designed, gallants could sit on stools against the side walls, even three or four rows deep, without obstructing anyone's view of the action. At the Globe, however, they could sit nowhere on the platform without interfering with the view of patrons in the gentlemen's rooms, the lowermost

[2] *The Globe Restored* (1953), pp. 36-41. Pages 34 to 50 of the book were previously printed, in substantially identical form, under the title of "Unworthy Scaffolds," in *Shakespeare Survey 3* (1950), pp. 83-94.

gallery, or the yard; and the resentment which they aroused is reflected in *The Malcontent* (a play first performed at the Blackfriars and later by the King's Men at the Globe), in a line which suggests that those who sat on the Globe's stage could expect hisses from the groundlings. *The Malcontent* reveals the further fact that the granting of permission to occupy a stool on the stage was a perquisite of the actors; for it was a tireman, an employee of the actors, who refused permission in the Induction to the actor who impersonated a would-be stage-sitter. Gallants on the stage at the Globe must always have been a thorough-going nuisance. It is not likely that they were permitted to become so numerous as to have extra space provided for their benefit, particularly at the downstage corners of the projecting platform.

But the most potent argument against the doctrine of the rectangular stage lies in the fact that it would greatly reduce the capacity of the yard; the areas on the two sides would be cut down by a half. Further, the compacter shape of the tapered platform would more nearly conform to the space most used by the actors, who would tend to avoid deep downstage corners and to prefer downstage center.

While conceding that the case for a tapered stage at the Globe is by no means conclusive, Dr. Adams nevertheless prefers it to the rectangular, and for its forward edge he assumes a width of 24 feet. He adopts this figure on the theory that the platform in the dismantled Theater was rectangular and 24 feet wide—the width of one section of the octagonal frame—and that the original width of the front edge was retained at the Globe even when the rear of the platform was widened. Such a platform would have an area of 942½ square feet, a large stage even by the standards of today.

THE PLATFORM PALING AND RAILS

Beneath the stage was an excavated cellar usually referred to as the "hell," whence rose devils, ghosts, smoke, mists, and other emanations appropriate to an infernal region. To screen the sub-stage activities from too-curious eyes, the three sides of the projecting platform had a paling of boards. The Fortune contract is specific: "The same stage to be paled in below with good, strong and sufficient new oaken boards." The probability is that the paling at the Globe was merely of smooth boards set vertically: recessed panels and protruding mouldings would afford toe-holds to groundlings who might be tempted to climb to the stage, and were therefore probably avoided. Just such plain smooth palings seem to be shown in three out of the four drawings of early stages.[3]

Along the edges of the Globe's platform was a low balustrade of turned spindles, spaced well apart and capped with a rail. The balustrade probably served primarily to keep groundlings from climbing to the stage; and if in fact gallants ever sat on the outer stage at the Globe, it served too as a back-rest and guard-rail to keep them from tumbling into the yard. It would need to be sturdily built, and was probably of oak. Stage rails are clearly shown in the *Roxana* and the *Messallina* vignettes and in the plans for the Cockpit-in-Court, where they appear to be about 18 inches high.[4]

The earliest reference to the stage rails at the Globe occurs in Thomas Middleton's *Black Book* (1604), in which, seemingly after having made a startling entrance by vaulting from the yard to the platform, Lucifer says:

> And now that I have vaulted up so high
> Above the stage rails of this earthen globe
> I must turn actor and join companies,
> To share my comic sleek-ey'd villainies.

Shakespeare seems to refer both to the stage rails and to the palings in a single passage in *Henry VIII*. At the end of Act V Scene iv, a Porter is required to clear a path for a procession. In his efforts to restrain the surging crowd of citizens, he calls out:

> You i' th' chamblet,
> Get up o' th' rail. I'll peck you o'er the pales else!

[3] Hodges suggests the possibility that the Globe's stage was not boarded in with palings, but hung round with a skirt of cloth. He cites several references which seem to indicate that draped stages were to be found in at least some Elizabethan playhouses, and he contends that the Fortune contract, in specifying a paled stage, was deliberately departing from conformity with the Globe. In support of his contention, he italicizes the word "other" in the provision that the Fortune's stage was to be "in all *other* proportions contrived and fashioned like unto the stage of the said playhouse called the Globe" (*The Globe Restored*, pp. 46-50). It is however noteworthy that none of the contemporary drawings shows a draped stage, and it seems improbable that the Globe should have nothing more substantial that a cloth hanging to keep groundlings from invading the "hell."

[4] The balustrades in the model and in the scale drawings accord with the Cockpit plan in scaling at 18 inches in height. They follow the *Roxana* engraving in the pattern of the individual balusters, and both that and the *Messallina* in having plain unturned posts at the stage's forward corners.

RUSHES ON THE PLATFORM

The outer stage was painted, if only to protect it from the weather, and here and there was strewn with rushes. The practice of strewing rushes on the floor originated in the home. In the humbler dwellings moist green rushes helped to conceal and to lay the perpetual dustiness of floors which often were made of nothing more than beaten earth; and in great houses rushes were still the normal floor covering in Elizabethan times, with carpets serving usually to cover tables and chests. Shakespeare indicates that rushes were spread even on the dance-floor. Romeo, on his way to the masquerade at the Capulet house, tells of his reluctance to take part in the evening's festivities (*Romeo and Juliet*, I iv 35-38):

> A torch for me! Let wantons light of heart
> Tickle the senseless rushes with their heels; . . .
> I'll be a candle-holder and look on.

As transferred to the stage, therefore, rushes represented an accustomed item of domestic furnishing in indoor scenes, and served equally well to suggest the greensward when the action was outdoors. Shakespeare makes use of them in both environments. Examples of their use in interior scenes are to be found in *Cymbeline*, II ii 12-14, when Iachimo, climbing from his trunk in Imogen's bedchamber, says:

> Our Tarquin thus
> Did softly press the rushes ere he waken'd
> The chastity he wounded.

and in *The Taming of the Shrew*, IV i 47, in Grumio's

> Is supper ready, the house trimm'd, rushes strew'd,
> cobwebs swept . . . ?

and again in *1 Henry IV*, III i 213-214, when Glendower says:

> She bids you on the wanton rushes lay you down
> And rest your gentle head upon her lap.

Rushes are strewn in the street in *2 Henry IV*, V v, in preparation for the procession to Westminster Abbey for the coronation of King Henry V. The scene opens with the stage-direction *"Enter three Grooms, strewers of*

PLATE 17. The DeWitt sketch of the Swan Playhouse, c. 1596. The sketch was actually made by Arend van Buchell, who presumably copied a drawing by DeWitt.

PLATE 18. The vignette from the title-page of *Roxana*, 1632.

PLATE 19. The vignette from the title-page of *Messallina*, 1640.

PLATE 20. The frontispiece to *The Wits, or Sport upon Sport*. 1662.

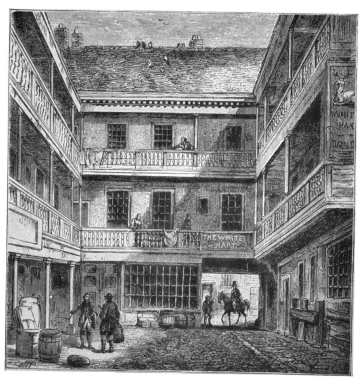

(Left) PLATE 21. The courtyard of the White Hart Inn in Southwark.

(Below) PLATE 22. The architect's designs, formerly attributed to Inigo Jones, for the Cockpit-in-Court, c. 1632.

By courtesy of Worcester College, Oxford.

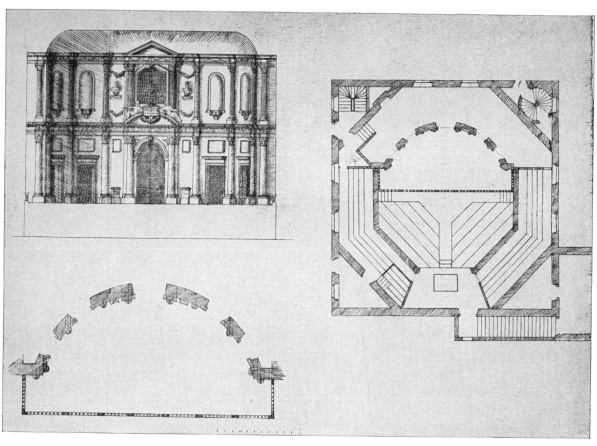

PLATE 23. Flying apparatus used in an Italian theatre in the 17th century.

PLATE 24. Henry Peacham's drawing of a performance of *Titus Andronicus* in 1594 or 1595. This is the earliest known illustration of a Shakespearean play.
By courtesy of the Marquess of Bath.

PLATE 25. English costumes of the Elizabethan period, from Abraham de Bruyn's *Omnium Pene Europae, Asiae, Aphricae atque Americae Gentium Habitus,* 1581.
The Victoria and Albert Museum. Crown copyright.

rushes," and with the line "More rushes! more rushes!" They probably served for the grassy carpet in *Richard II*, III iii 49-50:

> Go signify as much, while here we march
> Upon the grassy carpet of this plain.

and for the grass-plot in *The Tempest*, IV i 70-74:

> The queen o' th' sky,
> Whose wat'ry arch and messenger am I,
> Bids thee leave these, and with her sovereign grace,
> Here on this grass-plot, in this very place,
> To come and sport.

But in the use of rushes on the stage, scenic verisimilitude was of secondary importance; their primary purpose was the utilitarian one of protecting theatrical costumes. Nearly every Elizabethan play had scenes in which actors sat, lay, wrestled, or died upon the floor; and since at that period costumes were magnificent and costly, some outer-stage areas were strewn with a carpet of rushes so that actors could recline or die on them without damage to their finery. Other parts of the stage, however, were probably left uncovered. Bare boards are implied in *Troilus and Cressida*, I iii 153-156, when Ulysses speaks of

> a strutting player—whose conceit
> Lies in his hamstring, and doth think it rich
> To hear the wooden dialogue and sound
> 'Twixt his stretch'd footing and the scaffolage.

and, in the savage scene in *Titus Andronicus* in which Marcus and the mutilated Lavinia communicate with each other by writing in the sand (IV i), bare boards would suggest a "sandy plot" better than could rushes. Perhaps the usual practice was to strew the rear half of the outer stage midway between the doors, but with the areas around the doors left clear and the space around the platform trap, if the trap were to be needed in the play.

By the end of Elizabeth's reign, well-to-do households used plaited-rush mats instead of strewn rushes; and in reporting the first Globe's final performance, the performance which ended abruptly when fire broke out in the thatch, Sir Henry Wotton thought it a fact worth recording that the play "was set forth with many extraordinary circumstances of pomp and majesty, even to the matting of the stage."

THE STAGE POSTS

Two tall columns rose vertically from the stage of the Globe to sustain the weight of the "heavens" 32 feet overhead. Such posts were normal equipment in all the Elizabethan playhouses (except the Hope), for all had stage-covers and huts, and therefore the need that these superstructures should be supported. The supposition that stage posts were usually provided is confirmed by the fact that they were specifically excluded in the Hope contract. In the Hope, designed as it was both for plays and for animal-baiting, the stage itself was to be removable; logically enough, therefore, the contract provided that the heavens were to be "borne or carried without any posts or supporters to be fixed or set upon the said [removable] stage." Two round pillars, known to have been painted in imitation of marble, are shown as rising from square pedestals in the Swan sketch.

The Fortune contract gives specifications for "principal and main posts," but the probability is that the phrase does not apply to the two posts rising from the stage. Having again, and for the third time, insisted that the Fortune was to be finished according to the fashion of the Globe, the contract goes on to specify this exception:

> ... saving only that all the principal and main posts of the said frame and stage forward shall be square and wrought pilaster-wise with carved proportions called satyrs to be placed and set on the top of every of the same posts.

Chambers assumes that the passage in the Fortune contract refers to the stage posts.[5] Dr. Adams contends that it does not:

> Henslowe is here instructing Streete in a detail which is to give a distinctive finish to his playhouse. He wishes all the posts facing the audience on the inside of the building to be uniformly square, pilastered, and carved. His order refers not only to the posts of the tiring-house but also to the posts of the galleries. His particularized instructions regarding these inner or "forwarde" posts seem to indicate, first, that the corresponding posts of the Globe frame were shaped and decorated in some other fashion ... and, secondly, that the posts in the tiring-house sections of the Globe frame differed from the posts in the gallery sections. If this is the true meaning of the Fortune contract, as prolonged study has led me to believe, then no part of the phrase, "postes of the saide fframe and

[5] *Elizabethan Stage*, II, 545.

Stadge forwarde," relates to the free-standing pillars rising from the platform to support the stage superstructure.[6]

The posts on the facade of the Fortune's tiring-house, and the posts along
the inner frame of the galleries, were therefore to be square, wrought
pilaster-wise, and decorated with carved satyrs; but except for them, and
some other minor differences specified in the contract, the Fortune's stage
and tiring-house were to be "in all other proportions contrived and fashioned
like unto the stage of . . . the Globe." Neither the Fortune nor the Globe,
then, had square pilastered stage posts, but more than that we do not know.
The evidence of the Fortune contract is merely negative.

The stage posts at the Globe may have been round, like those in the Swan
drawing; timbers so tall would have been easier to obtain in the round than
in any other shape, and a pair of ship's masts may have been used: the ships
anchored in the Thames would unfailingly have suggested the idea of masts
to men who were building a playhouse on the Bankside. Or perhaps, in
conformity with the Globe's over-all plan, the posts were octagonal in cross-
section. They are so represented in the model and in the scale drawings.[7]

The position of the posts was of course determined by the position of the
"heavens" which they supported; for reasons later to be given, it therefore
appears that they stood about 17 feet forward of the scenic wall. Wherever
placed, they would cause some obstruction to visibility, and in this regard
no one position would be appreciably better than another. For the most
part they were ignored as a necessary evil, but occasionally they were pressed
into the service of the scene. In some plays the columns served as trees, and
sometimes they were climbed by actors. With the initial help afforded by a
pedestal such as that shown in the DeWitt sketch, an actor could easily
climb high enough to meet all the requirements of theatrical illusion. The
pillars served as the yew-trees under which Paris's page and Romeo's man
waited near the Capulet burial vault, in *Romeo and Juliet,* V iii. On one of
them Orlando hung his verses, in *As You Like It,* III ii; and to one of them
Posthumus was bound, in *Cymbeline,* V iv. The comedian Kempe, one of
the Globe's original housekeepers, relates that pickpockets were pilloried by
being tied to them: "I remembred one of them to be a noted Cut-purse,

[6] *Globe Playhouse,* p. 109. Hodges agrees with Dr. Adams in assuming that the principal
and main posts did not include the stage posts, but he relates the words rather to the
sub-stage posts which supported the platform floor (*The Globe Restored,* pp. 45-46).
[7] Scale Drawings X, XII, XIII and XIV, and the title-page.

such a one as we tye to a poast on our stage, for all people to wonder at, when at a play they are taken pilfring."[8]

THE PLATFORM TRAP

The largest and most important trap in the playhouse was, naturally enough, located in or near the center of the platform. Its central position is clearly indicated by stage-directions which incorporate such phrases as *"in the midst of the stage"* or *"in middle of the Stage."* Its size, and the efficiency of its raising-and-lowering apparatus, are suggested by the bulk and weight of objects which it was called upon to lift from sub-stage to platform level; such things, for instance, as are mentioned in the following stage-directions:

From *A Warning for Fair Women,* a play certainly acted by the King's Men, and probably at the Globe:

> *They offering cheerefully to meete and embrace, suddenly riseth up a great tree betweene them, whereat amazedly they step backe.*

From *The Devil's Charter,* another play acted by the King's Men:

> *Fiery exhalations lightning thunder ascend a King, with a red face crowned imperiall riding upon a Lyon or dragon.*

From Chapman's Blackfriars play, *Caesar and Pompey:*

> *Thunder, and the gulf opens, flames issuing, and Ophioneus ascending, with the face, wings, and tail of a dragon . . .*

From Peele's *The Arraignment of Paris:*

> *Hereuppon did rise a Tree of gold laden with Diadems & Crownes of golde. . . . The Tree sinketh.*

From Rowley's *The Birth of Merlin:*

> *Merlin strikes his wand. Thunder and Lightning, two Dragons appear, a White and a Red, they fight a while and pause.*

From *A Looking Glass for London and England:*

> *The Magi with their rods beate the ground, and from under the same riseth a brave Arbour.*

[8] Kempe, *Nine Days Wonder,* quoted by Chambers, II, 545.

In *The Silver Age,* Pluto says:

> Cleave, earth, and when I stamp upon thy breast
> Sink me, my brass-shod wagon, and my self,
> My coach-steeds, and their traces altogether
> O'er head and ears in Styx.

and upon his stamping on the stage, Pluto, Proserpine, the four devils who serve as coach-steeds, and the brass-shod wagon, all descend to eternal darkness. In certain other scenes, no fewer than eight actors descend together.

The "great tree," the "brave Arbour," the eight actors, and the "two Dragons," each presumably equipped with wings and tail, would call for a trap-cover certainly not smaller than $7\frac{1}{2}$ or 8 feet long by 4 feet wide. It was probably rectangular in shape (as in the *Messallina* vignette) with its long axis parallel to the front edge of the stage, so that persons standing and properties placed upon it would face the greater part of the audience.

The last three of the plays cited above provide in stage-direction or dialogue for a rapping or stamping upon the floor. From these and other instances it is clear that rappings or stampings normally served as cues to actors or stagehands below, so that they would know when to raise or lower the trap. Abundant evidence shows further that the trap was equipped with a mechanism capable not merely of lifting and lowering heavy loads, but of doing so either swiftly or slowly, as the requirements of the current scene might dictate. In the stage-direction previously quoted from *A Warning for Fair Women,* the great tree *"suddenly riseth up . . . betweene them";* in *Messallina,* on the other hand, *"Earth gapes and swallowes the three murder[er]s by degrees,"* and a little later Saufellus sinks even more slowly, with some twenty-four lines intervening between the time the trap begins to descend and the time he is lost to sight. Normally, however, the trap's cycle of rise and fall was brief, for theatrical illusion would not be helped by exposing the cellar beneath the platform to the gaze of spectators in the upper galleries.

When the platform trap was to be used for the entrance of a nether-world creature, the Elizabethan dramatist commonly called for thunder and lightning, "hellish musicke," trumpet blasts, falling chains, or other similar loud noises. Quite apart from the fact that such sounds helped to create an atmosphere of terror and torment, they served to drown out the noise made by the trap mechanism, which in its operation unavoidably voiced the complaints of creaking ropes and chafed timbers in the sub-stage "hell." Thunder is the sound most often called for in stage-directions, as in 2 *Henry VI*, with its *"It Thunders and Lightens terribly: then the Spirit riseth"* at I iv 25, and its *"Thunder and Lightning. Exit Spirit"* a few lines later. So needful and so usual were such "disguise sounds," as Dr. Adams calls them, in connection with trap operation, that the association of noise with the entrance of a ghost or fiend furnishes a clue to the original staging of many a scene. Whenever thunder and lightning, or other loud sounds, accompany the entrance of witch or spirit, devil or fury, it may be supposed that the entrance was made by the platform trap, even though no ascent be specified. One may therefore assume that the three Witches rose through the outer-stage trap in the first scene of *Macbeth*.

For similar reasons, the dramatists often specified such theatrical devices as the "fiery exhalations" of *The Devil's Charter*, the "flames issuing" of *Caesar and Pompey*, sulphurous smoke, or mist, as the trap opened. They thus achieved the dual objectives of contributing to the infernal atmosphere of the scene and of concealing the visual aspects of trap operation.

There are some indications that smaller traps, equipped only with steps or ladders rather than with raising mechanisms, were provided in each of the four corners of the stage. They are discussed in *The Globe Playhouse*, pp. 117-119, and shown in place on the platform floor in the model of the Globe. Dr. Adams's continuing studies, however, have led to the abandonment of his earlier theory that corner traps were a part of the first Globe's equipment when it was first erected. They are therefore not shown in the scale drawings. Dr. Adams believes that corner traps may have been installed in the first Globe at a later date, and that they were certainly present in the second.

THE "HELL"

The term "hell" was standard in Shakespeare's time for the cellar under the stage. Every Elizabethan playhouse had its "hell," as attested by Dekker in *News from Hell* (1606), when he spoke of "Hell being under every one of their Stages."[9]

The primary purpose of the "hell" was to serve the traps and to store

---

[9] The Hope, with its removable stage, can hardly have had a cellar except at the rear, under the tiring-house.

soon-to-be-needed properties. It underlay not merely the outer stage, but extended back under the tiring-house to underlie the rear stage also, which, as will later appear, had a trap of its own. At the Fortune it may have been walled in with downward extensions of the "good strong and sufficient new oaken boards" which formed the paling of the stage, but at the Globe, standing as it did on the marshy ground of the Bankside, the cellar walls were more probably of brick. Some sort of flooring was also needed, both as footing for the elaborately dressed actors, and as an underpinning for the posts—"a hundred posts," according to a line in *The Custom of the Country*—which rose from the cellar floor to provide support for the heavy platform with its three-inch flooring, upon which, in turn, rested the weight of the stage posts and some part of the superstructure.

Because of the marshy Bankside terrain, the Globe's "hell" was probably excavated to as shallow a depth as its functions would permit. Anything less than headroom would of course have been a constant annoyance; anything more would deepen the excavation by just so much, and would perhaps be bought at a heavy cost in dampness. But even a six-foot head-room, making allowance for 12-inch beams supporting the platform floor, would yield a seven-foot height in the spaces between the ceiling beams, and one foot more would yield eight; and a height of eight feet between the beams would seem to be enough to take care of even the tallest properties that needed to be sent up by the platform trap, especially if there were a sunken pit beneath the trap so that the trap door, when in the *down* position for loading, could rest level with the cellar floor.[10] And in saying that an eight-foot height could accommodate the tallest sub-stage properties, it is not necessary to except even such things as the "tree of gold laden with diadems and crowns," nor the "brave arbour"; for the property-maker undoubtedly had the limitations of his cellar in mind, and planned his properties accordingly. Such an eight-foot cellar would require an excavation of not more

[10] Cf. Scale Drawing XIV. The trap apparatus shown in the scale drawing is, it goes without saying, wholly conjectural; no drawing or verbal description of an Elizabethan trap mechanism is known to exist. This hypothetical reconstruction is based upon the following assumptions: (1) that stationary vertical timbers would be needed at the corners to guide the trap to its opening in the stage floor and to prevent swaying; (2) that, since the trap must be level at all times, it must be supported at all four corners by ropes leading from a single windlass; (3) that the windlass must be operable by several men, to handle the heavy loads sometimes placed upon the trap; and (4) that the mechanism would in all probability be an adaptation of shipboard apparatus.

than 5½ feet, for the platform floor already stood some 2½ feet above normal ground level.[11]

Shakespeare seems to have made use of the "hell" rather less than some of his contemporary dramatists, but when he did he used it with tremendous dramatic effect. The Ghost of Hamlet's father moved about "in the cellarage" at the Globe, calling upon Horatio and Marcellus, on the stage above, to "Swear!" In *Antony and Cleopatra*, IV iii, there occurs the stage-direction *"Musicke of the Hoboyes is under the Stage."* The elusive sound of the hautboys, seeming to come both from above and from below, mystified the soldiers who guarded Cleopatra's palace on the night before the decisive battle. Occasionally the "hell" assumed a dramatic character of its own, and represented places such as an underground cave, a dungeon, a wine-cellar, a grave, or perhaps, in the first scene of *The Tempest*, the hold of a ship.

THE PLATFORM IN USE

The outer stage had no curtain. Actors had to walk on at the beginning of an outer-stage scene, and walk off—if still alive—at the end. It was thus impossible for the dramatist to open a platform scene upon a group of characters already assembled, or to build up to a situation ending on the highest note with the sort of final tableau beloved by modern playwrights. With no front curtain, furthermore, dead bodies—and the Elizabethan drama is rich in them—presented a problem to the dramatist: one way or another, they must be removed from the stage. Shakespeare's variations upon the theme include such devices as Falstaff's prank with the body of Hotspur, Paris's entreaty to be laid in the tomb with Juliet, the burial of Oswald, the carrying off of Caesar's body by Antony and Octavius' servant, and the funeral marches which bring *Hamlet, Antony and Cleopatra,* and many other tragedies, to an end.[12]

[11] Hodges (*The Globe Restored,* pp. 41-43) contends that the builders of the Globe "may have dug down 1 foot or, with some ingenuity and a good deal of pumping, 2 feet," but not more than that, for "to have gone digging cellars on the Bankside of Shakespeare's day was to go digging for trouble." He would gain the necessary sub-stage headroom by having the platform floor higher than is usually postulated: as high, indeed, as the top of a spectator's head. Street and market-place stages, to be sure, were at least that high; but it is to be noted that none of the four drawings of early English stages shows a platform that seems to be more than 4½ feet high.

[12] Exceptions to this rule occur when death takes place in an inner stage, as in the final scenes of *Othello* and *Romeo and Juliet*.

The platform, when used alone rather than in association with the rear stage, characteristically represented an outdoor area under the open sky. Such scenes would include the island scenes in *The Tempest*, the heath in *King Lear*, the Field of Agincourt in *Henry V*, a public place or street in *Romeo and Juliet*, the Illyrian seacoast in *Twelfth Night*, and innumerable other streets, public places, forests, fields, and so on, throughout the range of the Elizabethan drama.

By its nature as a bare stage extending well forward from the scenic wall, the platform could function not only as an identified location, but also as an unlocalized playing area. Sometimes it served the dramatist's purpose to indicate to the audience precisely where the current action was supposed to be taking place; at other times such an indication was superfluous, for the action of the given scene was such as might with equal probability occur in any one of many localities, indoors or out, and there was no need to be specific as to place. These unlocalized scenes were normally staged upon the platform; its lack of restrictive architectural detail made it, so to speak, neutral ground.

It was probably an unformulated principle of Elizabethan staging that no given stage might be used in two successive scenes to represent two different places (see page 109 following). The platform, however, seems in some cases to have been excepted from a strict application of the rule. Because it was large, because it had widely separated points of entry, and above all because it was unrestricted and unlocalized, it could in effect serve as two different stages. A group of actors might occupy the stage as representing a certain locality, withdraw toward one side as the scene approached its close, and go out by the near-by stage door; upon their departure the deserted stage became for a brief moment a sort of no-man's-land, and then became a different place with the entrance of a new group of actors by the opposite door. Examples of this usage would include, for instance, the sequence in *The Merry Wives of Windsor*, in which the platform is successively a field near Windsor (II iii), a field near Frogmore (III i), and a Windsor street (III ii) ; or that in *Troilus and Cressida*, in which IV v is indefinitely somewhere in the Grecian camp, V i before the tent of Achilles at some distance away, and V ii before the tent of Calchas. Other illustrations are given in the note.[13]

[13] *Two Gentlemen of Verona*, IV i – IV ii; *2 Henry VI*, I iv – II i – II ii, IV i – IV ii, and

The most daring instance of Shakespeare's use of his platform to represent different places in consecutive episodes is to be found in the Tent Scene in *Richard III* (Act V Scene iii). Within the one scene there are seven alternations of place as between two distinct and relatively distant localities: the camp of King Richard's army, and the camp of Richmond's, on the night before the battle of Bosworth Field. From lines 1 to 18, the stage is King Richard's camp; from 19 to 46, Richmond's; from 47 to 79, the King's again; and from 80 to 118, Richmond's. For a space of about 60 lines the sense of separation is briefly lost, when the ghosts of Richard's victims appear to both men as they sleep in their respective tents; with the vanishing of the ghosts and Richard's awakening, the places become separate again. The stage is the King's encampment from 178 to 223, Richmond's from 224 to 271, and again the King's from 272 to the end of the scene. Theatrically speaking, Shakespeare has placed the tents of the two adversaries within a few feet of one another, but dramatically he has done no such thing. While the stage is occupied by the King, Richmond's tent simply does not exist; King Richard never speaks of it, never sees it: Richmond and his tent and his soldiers are perhaps miles away. Similarly, when the King goes out and Richmond enters, the stage becomes entirely Richmond's; Richard's tent in its turn ceases to exist. Never during the course of the long scene do the two men meet, nor any of their followers; never does either refer to the other as being close at hand. On the contrary, the implication is always that the two encampments are well out of sight of each other, as when King Richard asks, "Who hath descried the number of the traitors?" (line 9). And yet, distinct and distant though the places be, they are staged alternately upon the platform, with no possibility of a change of stage to mark the change of place.

The use of the platform as if it were two stages in one, to represent different places in two consecutive scenes, must, it would seem, be assumed also in many other less obvious instances, as for example in *Romeo and Juliet*, II iv–II v, and III i–III ii (see pages 169-170 following).

IV ix–IV x–V i; *Titus Andronicus*, V i–V ii; *Richard III*, III i–III ii, III v–III vi–III vii–IV i; *Richard II*, III ii–III iii; *Taming of the Shrew*, IV iv–IV v–V i; *Troilus and Cressida*, III ii–III iii–IV i; *Cymbeline*, III iii–III iv; *Hamlet*, I iv–I v; *Coriolanus*, I ix–I x–II i, and IV ii–IV iii; etc.

INDICATIONS OF PLATFORM PLACEMENT

Scenes which fall into the following categories may reasonably be supposed to have been staged on the platform:

Open-air scenes, in streets, forests, gardens, or on heaths, beaches, battle-fields, and the like;

Battle scenes, and scenes in which armies or drum-and-colors processions march across the stage;

Short scenes which contain no hint of location: *Macbeth*, III vi, *1 Henry IV*, IV iv, *2 Henry IV*, I iii, etc.;

Scenes in which a person appears at a house-window to talk with persons outside: *Romeo and Juliet*, II ii, *Othello*, I i, *Merchant of Venice*, II vi, etc.;

Scenes in which one or more persons appear on the walls of a fortified town or castle: *Coriolanus*, I iv, *1 Henry VI*, III ii, *Richard II*, III iii, etc.;

Scenes in which a person, *after entering*, knocks upon a door or calls for admittance to a house or garden: *2 Henry IV*, I i, *Comedy of Errors*, III i, *Richard III*, III ii, etc.;

Scenes in which ghosts, devils, etc., rise from the infernal regions to an accompaniment of thunder, music, etc., *Macbeth*, I i, *2 Henry VI*, I iv, *1 Henry VI*, V iii, etc.;

Threshold scenes (see pages 92-93 following);

Scenes whose stage-directions include the formula *"Enter at one door . . . at another"* or its variants (see pages 89 and 94 following);

Scenes in which dead bodies are removed from the stage; but this indication must be regarded with caution, for it has many exceptions, both in the removal of bodies in inner-stage scenes (*Richard III*, I iv, *Antony and Cleopatra*, IV xv and V ii, *King Lear*, III vii, etc.), and in their seeming non-removal in platform scenes (*Macbeth*, III iii, *1 Henry IV*, V iii, etc.).

ACTION IN THE YARD

At this point it may be well to mention those rare occasions on which the yard seems to have been brought into the sphere of dramatic activity, with actors making their entrances to the platform or their departures from it by way of the yard and the stage rails. J. W. Saunders, in an article entitled

"Vaulting the Rails,"[14] points out that in the early Miracle Plays there had been considerable freedom of traffic as between actors on the stage and the audience on the ground. He contends that the same conditions existed in the inn-yard theatres, and survived to some extent in the Elizabethan public playhouses.

Two of Shakespeare's plays, and two only, strongly suggest action in the yard. One of them is *Antony and Cleopatra*, in which Act II Scene vii takes place aboard Pompey's galley, lying off Misenum. As the scene progresses, twelve persons are concurrently onstage in a boisterous drunken ring-around-the-rosy dance which calls for space that only the platform could provide; and at the scene's end all of the participants, excepting only Enobarbus and Menas, make ready to climb down from the deck of the galley into a small-boat which will ferry them ashore. We find the following dialogue at lines 131 to 134:

> *Caesar* . . . Good Antony, your hand.
> *Pompey*   I'll try you on the shore.
> *Antony*   And shall, sir. — Give 's your hand.
> *Pompey*   O Antony,
> You have my father's house — but what? We are friends!
> Come, down into the boat.
> *Eno.*   Take heed you fall not.

Caesar's "Good Antony, your hand" is not a gesture of farewell, since he and Antony are not parting; it is rather a request for Antony to steady him as he feels for the steps down into the boat; so is Antony's "Give 's your hand." Shakespeare has dramatized the episode with such sure touches in the dialogue that one is forced to assume that the words were accompanied by appropriate action; and what more appropriate than that the actors should climb over the platform rail and down a short ladder to the floor of the yard, as into a small-boat moored beside the galley?

A similar situation occurs in *Pericles*, which is known to have been a Globe play. In V i, the scene is on board Pericles' ship off Mytilene, with a barge lying alongside. Again, the action of the scene, which demands a pavilion on deck and Pericles within it on a couch, seems clearly to require that the platform, rather than one of the smaller inner stages, should serve as the ship's deck. As the scene opens, several men board the ship as from

[14] *Shakespeare Survey 7* (1954), pp. 69-81.

the barge, and later Marina and her attendants; and at its end all of the principal characters enter the barge to go ashore. Lysimachus' "Sir, lend me your arm," addressed to Pericles, again suggests a precarious descent.[15]

The yard was perhaps used in yet another scene in *Pericles*. In Act II Scene i two fishermen throw a net into the sea and draw up a rusty armor. Since the platform's edge would suggest the seashore far better than could the platform trap, it would seem probable that the net was thrown from platform to yard, and that a stagehand in the yard loaded it with armor and sent it back.

Sir Edmund K. Chambers had just such situations as these in mind when he wrote:

> . . . It may perhaps be supposed that the episodes, in which personages pass to and from boats or fling themselves into a river, were performed upon the extreme edge of the stage rather than over a trap.[16]

The supposition that the yard was occasionally invaded by actors necessitates two further suppositions: first, that some way was found to keep spectators in the yard from interfering with the actors, and second, that the actors had some means of returning from yard to tiring-house. As for the first, it would seem possible that one of the backward-reaching arms of the yard could be roped off and closed to spectators temporarily. As for the second, perhaps stairs similar to the "ingressus" stairs in the DeWitt sketch served the purpose; and if not that, then perhaps the actors could climb down into the "hell" through a low door in the platform's side paling, and so get back to the tiring-house by sub-stage passageways.[17]

---

[15] It seems unnecessary to go as far as does Mr. Hodges in raising the possibility that the barge may have been "a practicable boat brought in through one of the gates of the yard and moored alongside the stage, which was the ship" (*The Globe Restored*, p. 49). Even for its "stunt value," this would seem to be carrying theatrical realism over-far.

[16] *The Elizabethan Stage*, III, 90.

[17] Since Dr. Adams does not accept the theory that action sometimes took place in the yard, no such stairs or door are shown in the model or in the scale drawings.

CHAPTER VII

THE TIRING–HOUSE EXTERIOR

WHEN Nick Bottom and the other Athenian rustics were preparing their Lamentable Comedy of *Pyramus and Thisby* for the entertainment of Theseus and Hippolyta on their wedding day, in *A Midsummer Night's Dream*, III i, Peter Quince said:

> . . . here's a marvail's convenient place for our rehearsal. This green plot shall be our stage, this hawthorn brake our tiring house.

and in the term "tiring house," he was using the designation regularly employed in Shakespeare's time for the backstage areas of a public playhouse.

"The Attyring housse or place where the players make them readye" was originally merely a makeshift enclosure set aside for costume changes. In the days of market-place performances, troupes had been small and each player had acted several parts; quick changes of costume had therefore been necessary, and a dressing room close at hand. In those days it had been a simple curtained booth set up at the rear of the trestle-borne platform itself. Later, in the inn-yards, a dressing room had been contrived by stringing a curtain from an overhanging balcony, or perhaps a near-by room had been used. The permanent playhouses of course provided special rooms for dressing; but by the time the first Globe was built, the terms "tiring-house," "tyring-house" and "tyre-house" had come to mean not a dressing room only, but the entire three-story section of the playhouse frame in back of the platform. In addition to the attiring-rooms which gave it its name, it contained the secondary stages, storage rooms for costumes and properties, and the necessary backstage passageways and stairs.

When the elder Burbage built the Theater in 1576, he probably devoted only one of the eight sections of the octagonal frame to tiring-house and stage. By the end of the century, however, the need for a larger and more adaptable stage had made itself felt; and when the Globe was erected in 1599, its designers seem to have enlarged their acting area by taking one bay (i.e., half a section) away from the spectator galleries on each side and incorporating it in the tiring-house, and by widening the rear of the platform correspondingly. The new tiring-house had twice the area of the old. Its façade no longer lay in a flat plane, but comprised a middle section 24 feet wide, flanked on either side by a 12-foot-wide half-section which joined it at a wide angle of 135 degrees. Stage doors and windows now slanted toward each other at a 90-degree angle, instead of facing directly forward, and so provided new opportunities for realistic stage business. All sections of the tiring-house façade were three stories high, a total of 32 feet from the platform to the "heavens."

The scenic wall formed a permanent backdrop for the outer stage. Its architectural details were those of contemporary London: black-and-white timbered walls, rich with carved oak and contrasting plaster-work; solid oak doors with wickets and heavy wrought-iron knockers; turned door-posts rising to support projecting bay windows with their practicable leaded casements. The habitual playgoer became accustomed to it, accepted it in scenes to which it was appropriate, forgot it entirely in scenes to which it was not.

THE STAGE CURTAINS

Three of the four drawings of early English stages show curtains at the rear of the platform. The *Roxana* vignette has curtains which extend across as much of the rear stage as the tiny engraving includes. The *Messallina* engraving shows similar curtains, hanging rather better than in *Roxana,* and decorated with figures. The Swan drawing shows none; but in view of the hundreds of references to "discovering" an inner-stage scene, many of which mention curtains or arras specifically, their omission in the Swan drawing weakens the case for curtains less than it does the case for the accuracy of DeWitt's sketch. Still other pictorial representations of stage curtains are to be found on the title-page of *The Bloody Almanack* (1643) by John Booker, in a Cavalier cartoon of 1649 entitled "The Curtain's drawne, all may perceive the plot,"[1] and in *The Wits* drawing of 1662. On the evidence of the drawings and of two early lists of property-maker's supplies, it can be said with assurance that each curtain was made in two sections that met in the middle, that they were suspended from rings sliding upon a horizontal rod, that they could be drawn by cords and pulleys, and that they opened laterally. They were a source of great pride to the Elizabethan theatrical companies, and were replaced from time to time with ever more

[1] Reproduced by Hotson, *The Commonwealth and Restoration Stage,* facing p. 30.

colorful and richer tapestries and fabrics. There is a record of silk tapestries at the Blackfriars in 1600, and of similar extravagance at a public playhouse not long after.

Stage-directions and dialogue in the plays of the period make it clear that the curtains could be drawn either by an actor visible on the stage, or by an invisible agent or means. References prior to 1603 are about equally divided as between the two alternatives. After 1603 the stage-directions increasingly omit mention of the curtains themselves and mention merely the person or thing discovered, as in the stage-direction in *The Tempest*, V i, which reads *"Here Prospero discovers Ferdinand and Miranda, playing at Chesse."* Dr. Adams cites some 35 or 40 applicable stage-directions, from among a host of others, on pages 139 to 144 of *The Globe Playhouse*.

The curtains served several purposes. Sometimes, as in the *Tempest* scene, they opened merely to effect an incidental disclosure. In "split" scenes they often parted to reveal the rear stage as a place associated with, but distinct from, the area represented by the platform: a smaller room adjoining a larger, perhaps, or an interior related to an exterior, as will be discussed in the pages of this book which deal with the combined stages. Occasionally the curtains assumed a dramatic character in their own right, as for instance when they served as the flap of Brutus' tent in *Julius Caesar*, IV ii-iii, or successively as the tent-flaps of Agamemnon, Achilles, and Calchas, in *Troilus and Cressida*, I iii, II iii, III iii, V i and V ii. For the most part, however, the opening of the curtains accompanied and indicated a change of place, with the ensuing inner-stage action ostensibly occurring in a location different from that of the preceding scene; similarly, their closing at the end of the inner-stage scene marked a change of place for the action which followed. And always, of course, the curtains, when closed, concealed from the audience the activities of the stagehands who were dressing the rear stage in preparation for the next inner-stage scene.

My own studies have led me to believe that the Globe had a pair of stage "gates" which could, on occasions to which they were appropriate, be set in place to span the forward aperture of the rear stage (Figure 8). They were of course temporary properties, readily installed in preparation for a scene that required their use, and as readily removed when they were no longer needed. When in place, they stood just behind the curtain line. They could therefore be set in position while the curtains were closed, revealed to the

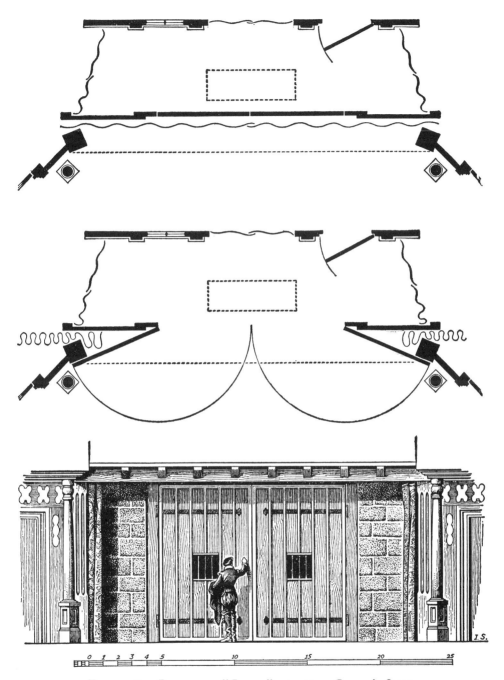

FIGURE 8.   PROPERTY "GATES" FOR THE GLOBE'S STAGE

The first two drawings show floor-plans of the rear stage, with the gates closed in the first drawing, open in the second. The drawing at the bottom shows the aperture of the rear stage in elevation, with curtains parted to reveal closed gates.

audience by the curtains' parting, and (if not needed in a later scene) taken away when the curtains closed again. The two leaves were hinged at their outer edges, and swung outward, toward the forestage, when they opened; each leaf was pierced by a barred wicket at eye-level. The gates were used most often in the historical plays, in scenes before the walls of fortified castles and towns. They served as the gates of the Tower of London in *1 Henry VI*, I iii; as the gates of Orleans in I v, I vi, and II i; of Rouen in III ii, and of Bordeaux in IV ii. They were the gates of York in *3 Henry VI*, IV vii, and of Coventry in V i. In *King John*, Act II, they were the gates of Angiers; in *Henry V*, III iii, of Harfleur; in *Coriolanus*, I iv, v, and vii, they were the gates of Corioles, and in IV i the gates of Rome. They served as the gates of Cleopatra's monument in *Antony and Cleopatra*, IV xv and V ii, as the gates of the Capulet burial vault in *Romeo and Juliet*, V iii, and as the gates of Vienna in *Measure for Measure*, V i. Possibly, though less clearly, they were used in other plays as well, as for instance in *Richard II*, III iii, as the gates of Flint Castle, and as those of Gloucester's Castle in *King Lear*, II ii and iv.

The use of solid gates in the scenes mentioned seems probable because in many of them an illusion of security or defensibility underlies the action, and that illusion would tend to be stultified if mere fabric curtains were all that barred entrance to the stronghold. In other of the scenes the gates are knocked upon, threatened with being broken up or burst open, unlocked with keys, or forced with a wrenching iron. All such scenes demand hard gates of wood; in all of them curtains would be manifestly unsuitable. Quite apart from their use in connection with the drama, it is possible that the gates served also a purely utilitarian purpose, in protecting the interior of the tiring-house from rain and winter's snow and cold.[2]

THE OUTER-STAGE DOORS

The aperture of the inner stage occupied the entire central section of the tiring-house wall on the first level. In the oblique walls at either side of it were two large doors. There are abundant contemporary references to the doors, and abundant proofs that there were two of them.

The usual formula when both doors were used at the same time was

[2] For a fuller discussion of the subject, see my article entitled " 'Gates' on Shakespeare's Stage," *Shakespeare Quarterly*, Vol. VII, No. 2 (Spring 1956).

"Enter A and B at two doors," or *"Enter at one door A, at another B."*
The formula has many variants; and from among forty or fifty Shakespearean stage-directions which specify or imply the use of two doors, the
following are quoted as examples:

From *3 Henry VI*, II v:

> *Enter a Sonne that hath kill'd his Father, at one doore: and a Father that
> hath kill'd his Sonne at another doore.*

From *Richard III*, III vii:

> *Enter Richard and Buckingham at severall Doores.*

And from *Antony and Cleopatra*, III ii:

> *Enter Agrippa at one doore, Enobarbus at another.*

A somewhat smaller group of directions makes it evident that there was
yet a third entrance, the usual formula being *"Enter at three several doors
A, B, and C,"* or *"Enter A and B at several doors, C at the middle door."* At
first glance such directions seem to imply a permanent door located in the
center of the scenic wall, but such a door is wholly out of the question. What
is meant by an entrance through the "middle door" is an entrance either
through the closed curtains where they overlap in the middle, or, if the
curtains are opened and the inner stage exposed, through an actual door
in the rear wall of the inner stage.

Sir Edmund K. Chambers has suggested (but without supporting the
suggestion whole-heartedly) that there may have been not merely three, but
five means of passage through the scenic wall, as in the early neo-classic
theatres based upon Vitruvius.[3] There was however no need for such supplementary doors, and the objections to them are insurmountable. Wherever
placed, whether in the central wall or in the oblique flanking walls, they
would overcrowd wall areas already used to the full. If placed in the central
wall, they would necessitate a narrowing of the inner-stage aperture, from
about 23 feet to perhaps 16, to provide space for them; and at a time when
greater rather than less width was sought to ensure full visibility for elaborate inner-stage spectacles, a narrowing of the aperture by 7 feet (it can
hardly have been less than that, with two doors involved) would be precisely

[3] *The Elizabethan Stage*, III, 84, 85, 100.

what the Globe's designers would seek to avoid. Besides, doors in the central wall at the sides of the aperture would interfere with the operation of the stage curtains. It would be equally impossible to put supplementary doors in the 12-foot-wide flanking side walls, already occupied by the wide stage doors with their door-posts. But the conclusive evidence *against* the existence of such supplementary doors is the absence of any evidence *for* them. There is no scene which requires simultaneous entrance through more doors than three, no scene which involves such situations as would inevitably arise if closely-neighboring doors existed.

Some idea of the size of the outer-stage doors is conveyed by the scenes in which processions pass with colors flying, or in which armies surge over the stage in attack or retreat. Even more informative are the things that must pass or be carried through the doors: a coffin as in *Richard III*, I ii, a triumphal chariot in which a conqueror rides standing, soldiers with pikes, scaling-ladders, and cressets on poles, and the dead at the close of a tragedy carried off on shields shoulder-high. (Never a horse, however; though Shakespeare often intimates that horses are near at hand, he goes out of his way over and over again to avoid bringing one of them upon the stage.) [4] Such doors could hardly be less than five feet wide, by perhaps eight or nine feet high.

In some plays the stage doors were pounded upon or violently assaulted. They must therefore have been solidly built, probably of oak, and heavily framed; and since on occasion they were required to represent either interior or exterior doors, they were perhaps of the vertically-boarded type that was suitable for either sort. They were hinged to the side of the frame nearest the corner post, and swung inwards, so that when open they would still screen the busy interior of the tiring-house from the view of the audience. Plays of the period make it clear that each stage door was provided with a knocker, probably mounted as today, breast-high and in the middle of the door. In certain theatres the knockers were iron rings, hanging at the top from a metal loop or eye-bolt, and striking against a flat metal shield or "boss." Several plays suggest also that the stage doors were furnished with locks. Since, however, a pretense of locking a door could be as convincing

---

[4] As for instance in *The Taming of the Shrew*, III ii and IV v; *Macbeth*, III iii and IV i; *King Lear*, II ii; *Cymbeline*, III iv and IV i; *1 Henry IV*, II i and II ii; *Henry V*, IV ii; and *Richard III*, V iv.

as actually doing so, it is probable that real locks were not provided; mere pretense would obviate the awkward situation that must arise if a door should be locked and its key lost among the rushes. On the inside of the door there was perhaps a heavy bolt, for use in scenes in which a door must stand up against assault.

In addition to knocker, keyhole, and inner bolt, at least one of the outer-stage doors had a wicket, or small barred opening, in its upper half. Such door wickets were not uncommon in Shakespeare's day, and their presence on the stage is attested by the many plays in which persons speak through a closed door to others within, or even thrust a staff or an arm through it. The wickets were probably about a foot square, and screened with a grid of vertical bars. Dr. Adams finds no play which demands wickets in both the outer-stage doors, but is inclined to believe that both doors had them as a matter of convenience and symmetry. Shakespeare makes use of just such a wicket in *The Comedy of Errors*, III i, a scene in which the two Dromios, on opposite sides of a locked house-door, exchange some thirty or forty lines of witticism and abuse through the wicket, and even blows with a staff.

But the primary purpose of the wicket was theatrical and practical, rather than dramatic: behind it stood the prompter, unseen by the audience but in a position to see and hear everything that took place on the platform and to make himself heard there if the need should arise. Well trained actors though they were, Elizabethan players had full need of a prompter, for they presented a different play each day; and one of the prompter's duties was to repeat to an actor the first few words of his speech just before he went out upon the stage. Shakespeare reflects the need for prompting in a line in the First Quarto of *Romeo and Juliet*, I iv, when he speaks of a "without-book Prologue faintly spoke / After a Prompter." The position of the prompter behind the wicketed stage door gave him the further advantage of being able to supervise the multitudinous backstage activities that accompanied every play.

Free-standing door-posts, of just such a sort as stood before many a London doorway in Shakespeare's time, rose on either side of each outer-stage door. Their incorporation in the scenic wall was perhaps the result both of a wish to reproduce a familiar architectural detail, and of the need to shore up the bay windows on the level above. Once they were there, however, they provided a convenient means by which an actor could stand concealed near the door. An instance of the use of a door-post as a hiding place occurs in *Othello*, V i, when Iago directs Roderigo to hide himself near the door of Bianca's house to await Cassio's departure after a supper within:

> Here, stand behind this bulk; straight will he come.
> Wear thy good rapier bare, and put it home.

and it was perhaps behind one of the door-posts that Paris hid when Romeo wrenched open the door of the Capulet burial-vault, in *Romeo and Juliet*, V iii.

The stage doors served in two distinct capacities. Sometimes they represented the actual doors of houses, castles, palaces; at other times, in unlocalized scenes or scenes in which doors would be incongruous (battlefields, forests, and the like) they were mere points of entrance or departure. In their first capacity they were treated *as doors:* knocked upon by a person desiring to enter the house and opened from within, opened from within by a person leaving the house and then closed again. In the second they were merely ignored. Of both sorts of scenes there are innumerable instances in Shakespeare's plays.

Doors of course play a role of special prominence in threshold scenes: scenes acted on the outer stage as before a house, with one of the two stage doors identified with the house throughout the scene as its entrance door, and the tiring-house serving as its interior. Two delightful examples of threshold scenes are to be found in the scene before Justice Shallow's house in *2 Henry IV*, III ii, and in the scene before Page's house, in *The Merry Wives of Windsor*, I i-ii. The probability is, however, that there are far more threshold scenes in the Shakespearean canon than are recognized as such in modern locality-notes. Chambers has stated his Threshold Theory as follows:

> I do not think that it has been fully realized how large a proportion of the action of Elizabethan plays passes at the doors of houses; and as a result the problem of staging, difficult enough anyhow, has been rendered unnecessarily difficult. Here we have probably to thank the editors of plays, who have freely interspersed their texts with notes of locality, which are not in the original stage-directions, and, with eighteenth-century models before them, have tended to assume that action at a house is action in some room within that house. The playwrights, on the other hand, followed the neo-classic Italian tradition, and for them action at a house was most naturally action before the door of that house. If a man visited his friend he was almost certain to meet him on the doorstep; and

here domestic discussions, even on matters of delicacy, commonly took place. Here too, of course, meals might be served.[5]

Many scenes which the editorial locality-notes allocate to interior rooms were, I strongly suspect, intended by Shakespeare to be enacted at the threshold. One such scene is that in which the County Paris calls upon old Capulet and his Lady to press for an early marriage with Juliet (*Romeo and Juliet,* III iv). An analysis of the sequence of scenes and of their respective stage placements makes it seem probable that the scene takes place not in a room in Capulet's house as modern locality-notes have it, but at Capulet's door and therefore under the window at which Juliet and Romeo will soon appear. The probability is, indeed, that on Shakespeare's stage the appearance of the two lovers in the window above followed Capulet's return into his house without a break (see pages 171–172 following).

Act II Scene iii of *The Merchant of Venice* is probably another unsuspected threshold scene. Modern locality-notes usually place it in a room in Shylock's house, as an indoor scene imbedded in a sequence of street scenes (II ii-vi) which eventually turn out to be before Shylock's door; but to move from outer stage to inner for the short 21-line scene would be to intimate a greater shift of location than is actually intended, perhaps suggest a lapse of time, and certainly break the flow of closely-knit episodes. There is no reason to doubt that the scene was originally played at the Globe on the platform as a threshold scene, before the door of Shylock's house. Another instance is provided by Act III Scene ii of *Much Ado About Nothing.* The editorial locality-notes assign it to a room in Leonato's house; the stage-placement of neighboring scenes seems to indicate, however, that no inner stage is available, and therefore that the scene is played upon the platform as at Leonato's threshold. On his way to church for Hero's wedding, Leonato is stopped by Dogberry and Verges, who come to report their arrest of Borachio; but in his haste to get away, he lacks time to hear the story which would have prevented his daughter's shame and changed the whole later course of the play.

At the opposite extreme from the threshold scene was the unlocalized scene or the scene to which a door of any sort would be incongruous. In such cases the actors probably entered the stage through portals which they did

---

[5] Op. cit., III, 59-60. This and other quotations from *The Elizabethan Stage* are reprinted by kind permission of the Clarendon Press, Oxford.

not treat as doors, went well forward on the platform so as to be free of association with the localizing features of the scenic wall, and departed, as they came, without recognizing the existence of the doors through which they passed. Under such conditions the outer stage of the Globe could, if desired, be as unlocalized as the stage of Carnegie Hall.

While the subject of incongruity is under discussion, let us return for a moment to the stage-directions mentioned on an earlier page, in which the simultaneous entrance of actors by two different doors is specified. In not a few cases Shakespeare uses the formula *"Enter at one door . . . at another"* in scenes as to which any sort of door would be totally incongruous. Such a scene is *A Midsummer Night's Dream*, II i, which takes place in a wood near Athens. Within the one scene we find these two stage-directions: *"Enter a Fairie at one doore, and Robin goodfellow at another,"* and *"Enter the King of Fairies at one doore with his traine, and the Queene at another with hers."* Other instances of the one-door-and-another formula in unlikely places are to be found in *Troilus and Cressida*, IV i (a street in Troy), *Coriolanus*, I viii (a field of battle), *King John*, II i (before the walls of Angiers), and *King Lear*, III i (a storm-lashed heath); and there are many more. Usually the inappropriate doors have been edited away in modern texts, and stage-directions such as *"Enter separately"* or *"Enter from opposite sides"* have been substituted for the more explicit words that Shakespeare wrote. The important thing to note is that the one-door-and-another stage-directions are never stated in terms of the dramatic environment, but in terms of the theatre; they speak not of the forest or the field, but of the stage. And since the literary formula remains always substantially the same, however much the dramatic *milieu* may vary, it may be supposed that whenever the formula is used it refers always to the same two outer-stage doors, and that the scenes involved are almost invariably staged on the platform.

THE OVERHANG OF THE TARRAS

The tarras will be discussed later, in the chapter dealing with the second-level stages; one aspect of it, however, needs to be mentioned here, in connection with the scenic wall on the lower level. As will be shown later, it projected forward some three or four feet beyond the plane of the curtains which veiled the lower inner stage. Its overhang therefore faintly resembled a "penthouse" (in Elizabethan times a sloping tiled ledge extending over a shop-front to protect the counters from the rain),[6] and was twice drawn into the sphere of dramatic action by Shakespeare, first in *The Merchant of Venice*, II vi, when Gratiano said:

> This is the penthouse under which Lorenzo
> Desir'd us to make stand,

and again in *Much Ado About Nothing*, III iii:

> Stand thee close then under this penthouse, for it drizzles
> rain, and I will, like a true drunkard, utter all to thee.

---

[6] Cf. *Love's Labour's Lost*, III i 18: ". . . with your hat penthouse-like o'er the shop of your eyes . . ."

CHAPTER VIII

THE INNER STAGES

HISTORICALLY, the platform was the first unit in the development of what eventually became the Elizabethan multiple stage. The second was the curtained recess at the rear of the platform. The third was the balcony, borrowed from the inn-yard. When the stage took final form, the last two units lay within the tiring-house, within the scenic wall, and they are therefore here referred to as the inner stages. The inner stage at first-gallery level lay in back of the platform, separated from it only by the stage curtains, and uniting with it when the curtains were opened. That on the second level was directly over the inner stage below. They were similar in size, in arrangement, and in some of their functions; in others they were very different, as later chapters will show. The lower inner stage is usually known nowadays as the rear stage or alcove or study, the upper as the chamber or (in connection with the tarras) as the balcony.

The size of each inner stage was necessarily determined by the dimensions of that section of the playhouse frame in which it was enclosed. The height of each was the height of its gallery: 12 feet in the lower, 11 in the upper. The width of each was the distance between the corner posts which framed its forward aperture: about 23 feet on the lower level, and (as a result of the "juttey forwards" in the second gallery) a few inches less in the stage above. The depth of each was the depth of its gallery minus the space for a passageway at its rear, by which backstage circulation could continue while an inner-stage scene was in progress; and if this passageway were 5 feet wide (nothing less would seem adequate, in view of the voluminous costumes of Elizabethan times), some 7 or 8 feet would be left as the depth of each inner stage. Each was therefore approximately three times as wide as it was deep, and nearly twice as high; nor was this relative shallowness a disadvantage, for each had a forward extension—the platform at lower level, and the tarras above—to increase the depth of its effective acting area.

The interior walls of the inner stages were made as alterable as possible. Each had a rigid rear wall of wood, pierced by a curtained opening in the middle, with a practicable door on one side and a window on the other (cf.

Scale Drawing XIV), all of them connecting with the passageway in back. These architectural features were appropriate to many an inner-stage scene, and could be concealed by hangings in others to which they were not. The sides or "ends" of the stages were closed by curtains. Each stage had a trap door in its floor, and another in its ceiling.

Each inner stage could be used alone or in combination with other stage units. Each could be disclosed to view, after having been set in advance with distinctive properties and scenic hangings, closed when the action moved else- where, refurnished with new properties and hangings behind closed curtains, and revealed again later as a different location. Herein lay the means by which the Shakespearean drama achieved its uninterrupted flow of action: when one group of actors brought a scene or sequence to its end in one stage unit, another group stood ready to pick up the action without pause in another unit; "the click of the completed rhyme of an exit tag was still audible, perhaps, as a new group took up the discourse."[1] There was, of course, no such regular alternation of scenes, as between the platform and a single inner stage, as was envisioned by the proponents of the now-discarded Alternation Theory, but there was nevertheless an infinitely variable rota- tion, as between the platform and some other unit or units of the multiple stage, which permitted each scene or sequence to be played on an appropriate stage unit and with suitable properties and trappings if need should be. The result was a continuity and pace found today only in motion pictures.

VISIBILITY OF INNER-STAGE SCENES

Nearly half a century ago, when the modern interest in the Elizabethan playhouse was first beginning to manifest itself, Professor George Pierce Baker contended that an inner stage would be "so far back that it must have been out of sight for many of the audience, and inaudible to even more."[2] A few other scholars, perhaps following Baker's lead, have tended to think of the inner stages as "remote," "dark," "obscure," "on dull days . . . almost invisible." But the facts are clearly otherwise. As for remoteness, the rear wall of the inner stage on the lower level was no more than 28 or 30 feet away from the nearest spectators, and 85 from those standing at the farthest remove against the back wall of the top gallery; the upper inner stage would

[1] Arthur Colby Sprague, *Shakespeare and the Audience*, p. 13.
[2] *The Development of Shakespeare as a Dramatist*, p. 88.

of course be farther away from those below, but correspondingly nearer to spectators in the higher galleries. As for illumination, both stages had the daylight which flooded the unroofed yard; and since they were nearly twice as high and three times as wide as they were deep, even the back walls must have been adequately lighted. Indeed, the provision of a roof extending over a part of the platform, and significantly called "the shadow" in contemporary terminology, perhaps indicates that the playhouse suffered from too much light rather than too little. Naturally, the light in the inner stages was more subdued than on the platform, as was entirely appropriate to the interiors which they usually represented.

No longer is it supposed that the torches, lanterns and candles called for in some inner-stage scenes were needed to supply supplementary illumination. They were used solely as an informative convention, to tell the audience that the current scene was taking place at night. If, as seems to be true, they were used more often in inner-stage than in outer-stage scenes, it was probably because night scenes were predominantly indoor scenes: Elizabethans went indoors at night, as we do, and even to a greater extent than we, for they regarded the night air as noxious. The assumption that the use of torches and lanterns was wholly conventional and in no wise utilitarian is confirmed by the fact that they were used in platform scenes also, where surely their feeble illumination was not needed: witness the torches carried by Paris and Romeo in the Verona cemetery (*Romeo and Juliet,* V iii), by Fleance on the night of Banquo's murder (*Macbeth,* III iii), and by the Greeks and their Trojan guests as they blundered toward Achilles' tent in *Troilus and Cressida,* V i.

To be sure, patrons sitting in the gentlemen's rooms could not, whatever the light, see the nearer corners of the inner stages (cf. Scale Drawings I and II), just as box-holders in a theatre of today are inconvenienced in this respect; but presumably they accepted this disadvantage as part of the price they paid for sitting where they could be seen as well as see. As for the vertical sight-lines into the lower inner stage, the sectional view of the playhouse (Scale Drawing XII) indicates that spectators in the yard or the lowest gallery could see the floor, walls, and ceiling, that those in the middle gallery could see all but the ceiling, and that those in the topmost gallery could see the back wall of the rear stage up to a height of about 8 feet above the floor, or well over the height of an actor's head.

The visibility of scenes in the inner stage on the second level, complicated by the possible existence of a protective balustrade, has been the subject of special debate. It is discussed on pages 126 to 129 following.

WALL-HANGINGS IN THE INNER STAGES

The Elizabethan public playhouse had no representational scenery in the modern sense of the word. Scenery of a sort was already in use on the Continent, and in England it later reached a high degree of development in Inigo Jones's designs for masques at Court, but it was not yet known to the public stage. Two question-raising items in Henslowe's inventories of properties owned by the Admiral's Men—"the sittie of Rome" and "the clothe of the Sone and Moone" would seem to contradict this statement; but if the entries do refer to painted scenery, they stand alone. One assumes that the public stages had at least such simple painted devices as a woodland cloth for the frequent forest and orchard scenes and a stone- or brick-work cloth for battlement and base-court scenes, but even for such easy and obvious contrivances no direct evidence can be cited. If they existed at all, they were symbolic rather than realistic, decorative rather than illusion-producing; and the normal background of the Elizabethan or Jacobean stage was still the conventional arras. Richard Flecknoe, writing in 1664, had this to say on the subject:

> Now for the difference betwixt our Theaters and those of former times, they were but plain and simple, with no other Scenes, nor Decorations of the Stage, but only old Tapestry, and the Stage strew'd with Rushes (with their Habits accordingly) whereas ours now for cost and ornament are arriv'd at the heighth of Magnificence.

Curtains played a large part in the operation and decoration of the Elizabethan stage. They stretched across the apertures of the inner stages to screen backstage activities and to permit discoveries. They hung at the sides of each inner stage and at the opening in its rear wall, and on occasions also in front of the rear wall's door and window, to hide them in scenes to which window or door would be incongruous. But though curtains were ever-present features of the stage, the role they played in the theatre was hardly greater than the role they played in the home, for wall-hangings were items of normal everyday domestic furnishing. They did not then, as they do now, serve merely or even primarily for decoration; in the main their purpose was functional—to conserve heat, eliminate drafts, and conceal a rough, unfinished wall. They were supported at their top edges by "tenter-hooks" fastened over a rod or a wooden frame, and were hung several inches out from the wall, to prevent their taking stain or mildew from the wall's dampness. They extended clear to the floor, and often from one end of the room to the other, covering doors and other recesses. In the playhouse, therefore, inner-stage "walls" formed in part of hangings resembled closely what spectators were familiar with at home. Actors entering between a pair of hangings at the side of an inner stage emerged as from an adjoining room beyond. On the stage, as in homes, curtains offered ready hiding places, and a Polonius or a Falstaff who hid behind the arras was merely reflecting a situation familiar enough in real life. Incidentally, of Shakespeare's eleven references to arras, nine allude to it as a means of concealment.

Tapestries or arras were the more splendid and expensive of the wall-hangings; they were used in the palaces of the nobility and in the superior rooms of the well-to-do. Painted cloths, their poor relations, were used in inferior apartments and in bedchambers. Even so modestly situated a person as Mistress Quickly, however, had tapestries in her dining-room—tapestries which Sir John persuaded her to pawn for his benefit and to replace with less expensive painted cloths.[3] In upper-class houses the hangings were frequently changed, as for instance in honor of a guest. A between-scene change of tapestries on the stage would therefore again merely reflect a normal and familiar custom in the home.

The plays of the period contain many a reference to wall-hangings on the stage, several of which are cited on pages 178 to 189 of *The Globe Playhouse*. One can only guess whether the tapestry in Imogen's bedchamber, as described by Iachimo in *Cymbeline*, II iv, was an actual wall-hanging available for use at the Globe:

> It [the chamber] was hang'd
> With tapestry of silk and silver; the story
> Proud Cleopatra, when she met her Roman
> And Cydnus swell'd above the banks, or for
> The press of boats or pride: a piece of work
> So bravely done, so rich, that it did strive
> In workmanship and value; which I wonder'd
> Could be so rarely and exactly wrought . . .

[3] *2 Henry IV*, II i 152 ff.

There are several contemporary allusions to the custom of hanging the stage with black for tragedies, in lines such as

> The stage is hung with black, and I perceive
> The auditors prepar'd for tragedy;

> Let here be made the sable stage, whereon
> Shall first be acted bloody tragedies;

> The stage of heaven is hung with solemn black,
> A time best fitting to act tragedies;

and

> . . . . our black-hung stage.

Shakespeare has "Hung be the Heavens with black" in *Richard III*, I i, and "Black stage for tragedies and murthers fell" in *Lucrece*, 766. There is no clear indication of the place or places where the sable hangings were draped, though there seems to be some slight emphasis upon the heavens, as implying perhaps a conventional draping along the edges of the stage-cover or "shadow." In any case, it seems improbable that the black draperies were hung in either of the inner stages. Hodges suggests that they may have been the platform "skirts" mentioned on page 69 above.[4]

DISCOVERY SCENES

An Elizabethan play seldom states specifically that a given scene is to be enacted in an inner stage. The indications of inner-stage placement are few and ambiguous, and introduce the problem of staging upon which Shakespearean scholars differ most widely; for the very scenes which to one scholar are clearly inner-stage scenes, appear, to another scholar, to call for the open platform. The indications, such as they are, will be discussed later in the chapters devoted to the two inner stages separately. It is however necessary to state at this point that the presence of the word *"enter"* in a stage-direction does not preclude the possibility that the person "entering" is actually revealed, already in place on the stage, by the opening of curtains. To modern ears "enter" implies motion; it did not necessarily do so in the context of an Elizabethan dramatic script. In Shakespeare, for instance, we find such stage-directions as these:

[4] *The Globe Restored*, pp. 47-48.

In *Othello*, I iii (Q2):

> *Enter Duke and Senators, set at a Table, with lights and Attendants.*

and at V ii of the same play:

> *Enter Othello with a light, and Desdemona in her bed.*

In *The Winter's Tale*, V iii:

> *Enter Leontes, Polixenes, Florizell ... Hermione (like a Statue) Lords, etc.*

and in *Cymbeline*, II ii:

> *Enter Imogen, in her Bed, and a Lady.*

All of these scenes begin with the word "enter" and yet all of them involve inner-stage discoveries. An understanding of this point is vital to any attempt to reconstruct the original staging of Elizabethan plays. Unless it be kept in mind, the modern reader is apt to assign to the platform, scenes that were originally enacted in one of the inner stages.

PLATE 26. A modern reconstruction of the interior of the Globe Playhouse. This and the following plates are photographs of the model built by John Cranford Adams with Irwin Smith assisting. The model is now in the Folger Shakespeare Library, Washington

Photograph by Wendell Kilmer

PLATE 27.   The multiple stage in the Adams model.

PLATE 29.   The entrance door and sign-board.
Photograph by Wendell Kilmer.

PLATE 28.   The superstructure or "huts".
Photograph by Wendell Kilmer.

(Left) PLATE 30. The inner stages, with the lower stage open, the chamber curtained.

Photograph by Library of Congress.

(Below) PLATE 31. The "heavens", decorated with zodiac and stars.

Photograph by Wendell Kilmer.

CHAPTER IX

THE REAR STAGE

THE inner stage on the lower level was referred to by Greene in 1589 as "the place behind the stage." At about the same date Marlowe's *Doctor Faustus* was first performed, and its famous opening scene, starting with the stage-direction *"Enter Doctor Faustus in his Study,"* gave to the rear stage a name—"the study"—by which it has since often been known, and by which Dr. Adams designates it throughout his book. But because "study" refers to a dramatic rather than a merely theatrical placement, because it suggests that the rear stage was restricted to the representation of interiors, and because in Shakespeare the word invariably means a place other than the lower inner stage,[1] I prefer to use the more non-committal term "the rear stage."

THE PHYSICAL FEATURES OF THE REAR STAGE

In the first years of permanent playhouses, both the back walls and the side walls of the rear stage were probably formed entirely of cloth hangings. Later, references to a practicable door began to appear, and still later to a window, carrying with them the implication that at least some part of the hangings in the back wall had been replaced by a rigid partition in which door and window could be framed. Even then, however, curtains seem to have persisted in the back wall, presumably in a central aperture between window and door. Each of these features will be considered separately.

The normal use of the window was to enable those inside the rear stage to recognize persons approaching the house from the back, as in *Romeo and Juliet*, IV i, in which Friar Laurence sees Juliet coming toward his cell, and perhaps *The Merry Wives of Windsor*, I iv, in which Mistress Quickly bids Rugby "go to the casement, and see if you can see my master, Master Doctor Caius, coming."[2] Shakespeare seems to have made no further use of the

---

[1] Cf. *Titus Andronicus*, V ii, in which Titus's study is on the upper level; *Romeo and Juliet*, III iii, in which Friar Laurence's study is off-stage in the tiring-house; and *Julius Caesar*, II i, in which Brutus's study also is off-stage.

[2] There is a possibility that Rugby watched from an imaginary window off-stage, and many editors have assumed so, probably because he takes no part in the 25-line conversation that follows. It seems more likely, however, that he watched at the casement in the rear wall, the more so since Dr. Caius undoubtedly entered by the rear door.

rear window, though other dramatists used it with some regularity after 1600. In no instance is the window opened.

The presence of the window suggests that the wall itself was thought of, dramatically speaking, as being an exterior wall. By association, therefore, the corresponding door seems normally to have been thought of as an exterior door, and to have been used for entrances from or exits to points outside the house. It was clearly that door on which the Nurse, in *Romeo and Juliet*, III iii, knocked again and again before she was admitted to the Friar's cell, and that on which Aeneas knocked repeatedly before Pandarus opened it to him in *Troilus and Cressida*, IV ii. Occasionally, however, and notably in sequences in which the backstage stairway was brought into the sphere of dramatic action (*Romeo and Juliet*, IV ii-iii and IV iv-v, *The Merry Wives of Windsor*, III iii and IV ii, etc.), it was treated as an interior door which led to other parts of the same house.

The door, of course, opened upon the passageway at the back of the rear stage. It was presumably of normal domestic size, and swung forward into the room. There is no reason to believe that it had a wicket. It did, however, have a practicable lock and key visible on the inside, as evidenced in *Richard II,* V iii:

> *Aumerle*   Then give me leave that I may turn the key,
> That no man enter till my tale be done.
>   *King Henry*   Have thy desire.
> [*Aumerle locks the door.*] *The Duke of York knocks at the door and crieth.*

and in *Measure for Measure,* I iv:

> *Lucio (within)*   Ho! Peace be in this place!
> *Isabella*   Who's that which calls?
> *Nun*   It is a man's voice. Gentle Isabella,
> Turn you the key and know his business of him.

The curtains at the ends of the rear stage, when used as points of entrance or departure in interior scenes, were always presumed to lead to other parts of the house, such as the Friar's study in *Romeo and Juliet*, III iii, the "fat-room" or "by-room" in *1 Henry IV*, II iv, the counting-house in *The Merry Wives of Windsor*, I iv (Q1), Cressida's chamber in *Troilus and Cressida*, IV ii, and so on. Often serving-men crossed the inner stage, in at one end curtain and out at the other as from kitchen to dining-hall, carrying dishes and service for an off-stage banquet, as in *Romeo and Juliet*, I v, *Macbeth*, I vii, and *Coriolanus*, IV v.

The end curtains were sometimes used for concealment and eavesdropping, but probably not as frequently as the curtain in the middle of the rear wall. In spite of the fact that the end curtains approached the back wall at a broad angle which to some extent eliminated blind corners, they were nevertheless less visible to all the audience than the centrally-placed rear curtain. The latter, therefore, was presumably used in concealment episodes which must be in full view of the spectators, such as that in which Falstaff, hiding from the Sheriff, fell asleep behind the arras and had his pockets picked by Peto, in *1 Henry IV*, II iv.

The rear curtain, hanging as it did between the door and the window, was presumed to front a solid wall. Persons who hid behind it, therefore, must always eventually return from their place of hiding; and for the same reason it was never used as a means of entrance or exit. Under special conditions the curtain could, of course, be withdrawn to reveal the passageway beyond, and Dr. Adams believes that the "Shew of eight Kings," in *Macbeth*, IV i, was staged at the Globe by having the eight Kings, one at a time, file past the aperture in the rear wall in slow procession (*Globe Playhouse*, pp. 189-191). Theoretically, the rear curtain could also have been used to conceal Portia's three caskets in *The Merchant of Venice*, and Hermione as a statue in *The Winter's Tale*, but in both plays it would seem more likely that supplementary curtains were used, so as to bring the action of these climactic scenes farther front on the inner stage.

Such supplementary hangings, sometimes known as "traverses," were strung up in several plays. In Jonson's *Volpone*, for instance, Volpone stood "behind the curtain, on a stool," and peeped over it to watch the reactions of his acquaintances when they received the false news of his death. On other occasions they were hung at a right-angle to the back wall, so as to divide the rear stage into two compartments which might serve as a pair of shops or madmen's cells, or, as in *Richard III*, V iii, as separate tents for Richard and for Richmond.

The trap in the floor of the rear stage was the most often used and versatile trap in the playhouse. Its position in an inner stage gave it some special advantages. For one thing, it could be viewed by the audience only at an oblique angle, not looked into directly like the platform trap, and could therefore be left open indefinitely. For another, it could be veiled from the spectators by closed curtains, and so prepared in advance with properties such as a well-head or a mound of freshly-dug earth. It served sometimes as a pit or an open grave (as for instance the grave of Ophelia in *Hamlet*, V i), sometimes as a well or river bank, and often as an infernal area from which ghosts could rise. It was through the rear-stage trap that the ghost of Caesar entered in *Julius Caesar*, IV iii, the ghost of Banquo in *Macbeth*, III iv, and the ghosts of the parents and brothers of Posthumus in *Cymbeline*, V iv. The trap was silent in operation, and therefore needed no disguise sounds: note that Macbeth had no warning of the appearance of Banquo's ghost, and that neither Lucius nor Posthumus was wakened from sleep in the other instances mentioned.

Overhead, in the ceiling of the rear stage, there was another trap, sometimes used as a means of eavesdropping on an inner-stage scene below. Although at least thirty plays written between 1599 and 1639 made use of the ceiling trap, there is no clear evidence of its having been used in any play by Shakespeare. As suggested by the late W. J. Lawrence, it may have served the secondary purpose of providing a convenient means by which heavy properties could be moved from one level of the playhouse to another during the morning hours of preparation for the afternoon's play.[3] In Scale Drawing XIV, the ceiling trap is pictured as one of a series of traps which run in vertical sequence from sub-stage to superstructure, with a winch and tackle above them.

THE REAR STAGE IN USE AS A SEPARATE UNIT

The special value of the rear stage lay in these three things: (1) by virtue of the fact that it was itself a walled-in area, it could serve appropriately to represent a room or other enclosure; (2) because it could be concealed from the audience by curtains, it could be fitted out with properties and wall-hangings to give color and to suggest a definite locality; and (3) because it lay at the rear of the outer stage, it could be used in combination with the platform, either as a single large stage or as two separate but related stages, and by its setting could give localization to the two together.

When used as a stage in its own right, the rear stage characteristically

---

[3] *Pre-Restoration Stage Studies*, p. 147.

represented an enclosure or restricted area of some sort, man-made or natural, at ground level. It might be a hall at Elsinore or Belmont, a room in Windsor or Verona, a tavern, a church, a farmhouse near Dover, a cavern in Scotland, a cell for Prospero or Friar Laurence, a tent for Brutus or Coriolanus, a monument for Cleopatra, or a tomb for Juliet; a hawthorn brake for Bottom or a bower for Titania, a wooded glade, a formal garden, or the corner of a churchyard.

Even when the rear stage was used by itself alone, without reference to the platform, it is improbable that the action was restricted to its relatively shallow depth, for actors of the rhetorical school needed plenty of elbow room. They made their initial entrances through the inner-stage doors, so as to establish the rear stage as the setting for the scene, but thereafter they felt free to advance to the forestage, where their movements would be less cramped and where they would be in closer touch with their hearers. One need not suppose that Elizabethan actors ever saw the division between the inner stage and the outer as a fixed boundary; once the curtains were thrown wide, indeed, no boundary existed, and the platform could serve as a forward extension of the rear stage without having an identity of its own. Sometimes, of course, the actors were pinned to the properties in the inner stage; and although Brutus and Cassius probably went to the forestage for their quarrel, Brutus returned to the inner stage when he sat down to read by the light of a taper (*Julius Caesar*, IV iii). In any event, as the inner-stage scene drew toward its close, it was perhaps conventional for the last actors to move back into the rear stage for the final twenty lines or more of dialogue, and to depart through the rear-stage exits. They thus restored the theatrical illusion that the entire scene had passed within the confines of the inner stage, and when the curtains closed at the scene's end permitted the action of the next scene to start upon the platform as in a different place.

INDICATIONS OF REAR-STAGE PLACEMENT

Scenes in the following categories may be presumed to have been placed in the rear stage. In some instances the platform was used in combination with the inner stage, either as a forward extension of it or as a separate but related place.

> Lower-level scenes which involve discoveries: *Tempest*, V i (the discovery of Ferdinand and Miranda); *Othello*, I iii (the opening of the scene); *Hamlet*, V ii (beginning with line 235), etc.

Lower-level scenes which involve the extensive use of properties: *Merchant of Venice*, IV i; *Henry VIII*, I iv, etc.

Scenes in which a person knocks on a door, or is descried offstage, *before entering: Romeo and Juliet*, III iii and IV i; *Troilus and Cressida*, IV ii, etc.

Scenes which refer to a door or stairway as leading to rooms above: *Merry Wives of Windsor*, III iii and IV ii, etc.

Scenes in which a large group of persons is seated formally, such as a senate, parliament, council, or the like: *Julius Caesar*, III i; *Othello*, I iii; *Richard III*, III iv, etc.

Scenes in which ghosts or apparitions rise to the inside of a room, tent, or cave: *Macbeth*, III iv; *Julius Caesar*, IV iii, etc.

Generally speaking, all indoor scenes at ground level, particularly when a part of the stage is supposed to be *in* and the rest *out: Romeo and Juliet*, V iii; *Julius Caesar*, III i and IV ii-iii, etc.

Outdoor scenes which require specific localization or properties: *Midsummer Night's Dream*, III i; *2 Henry IV*, IV i; *Richard II*, III iv; *Hamlet*, V i, etc.

COMBINED-STAGE SCENES

Sometimes, in larger scenes, the rear stage and the platform merged to form a single great stage, with many points of entry, space enough for free movement and a full company of actors, and a prepared setting in the inner stage to give color and character to the whole. So used, the combined stages might represent a single large interior, such as the court of justice in *The Merchant of Venice*, the council chamber in *Othello*, the throne room in *Hamlet* or *King Lear*, or a ballroom in the home of Leonato or old Capulet; or they might serve for a single large exterior: the Forest of Arden in *As You Like It* or Gaultree Forest in *2 Henry IV*, Olivia's garden in *Twelfth Night*, or a churchyard in *Hamlet*. In such cases it was not necessary that initial entrances be restricted to the inner stage nor (unless the scene following was to open on the platform) that the scene close there, for the outer stage, as well as the inner, was recognized as part of a single locality.

At other times the combined stages represented two distinct but logically related places rather than one locality. They might be two adjoining rooms, as in *2 Henry IV*, IV iv-v, in which the platform serves for the Jerusalem Chamber and the rear stage for a neighboring room, or *Hamlet*, II ii, in

which the inner stage is the King's private room and the outer stage an ante-
chamber or lobby adjoining it. Or the combined stages might be used to
represent an interior associated with a larger exterior. There are many
examples of this bold device. In *Romeo and Juliet,* for instance, the platform is a Verona graveyard, and the rear stage a burial vault within it; in
Julius Caesar, III i, the outer stage is a street in Rome and the inner stage
the interior of the Capitol. In *Julius Caesar,* again, the rear stage is the
interior of Brutus' tent, and the platform a battlefield near Sardis (IV ii-iii) ;
in *King Lear,* II ii, the inner and outer stages serve respectively for the base-
court of Gloucester's castle and the adjacent parklands; and in *Antony and
Cleopatra,* IV xv and V ii, in a complicated staging on two levels, the two
inner stages serve for the interior of Cleopatra's monument, and the outer
stage for the land outside. In such cases, entrances and exits were of course
governed by dramatic fitness: the stage doors in the scenic wall were used by
actors who entered the area which the platform represented, and the rear-
stage door by those who entered the area represented by the inner stage.
Invariably, however, unless the scene happened to be the final scene of the
drama, the action ended either on the outer stage or the inner stage alone—
and usually the inner—as a means of creating the illusion that the entire
scene had been enacted upon that one stage, and of permitting the next to
open upon the other as in a different place.

Normally, as we know, a change of dramatic place was accompanied and
indicated by a change of stage. The practice was necessary and logical, for
under the conditions of continuous action two consecutive scenes upon the
same stage would be virtually indistinguishable from a single scene, and
the idea of a removal from one place to another within their uninterrupted
course would be precluded; and the fact that the platform was occasionally
treated as if it were two stages in one does not impair the validity of the
rule nor suggest that it was not generally followed. In the case of combined-
stage scenes, however, a strict application of the rule would impose a severe
restriction, for it would forbid the use of either the rear stage or the platform—by far the most useful of the stage units—in the scene to follow.
And therefore dramatists devised a means of circumventing the restriction.
In combined-stage scenes, they commonly had the actors move back to the
inner stage for the final twenty lines or more of dialogue, thus creating
the illusion that the entire scene had passed there and releasing the platform

for the beginning of the next scene; or, conversely and less frequently, they had them advance to the platform and the stage curtains close behind them, thus making the closing passage the technical equivalent of a platform scene and permitting the next to open in the inner stage.

The device of retirement to the rear stage at the end of combined-stage scenes seems to have been used in a large proportion of the "big" scenes in Shakespeare's plays (except, of course, final scenes in which no provision had to be made for a scene to follow). If their texts be examined with this in view, it will be found to be the rule, rather than the exception, for the greater part of the actors to depart from the stage at least one full minute before the scene reaches its end, leaving perhaps only two or three, and never more than can be accommodated within the confines of the inner stage, to bring the scene to its end. Because of the importance of this convention in the staging of Elizabethan plays, more than the usual number of instances will be cited.

In *Othello*, the first combined-stage scene is in the council-chamber (I iii); it closes with 109 lines of dialogue between Iago and Roderigo, and is followed by a scene on the platform as representing the seaport in Cyprus. The second is a hall in the castle (II iii), which ends with 53 lines of duologue and soliloquy and is followed by a platform scene as in an open place before the castle's door. The third is the great scene in Othello's garden (III iii); it ends with 159 lines of duologue, and again the platform represents the open place before the castle in the scene that follows.

In *Romeo and Juliet*, the ballroom scene (I v) ends with the departure of the guests and with Juliet and the Nurse alone in the inner stage for the final 17 lines of dialogue; it is followed by a scene in which the platform represents a lane near Capulet's orchard.

Julius Caesar uses the combined stages twice. In III i the platform serves for 12 lines as a street before the Capitol, and thereafter the rear stage, with overflow to the platform, serves for the Capitol itself; the scene ends with 44 lines of soliloquy and duologue, and is followed by the Forum Scene on the platform. In IV ii, the forestage is the ground before Brutus' tent; with the parting of the inner-stage curtains at IV iii, the rear stage becomes the tent's interior. The sequence comes to an end with 70 lines of dialogue during which not more than five persons are on the stage. A platform scene follows, as on the battlefield near Philippi.

The four-scene murder sequence in *Macbeth* is, of course, acted on the combined stages; it ends with 12 lines of conversation between Malcolm and Donalbain, and is followed by an exterior scene. The Banquet Scene at III iv shows Macbeth and his lady alone for 23 lines after the guests and attendants have departed; it is followed by a scene on the Scottish heath.

The churchyard scene in *Hamlet* (V i) ends with a small group of five or six persons clustered about Ophelia's grave in the inner stage. It is followed by a scene which begins on the platform, but which after 235 lines becomes another and different combined-stage scene with the opening of the stage curtains. This is but one instance of the extraordinary fluidity which characterizes the entire staging of *Hamlet*.

Nine instances have been cited in which the number of actors has been reduced to a small group at the close of a combined-stage scene, and an outer-stage scene has followed. The list could be extended indefinitely. It is my contention that in each instance the actors have retired to the inner stage as the scene approached its close, and that the concluding passages of dialogue, lasting at least a full minute in all but two of the cases cited, became the technical equivalent of a rear-stage scene and thus permitted the dramatist to open his next scene on the platform as in a different place.

Occasionally the procedure is reversed. At some point in the course of the combined-stage scene most of the characters on the stage—perhaps a king and his courtiers—depart, and at the same moment the stage curtains close. A few actors have however already advanced to the outer stage, and their subsequent dialogue constitutes the equivalent of a forestage scene, and permits the next scene to open in the inner stage. In *1 Henry IV*, I iii, for example, the King and his train leave the stage at line 124, and the curtains are drawn together. Hotspur and Northumberland are left alone on the platform, to be joined a moment later by Worcester. They continue the action on the outer stage, while behind closed curtains the appurtenances of a royal palace are being replaced by those of an inn-yard at Rochester. Here the transfer of action not merely permits the next scene to open in the inner stage, but also provides nearly 180 lines for the change of inner-stage setting.

Usually, in such cases, the combined-stage scene in question is followed by another combined-stage scene in a different place, and the premature closing of the curtains is primarily due to the need to provide time for a change of properties and hangings in the inner stage, as in the instance just cited. Another example is furnished by *Much Ado About Nothing*, II i. The scene is a hall in Leonato's house, and the occasion a masked ball—an occasion calling for the pageantry of lights and music and rich color. At line 160 the stage-direction reads *"Dance. Exeunt [all but Don John, Borachio, and Claudio]."* As the music and the dance end and the dancers depart, the curtains close, and the action thereafter continues on the outer stage, while behind the curtains the ballroom properties are being replaced by others appropriate to a garden with pleached bower. About 240 lines are thus provided for the change.

The device is used twice in *A Midsummer Night's Dream,* in I i and IV i. In the first instance it is used to provide time for a change of setting from the Palace of Theseus to a wood near Athens; in the second instance, for a reversal of the change; and each time the closing of the curtains is heralded by the departure of the Duke and Hippolyta and their trains.[4] I shall cite just one more example, the Court of Justice scene in *The Merchant of Venice.* It is, of course, acted on the combined stages; the inner stage has been set in advance with a judicial bench and bar, a dais and canopy for the Duke, and tapestries on the walls. But in a few minutes the inner stage must serve as background for a new combined-stage scene, this time to represent Portia's moonlit grounds at Belmont. To provide time for the necessary change, the action transfers to the platform at line 407, where the stage-direction reads *"Exeunt Duke and his train."* As the court breaks up and the dignitaries retire, the curtains are closed, with Antonio, Bassanio, Gratiano, Portia and Nerissa in front of them as on a street before the courtroom, for the final 50 lines of IV i and the 19 lines of IV ii. Instantly, as soon as the curtains are at rest, the stagehands must begin their task of removing the trappings of the court of justice and substituting those of the garden at Belmont: they have only 69 lines, far less time than is usually allowed, to make the change.

---

[4] Each time also an upper-stage scene (in Quince's house) intervenes between the end of the earlier combined-stage scene and the beginning of that which follows. The intervening scenes are too short, however (114 and 46 lines respectively), to allow adequate time for a major change of setting, and therefore it is necessary to transfer the action to the forestage to permit the change to get under way behind closed curtains. In the second instance, still further time is gained by having V i begin on the outer stage, with the curtains remaining closed until line 84 (". . . and take your places, ladies").

It has often been remarked that Shakespeare habitually ended his big scenes with a relaxation of tension, rather than with the heightened intensity characteristic of scenes on the modern stage. The relaxation was in part due to the absence of a front curtain (see page 78), but not less to the practice of withdrawing most of the actors from the stage before the scene came to an end. But, one may ask, would he not in any event have withdrawn the actors, would he not in any event have relaxed the tension, even if purely theatrical pressures had not been present? It is, of course, impossible to be sure; but it is perhaps significant that the final scenes of his plays, when he had no need to think of a change of setting, almost invariably close with a crowded stage. This is true in *Hamlet*, in *King Lear*, in *Romeo and Juliet*, in *The Merchant of Venice*, in *Twelfth Night*, in *As You Like It*, in *Macbeth*, in *Julius Caesar*, in *Antony and Cleopatra*, in *Cymbeline*, *The Winter's Tale*, *Measure for Measure*, *All's Well That Ends Well*, *Much Ado About Nothing*, and most of the others.[5] The plays themselves thus furnish strong internal evidence in support of both the major and the minor premises. They indicate that combined-stage scenes usually ended with a reduced number of actors on the stage if there was need of a platform scene to follow on the one hand, or of an inner-stage scene or change of setting on the other; and conversely, that the scene normally ended with a crowded stage if no such needs existed.

CONTINUITY OF ACTION

There can be little doubt that Shakespeare intended his plays to be performed substantially without a break. The premature closing of the stage curtains, in the instances just mentioned, is only one evidence of his concern to provide adequate time to permit inner-stage changes of setting to be effected without necessitating even a momentary pause in the action. And there are others, as for instance his occasional resort to "padding" to eke out the time, and his care to allow time for an actor to make a backstage trip from one stage unit to another.

Study of the plays themselves seems to show that a major change of setting called for a time-allowance of about 200 lines of dialogue, or (at the

[5] *Othello* is an exception; it ends with perhaps nine persons on the stage. But that is because the final scene is played in an inner stage, which can accommodate only a relatively small group of actors.

rate of 20 lines per minute), 10 minutes; a simpler change, particularly in the upper stage, might need no more than 75 lines or 3½ minutes. Normally, of course, the requisite time was provided by the interposition of a platform scene or a scene in the other inner stage; once in a while, however, Shakespeare seems to have found himself compelled to devise action or dialogue specifically for the purpose of covering an inner-scene change. Usually the covering passages are so brilliantly contrived, so apt and inevitable dramatically, that their dual purpose passes unsuspected. This is conspicuously true of the first 235 lines of *Hamlet*, V ii. In the previous scene, the rear stage has served for the corner of a churchyard, and its trap for Ophelia's grave; it must be converted to a hall at Elsinore for the final scene of the tragedy. Time must be provided to clear away all traces of churchyard, grave, and mound of earth, and to dress the stage as a room in the palace with a royal "state"; and therefore now, and not until now, Hamlet relates the story of his voyage and of the King's plot against his life. He had previously been so impatient to tell Horatio of his dreadful adventure that he had bidden him "repair thou to me with as much speed as thou wouldest fly death." Horatio had presumably done so, but the story had not been told; he has been with Hamlet throughout the Graveyard Scene, but still the story has not been told. Why? Perhaps because, on purely practical grounds, the insertion of the narrative at any point before the end of the Graveyard Scene would not have aided in providing time for the change of inner-stage setting; and the unexplained delay inevitably suggests the thought that Shakespeare, having originally intended to use Hamlet's recital earlier in the play, may have postponed it, or even have lifted it from its original context, to help in solving a theatrical problem. Hamlet's report takes up 80 lines, but 80 are not enough; and therefore Shakespeare creates the waterfly Osric, whose lengthy embassy takes another 110 lines, and then a Lord who repeats Osric's message in 16 lines more. The inner stage is now ready, and at line 235 the curtains open to reveal the King and Queen and "*a table and flagons of wine on it.*"[6] Similarly, one may suspect that the first 85 lines of *Romeo and Juliet*, V iii, including the wanton slaughter of Paris, are related to the need for time to change the rear-stage setting from Friar Laurence's cell to Capulet

---

[6] Cf. Granville-Barker, *Prefaces to Shakespeare*, III, 165 n. 1, 170; W. W. Greg, *The Editorial Problem in Shakespeare*, p. 68; L. L. Schücking, "The Churchyard-Scene in Shakespeare's *Hamlet*," *Review of English Studies*, Vol. XI (April 1935).

burial vault, and that the lengthy description of the storm in *Julius Caesar*, I iii, permits the inner stage to be set as Brutus' orchard.

A more obvious, and therefore less happy, instance is found in *The Merchant of Venice*, III v. The lower inner stage has been used throughout the play as background for a hall in Portia's house in Belmont; it will now shortly be needed for the court of justice in Venice, and action must be provided to cover the change of setting. Perhaps at a loss for dramatic material (for no problems remain to be resolved except those which the trial itself must resolve), Shakespeare inserted the Launcelot-Jessica-Lorenzo scene, which involves none of the principal characters of the drama and advances the plot not one whit. It has been suggested that the practical purpose of the scene is to give Portia and Nerissa time to change their costumes to those appropriate for a young Doctor of Laws and his clerk; but this supposition is disproved by the fact that their delayed entrances in the Trial Scene give them 8 and 6 minutes respectively for the purpose, as contrasted with the mere $4\frac{1}{2}$ minutes which suffice for the rechange. One justification for the scene is that it provides dramatic time for the journey from Belmont to Venice; but basically the scene is, to quote Granville-Barker, "padding unalloyed, and very poor padding at that."[7]

The structure of the plays affords still another proof of the dramatist's concern to avoid a break in the action. Sometimes an actor who has appeared on a given stage in one scene is required to appear on another stage in the scene following, as in a different place. If he were kept on the first stage until the very end of the scene and then were required to be on the second stage for the opening lines of the new scene, there would be an inter-scene pause while he made his backstage passage from one stage unit to the other (unless, of course, they happened to be adjacent the one to the other). Shakespeare's care to avoid such an inter-scene break is proved by his almost invariable practice of withdrawing the actor from the stage at least half a minute before the end of the earlier scene, or delaying his entrance to the later scene by at least half a minute, or both. This practice has been noted by Shakespearean scholars as a dramatic principle, and has been called the Law of Re-Entry. It may be stated as follows:

> If any character appears in two consecutive scenes which occur at places presumed to be at some distance from one another, he must, in order to

[7] *Prefaces to Shakespeare*, II, 107.

make his remove seem credible in a scheme of dramatic time, either make his exit from the stage at least ten lines before the close of the earlier scene, or delay his entrance to the later scene by at least ten lines.[8]

In observance, the Law of Re-Entry served the dramatic purpose of providing time for an inter-scene journey; but not less it served the purely theatrical purpose of preventing an interruption in the smooth flow of action.

All the examples previously cited have tended to suggest that Shakespeare sought to avoid breaks or pauses in the performance of his plays. Is it, however, possible that he did in fact intend one or more intermissions in each play? The question is one upon which scholars are sharply divided. Some adhere strongly to the doctrine that there were no intermissions of any kind on the public stage in the period under discussion. Others incline to the idea that the actors gave their audiences an occasional respite from the strain of attention. Many factors are involved—the question of act-divisions and their validity, the length of time needed for a performance, the prevalence of interludes in the private theatres, etc.—and the matter cannot be adequately examined here. At the present time I wish merely to point out that in their provision of time for a change of inner-stage setting, the plays themselves, while affording many instances of continuity, afford also a few of discontinuity. As a case in point, Act III Scene iv of *Richard II* takes place in the Duke of York's garden, and requires properties in the inner stage, such as "yon dangling apricocks," to give it locality and meaning. It is followed by the Abdication Scene in Westminster Hall (IV i), which, with its crowds and its regal throne, clearly calls for the combined stages. But no time is allowed for a change of setting. Can it be that there was an intermission which provided time for the change? Again, in *Henry V*, the 67 lines of II iii would seem to be inadequate to cover the change of setting from the English council chamber of II ii to the French King's hall of state in II iv. Scene iii, as it happens, is the last scene on English soil; beginning with iv, the action is in France. May one suppose that between those scenes Shakespeare intended an intermission, both to mark the crossing from England to France and to give added time for a change of setting?

[8] Cf. John Cranford Adams, "The Original Staging of *King Lear*," *Joseph Quincy Adams: Memorial Studies* (1948), p. 323. The so-called Law was first expounded by R. Prölss in his *Von den ältesten Drucken der Dramen Shakespeares* in 1905. It has been commented upon by several writers, including W. J. Lawrence, *Shakespeare's Workshop* (1928), pp. 17-18, and C. M. Haines, "The 'Law of Re-Entry' in Shakespeare," *Review of English Studies*, Vol. 1 (1925), 449-451.

And may not a similar intermission have been introduced in *The Merchant of Venice*, at the close of the two brief outer-stage episodes following the trial, to give opportunity for a readjustment of mood after the tensions of the Trial Scene and Shylock's final departure, and at the same time to augment the mere 69 lines provided for the removal of courtroom properties and the substitution of others appropriate to Portia's garden? There are other instances, none of them conclusive, which point in the same direction. The question merits more study than it has yet received.

CHAPTER X

SECOND-LEVEL STAGES

THE TIRING-HOUSE STAIRS

THE multiple stage of the Globe Playhouse occupied five levels, from sub-stage to superstructure, and needed stairways to enable actors, musicians, and stagehands to get from one floor to another. The stairs which led down from ground level to "hell," and those which led up from second-gallery level to third and thence to the huts, are presumed to have existed merely because they would have been indispensable. No contemporary documents mention them. They were mere utility stairs, at all times wholly concealed from the audience and never involved in theatrical action. It is idle to speculate as to their location: any place would do for them, if reasonably accessible and yet out of the lanes of heavy traffic.

The stairs leading from first level to second were, however, a very different matter. They were used and referred to in many a Globe play, and their position is therefore of importance in any reconstruction of the Playhouse. These facts about them can be deduced from stage-directions and dialogue in the plays of the period:

First, there was only one stairway from lower stage to upper. Even when, as in *The Devil is an Ass*, two two-story houses were represented on the stage, or, as in *Two Lamentable Tragedies*, at least three, in only one of the houses do actors move up or down stairs. If two stairways had been available, we might expect scenes to have been devised to take advantage of that fact; but no such scenes exist. We are therefore probably justified in assuming that only one stairway connected the first floor of the tiring-house with the second.

Secondly, the stairway was not on the front of the tiring-house façade, or elsewhere in full view of the audience, for whenever an actor went from one floor to another he disappeared from view. This fact is indicated by the many stage-directions which give an "exit" to an actor when he takes to the stairs, and an "enter" or "re-enter" when he appears at the new level. The stairs therefore were off-stage, behind the scenic wall.

They were not, however, constructed wholly or even partly within the inner stages on the first and second levels. If they were, the "exit" and "re-enter" would perhaps not be necessary; more importantly, they would destroy any illusion of privacy or security in scenes in which doors are locked, and would rule out all scenes in which upper and lower rooms are treated as having no means of communication; and finally, in scenes in which either inner stage was open to the audience's view, all backstage movement of actors, musicians and stagehands by way of the stairs would have to cease until the scene came to an end and the curtains closed.

And yet some part of the stairway—perhaps only a step or two and a bit of handrail—was occasionally, and under some conditions, visible to actors in inner-stage scenes. This assumption is based upon the frequent use of phrases such as "those stairs," "yonder stairs," etc., spoken presumably with an accompanying gesture to direct the attention of the spectators to something which they, as well as the actors, could probably see. Though not actually *in* the inner stages, the stairs were therefore close at hand; and other phrases and bits of stage business establish a close relationhip between the stairway and the rear doors of the upper and lower inner stages. It may therefore confidently be assumed that the foot of the stairway was near to the door in the back wall of the lower inner stage and visible through it when the door was fully opened, and that the head of the stairs was placed in a similar position with reference to the upper-stage door. The probability is that the 12-foot-high stairway was a single straight flight, as being the cheapest to build and the easiest to climb; and since in a straight flight the head of the stairs cannot be over the foot, it follows as a consequence that the relative doors could not be over one another. On one level, therefore, the door was at the left of the aperture in the rear wall, and on the other level at the right, with each door balanced by a window on the opposite side. The rear walls of the inner stages are so shown in Scale Drawing XIV.

With the doors and the stairway thus closely associated, the business of going to a door and calling up or down to someone on the other stage would seem entirely natural. An instance of this is to be found in *The Merry Wives of Windsor,* IV ii:

> *Mrs. Ford* What, ho, Mistress Page! Come you and the old woman down. My husband will come into the chamber. . . .
> *Ford* Come down, you witch, you hag you! Come down, I say!

In *The Globe Playhouse,* Dr. Adams assumed that the stairs were constructed in the passageways at first and second level.[1] In building the model of the Globe, however, he realized that stairs so placed would leave the passageways too narrow, and would be too narrow themselves. He therefore moved them to a shaft outside the rear wall of the playhouse, as in Scale Drawings I, II, IX, XII and XIV.

THE TARRAS

The Globe Playhouse had four related acting areas on the second level: a curtained inner stage directly over its counterpart on the lower level; in front of it a long shallow balcony projecting forward over the opening of the rear stage below; and a pair of window-stages, one at each end of the balcony and above an outer-stage door.

The balcony was, as has already been said, historically the third oldest unit in the development of the multiple stage. It went back to the inn-yards, with their encircling galleries giving access to upper rooms (cf. Plate 21). Strolling players had set up their improvised platforms at one side of the yard, with a curtained space behind to serve as dressing-room, and with a section of railed gallery overhead. Inevitably they had accepted the invitation which the gallery offered, and had pressed it into the service of the play. Upon it they had appeared as on the battlements of a castle or the walls of a city, or in the upper room of a house; and so useful had it proved to be, particularly in the heyday of the historical play, that when James Burbage designed the first permanent playhouse in 1576, he reproduced a section of gallery in the second level of his tiring-house. In Burbage's Theater the gallery was probably no longer, from side to side, than the aperture of the inner stage below it, and did not project appreciably from the scenic wall; it was presumably enclosed at the back by curtains which permitted ready entrance from the rear, and which at the same time screened a dressing room behind. The rough-and-tumble battles that were staged upon it in some of the earlier historical plays suggest that it was fronted by a sturdy balustrade, or even (as in the DeWitt drawing) by a solid parapet. When not called for by the action of the play, it seems (again as in the DeWitt drawing) to have been made available to privileged spectators. This custom is reflected in *The Taming of the Shrew,* when at the end of the Induction Christopher Sly

[1] Pp. 237 and 237 n. 8, and floor-plan, p. 242.

and his "wife" move forward to the balcony to watch the play unfold on the stage below.

The evolution of the second level of the tiring-house brought changes in the design of the balcony. A curtained inner stage on the upper level, inspired perhaps by the success of that on the level below, was felt to be necessary. The depth of the playhouse frame, however, was a fixed dimension; it could not contain a balcony, plus an adequate inner stage, and a passageway at the rear besides. The balcony therefore gave way; it was pushed forward so that it projected from the scenic wall by some three or four feet. Not until the last decade of the 16th century did references to an upper inner stage begin to appear, and at about the same time actors began to speak of the balcony as an overhanging structure, in such phrases as "beneath this tarras" and "under this penthouse." The curtains at the rear of the balcony were retained, but now they served a new purpose in addition to the old, that of permitting discoveries in the upper rear stage; and the new need for visibility for inner-stage scenes demanded further that the old heavy balustrade, which in the past had withstood so many assaults, should be replaced by a lighter (and perhaps removable) one, with balusters slender and widely spaced.

The word "balcony" was as yet little used; its first appearance in print did not come until 1618. The term that late 16th- and 17th-century dramatists used for their projecting balcony was "tarras," with, of course, several variant spellings. The relationship of "tarras" to the present-day "terrace" is of course immediately obvious, but the old spelling is here retained to avoid the modern association of the word "terrace" with a raised level or platform of earth. Shakespeare employs the word "tarras" only once, in the stage-direction *"Enter King, Queene, and Somerset on the Tarras,"* in *2 Henry VI*, IV ix; other dramatists of the period use it often, both in stage-directions and in dialogue.

Some of the scenes enacted on the tarras suggest that it was of considerable length, and of depth enough to accommodate a lively tussle on the walls. Such a scene is Act II Scene i in the pre-Globe play *1 Henry VI*, in which Talbot, Bedford and Burgundy and their men enter with scaling ladders to attack the "flinty bulwarks" of Orleans:

> *Bed.* Ascend, brave Talbot. We will follow thee.
> *Tal.* Not all together. Better far, I guess,
> That we do make our entrance several ways;

> That, if it chance the one of us do fail,
> The other yet may rise against their force.
> *Bed.*   Agreed. I'll to yond corner.
> *Bur.*   And I to this.
> *Tal.*   And here will Talbot mount, or make his grave.

They scale the walls, engage the French garrison, and *"The French leap o'er the walls in their shirts."* The length of the tarras is further suggested by scenes in which defenders to the number of twelve or more appear on the walls to parley with besiegers on the outer stage below, or in which a person at one end is presumed to be inaudible to a person at the other. Its depth is indicated not only by the space needed for skirmishes on the walls, but even more specifically by the chair and cushion placed "in the gallerie" for the King in *The Spanish Tragedy,* IV iii. Yet other scenes (though none by Shakespeare) show that it was possible for an actor to climb from the tarras through the casement of a window-stage. The tarras, therefore, must have extended all the way across the mid-section of the tiring-house façade, a distance of 22 or 23 feet, and terminated at the side walls of the projecting window-stages.

The tarras usually served to represent an elevated area out of doors. Its traditional and most frequent use was, of course, as the top of a defensive wall. It was so used by Shakespeare again and again, particularly in the earlier plays. Five times it served for castle or city walls in *1 Henry VI:* as the walls of Orleans in Acts I and II, of Rouen in III, of Bordeaux in IV, and of Reignier's castle at Angiers in V. Three times it served so in *3 Henry VI,* twice in *2 Henry VI,* and one or more times in *Titus Andronicus, Richard II, King John, Henry V, Coriolanus, Timon of Athens,* and *Pericles.* In *Richard III,* III vii, it served as a balcony or something of the sort at Baynard's Castle, on which Richard appeared between two bishops; in *Julius Caesar,* III ii, as the public pulpit from which Brutus and Marc Antony addressed the Roman populace, and in V iii as the hill from which Pindarus watched what he believed to be the capture of Titinius. In *The Tempest,* I i, it probably served as the quarter-deck of Alonso's storm-tossed ship.

No such relationship existed between the tarras and the inner stage at its rear as that which existed between the outer and inner stages on the lower level. Platform and rear stage, as we know, were often used in combination with one another to represent adjoining rooms or an exterior related to an interior. No comparable correlation, however, was possible on the upper level, for when the curtains were open the shallow tarras lost its separate identity and became merely a forward extension of the stage behind it. Tarras scenes, therefore, were always played before closed curtains, and always in association with action on the platform. Inner-stage scenes, on the other hand, were seldom related to action on the outer stage below: they were usually presumed to be taking place in a fully enclosed room, with the window-stages providing the only means by which a person in the upper story of the house could communicate with one on the platform outside.

Almost never does action begin on the tarras and move thence to the inner stage, and rarely does it begin in the inner stage and then advance to the tarras. Each such generality has its exceptions, however. In *The Silver Age*, in a scene to be discussed on page 148, Jupiter alights on the tarras and then moves back to Semele's chamber; and in the second Induction Scene in *The Taming of the Shrew*, Christopher Sly clearly leaves the inner stage and goes forward to the tarras when the play itself begins.

In the last decade of the 16th century, the use of the tarras as a distinctive stage unit waned, for increasingly after that date the upper inner stage was in demand. During the period 1576 to 1599, the tarras was the most often used of the second-level stages; after 1600 it was the least used. By my reckoning, Shakespeare employed the tarras perhaps twenty times in plays of 1600 or earlier, as against only four times in plays of later date.

The existence of an upper stage is generally accepted by students of the Elizabethan drama, but few of them recognize the tarras and the inner stage as separate entities.[2] Basically, the difference of opinion revolves around little more than the position of the upper-stage curtain. Dr. Adams would hang it three or four feet behind the tarras' edge so as to permit battlement scenes to be acted before it in an appropriately shallow depth, properties to be set behind it in the rear stage, and inner-stage scenes to be discovered by its opening. Others would move the curtain either forward or backward so as to merge the two stages into one, under the single name of "balcony" or "gallery." But of the eight uses of the word "tarras" which Dr. Adams

[2] Cf. George F. Reynolds, "Was There a 'Tarras' in Shakespeare's Globe?", *Shakespeare Survey* 4 (1951), pp. 97-100. Professor Reynolds however is arguing less against the existence of a tarras than against a too literalistic interpretation of the plays as a basis for reconstructing stage and stagecraft.

quotes from contemporary dramatic dialogue or stage-directions, and two others that he does not, all suggest that the tarras represented a place out of doors, outside of a building, and therefore a sort of place quite different from that which the enclosed inner stage represented.

THE CHAMBER

The inner stage on the second level was similar to that on the first in all major respects except one: its curtains opened to the shallow tarras, rather than to the broad expanse of the platform. Its forward aperture was about 21½ feet wide; its height was that of the second gallery, 11 feet; its depth was approximately 8 feet behind the curtain line, or 12 feet if one includes the tarras which formed its forward extension when the curtains were opened. From his analysis of the scenes which he believes to have been enacted in the upper inner stage, Dr. Adams discovers that it had a rigid rear wall with a curtained opening in the middle, that on one side of the central opening there was a practicable door that could be locked, and on the other a window that could be opened, and that its ends or sides were closed off by hangings. More often than for anything else, it was used to represent an upper room; and more often than by any other name, it was called "the chamber."

Although the existence of an upper inner stage is now generally accepted by students of the Elizabethan theatre, there is much disagreement as to the nature and extent of its use by Shakespeare and his fellow dramatists; the chamber is as a matter of fact the subject of more controversy than all other units of the multiple stage combined. Dr. Adams states his own position thus (*Globe Playhouse*, p. 275):

> ... An upper stage similar to the study below [i.e., the lower rear stage] first made its appearance early in the last decade of the sixteenth century. This was the last major unit to be added to the Elizabethan multiple stage. Prior to its introduction all interior scenes had to be laid in the study, despite the fact that most London citizens utilized the ground floor of their houses for shops and had their living quarters above. The development, therefore, on the second level of the tiring-house of a sizable curtained stage which could be prepared in advance as a living room, a bed- or dressing-room, a private room in a tavern, and so forth, enabled dramatists to reflect London life with greater fidelity. In general after 1595 such scenes as would in reality have taken place in some room on the second level of an Elizabethan dwelling, tavern, prison, or palace were presented above.

To the chamber Dr. Adams assigns such climactic scenes as those of Juliet's interview with her father and her drinking of the potion, Hamlet's talk with his mother in her closet, the blinding of Gloucester, the violation of Imogen's bedchamber by Iachimo, and the boisterous scene in an upper room of the Boar's Head Tavern, in 2 *Henry IV*.

A contrary view is held by several scholars, for whom Granville-Barker may serve as spokesman:

> The upper stage is primarily a "practicability", a balcony or a city wall or something of the kind; and it is not likely to be used except in relation to some scene on the lower stage. . . . From below, balustrade or no, a view of any action taking place more than a few feet from the edge would necessarily be poor. The upper stage might be the same size as the inner stage below it; but from this the actors could step out on the main stage. To the upper stage they would be strictly confined. On all accounts they would not needlessly locate scenes there.[3]

In other words, Granville-Barker allows to the chamber no uses for which the tarras alone would not serve—scenes played in the flat rather than in depth, by actors standing near the rail, scenes therefore to which the balustrade would offer no obstruction. For these reasons he contends that in *Romeo and Juliet*, III v, "the last part of the scene, containing Capulet's outburst, could have been effectively played nowhere but on the lower stage"; and to this opinion he adheres so strongly that, since the scene unmistakably begins above, he sees no alternative to breaking the action in the middle and transferring it to the stage below, a device which he describes as "the present ensuing clumsiness that brings Juliet from upper stage to lower in the middle of a scene, her bedroom on her back, as it were."[4] Similarly, other of the scenes which Dr. Adams places in the chamber are placed below by writers who fail to share his conviction as to the adequacy of the upper inner stage for important scenes. The horrifying scene of Gloucester's blinding is placed on the lower stage by C. M. Haines when he says that in *King Lear* the upper stage "never comes into play."[5] The scene in which Iachimo enters Imogen's chamber is placed below by Thomas Marc Parrott.[6]

---

[3] *Times Literary Supplement*, May 30, 1936, p. 460.
[4] *Prefaces*, II, 33 and 33 n. 2.
[5] "The Development of Shakespeare's Stagecraft," *Shakespeare and the Theatre* (1927), pp. 56-57.
[6] *William Shakespeare: A Handbook*, p. 78.

Hamlet's talk with his mother in her closet would be staged in the lower rear stage by Granville-Barker[7]; and even the Boar's Head Tavern scene, which is repeatedly localized by the dialogue as taking place in an upper room, is moved by Granville-Barker to the lower stage.[8]

Such divergent points of view are possible only because solid facts are hard to come by; of the Shakespearean scenes that may have been enacted in the chamber, it is impossible to be certain of more than one or two. If the indications point merely to an inner stage, then doubt may still exist as to whether the stage was above or below. If the stage-directions place the action "aloft" or "above," the question may still remain as to whether the chamber was used, or the tarras or a window; and if upper-level placement is indicated by dialogue only, and not explicitly by stage-directions, as in the Boar's Head Tavern scene and the Garter Inn scenes in *The Merry Wives of Windsor*, it may yet be argued that the upper-level placement is a mere matter of theatrical illusion, and that the dialogue seeks to suggest a location that does not actually exist. In only two Shakespearean scenes is the chamber indicated beyond the possibility of dispute: in *Titus Andronicus*, I i, in which at line 63 "*They go up into the Senate House*," and in the second Induction Scene in *The Taming of the Shrew*, which opens with the stage-direction "*Enter aloft the drunkard . . . .*" Both scenes are aloft, and both require more space than either the tarras or a window-stage could provide. For future reference it should be noted that in the former scene the Roman senators probably constituted a considerable company, and that in the latter the chamber was called upon to accommodate a bed, perhaps a chair or two, six actors with speaking parts, and one or more attendants.

The reluctance of Chambers and Granville-Barker and others to accept the chamber as a stage in which important action might take place is based upon four contentions: first, the relative remoteness of the upper inner stage; second, its unfavorable sight-lines from yard and first gallery; third, its lack of a forestage upon which action could flow forward into the midst of the audience; and fourth, the impediment to sight and emotional contact which the balustrade provided.

As for the first of these contentions, it is of course undeniable that the

[7] *Prefaces*, III, 19.
[8] *Modern Language Review*, Vol. XXXIX No. 3 (July 1944), p. 298.

chamber was more remote from the groundlings and first-galleryites than the inner stage on the lower level; it was however actually nearer than that stage to patrons in the upper galleries—some 900 persons out of a total of 2,000. As for the sight-lines, no spectator standing in the yard or seated in the first gallery, obviously, could see the chamber floor; a ruler laid over the north-south sectional drawing (Scale Drawing XII) indicates that to a man standing in the center of the yard, as near as possible to the forward edge of the platform, the rear wall of the chamber would be lost to view up to a height of about 5 feet 4 inches. As he moved back in the yard he would see correspondingly more, and would actually see all but the lowest two feet when he stood against the back balustrade; on the other hand, if he moved into the wings of the yard at the sides of the projecting platform, his view into the chamber would become progressively worse. If he were seated in the back of the lowermost gallery, he could see the chamber's rear wall down to the final two feet; at the sides of the gallery his view would again be somewhat less favorable. But it should be remembered always that the Globe was a three-galleried octagon, and that the chamber was level with the middle gallery of the three and equidistant from the lowest and the highest. The preferred places of viewing were these galleries, not the yard; and if the penny-paying groundlings suffered some disadvantages on the score of sight-lines, their rights were still respected, for chamber scenes, unlike scenes in the rear stage below, seldom had stage business taking place at floor level.

The balustrade which Dr. Adams believes to have stretched across the forward edge of the upper stage has proved to be no less an obstacle to some writers than the matter of sight-lines, and notably so to Granville-Barker, who writes as a practical man of the theatre and whose opinion therefore merits the most respectful attention. He accepts the idea that the balustrade existed, and as a consequence rejects the idea that important scenes were enacted in the inner stage on the upper level:

> What could the groundlings, or even people in the lowest gallery, *effectively* see of scenes played three feet back or more behind that masking balustrade, and of seated figures particularly? Make them out, perhaps they could; but that is not enough. For scenes to be *effective*, especially if they are of emotional import, the actors of them must be able to dominate their audience. Juliet, leaning from her balcony, can do this. But

Hamlet and the Ghost, or Cleopatra with the dying Antony — put them behind a Venetian shutter of a balustrade, and the actors might as well be acting in a cage.[9]

Dr. Adams has sought to minimize the disadvantages of the balustrade by making the individual balusters few and slender; in his model of the Globe there are only eight of them, scaling at three inches at their thickest parts, and spaced $2\frac{1}{2}$ feet between centers (Scale Drawings X and XIV). But is it not also possible that the supposed balustrade was either removable or non-existent? Dr. Adams's assumption that it existed is one of his few conjectures—perhaps indeed the only one—in support of which he cites no direct evidence. He relies rather upon the supposition that a balustrade must needs have been provided to prevent actors from falling to the hard oak planks below: "A guard-rail was imperative there to remind actors of the 12-foot drop to the platform below and to prevent their accidentally falling off" (Globe Playhouse, p. 253), and upon the fact, which may or may not be applicable, that Henslowe bought "ij dozen turned ballysters" in 1592 when the Rose was being remodelled. As against his statement that a guard-rail was "imperative," one may cite the evidence of several contemporary engravings reproduced by C. Walter Hodges, which show elevated stages without any protective rail.[10] None of the stages, to be sure, is a second-level stage, and none is as high as the tarras in the Globe is presumed to have been, but all are well over head-level; and even if all but one of the engravings show Continental stages rather than English, the fact remains that stage-builders of the 16th and 17th centuries considered it safe to leave the stage's edge unguarded.

As between a removable guard-rail and no rail at all, some preference is perhaps to be given to the former, for there are many scenes which demand a tone of intimacy and privacy and enclosure, and some in which a retreat from the audience would be a dramatic advantage. A removable guard-rail would have presented no constructional difficulties to the Tudor craftsman. The ends of the horizontal cap-rail could drop into sockets affixed to the vertical posts at each end of the tarras. To keep the rail from sagging, balusters would support it at intervals, held in position by pegs projecting from each baluster's head and foot and designed to slip into sockets in the

[9] Modern Language Review, Vol. XXXIX No. 3 (July 1944), p. 298.
[10] The Globe Restored, Plates 16, 17, 19, 20, 21, 23, 26, 27, 28.

floor and in the under side of the cap-rail. Such a balustrade could readily be put in place in preparation for scenes to which it would be appropriate, in which its protection was needed, and in which it offered no obstruction to vision or to contact between actors and spectators; it could be removed as easily for static scenes and those in which any balustrade would impose a barrier to emotional contact, such as those of Antony's death and Juliet's drinking of the potion. I cannot believe that a guard-rail, some three feet above floor level, spanned the upper stage and marred the view of the seated figures during *Coriolanus*, I iii, a gentle domestic scene which opens with the unusually explicit stage-direction: *"Enter Volumnia and Virgilia, mother and wife to Martius: They set them downe on two lowe stooles and sowe."*

Let us return to the group of controversial scenes mentioned earlier. As for the much-discussed Act III Scene v of *Romeo and Juliet*,[11] I agree with Dr. Adams in believing that it was acted throughout upon the upper stage, both because a removal from upper stage to lower would involve the "clumsiness" which Granville-Barker admits, and because the text reveals no break in the dialogue during which Juliet could make a back-stage descent. And if III v was acted on the second level, then so too were IV iii and IV v, which, with IV ii and IV iv, form a sequence of four closely-knit scenes which Shakespeare seems to have planned as a contrapuntal interplay of poignant tragedy on the stage above and gay oblivious bustle on the stage below. None of the upper-stage scenes, it will be noticed, makes more demands upon the chamber than are made by the second Christopher Sly scene in *The Taming of the Shrew;* but all the staging of *Romeo and Juliet* is difficult on any theory, and completely satisfying answers are stubbornly elusive.

There are no clear indications of the stage-placement of the scene in Queen Gertrude's closet (*Hamlet*, III iv). Some writers, basing their opinions upon the fact that Polonius' body is later removed from the stage and upon the contention that so dramatic a scene must needs be played in close contact with the audience, favor the platform; others favor the rear stage on the lower level, and still others the chamber. But it is probably significant that Shakespeare uses the word "closet" three times as referring to

---

[11] See the correspondence of Dr. Adams, Granville-Barker, and W. J. Lawrence, in *The Times Literary Supplement*, Feb. 15, 22 and 29, and May 23 and 30, 1936, and Richard Hosley's "The Use of the Upper Stage in *Romeo and Juliet*," *Shakespeare Quarterly*, Vol. V No. 4 (Autumn 1954), pp. 371-379.

the room in which the Queen's interview with her son is to take place or has taken place (III ii 344, III iii 27, and IV i 35); and since a closet can only be a small private room, it may be supposed that Shakespeare intended an inner stage. And if an inner stage, then the chamber, for the rear stage on the lower level seems to serve as the King's personal room throughout a large part of the play. It is there, as I see it, that Hamlet finds the King at his prayers (III iii) and resists the impulse to kill him. Hamlet goes out by the rear door to the stairs; the King departs, leaving the lower stage empty but its curtains still open. The curtains on the upper level are drawn wide to reveal Polonius and the Queen (III iv), and four lines later Hamlet's voice is heard outside the chamber door. At the end of the stormy scene between mother and son, the Queen leaves by the stairs, and Hamlet drags away Polonius' body "into the neighbor room." The King enters the stage on the lower level (IV i), and the Queen descends the stairs to meet him there. This staging of the three scenes accords with the King's

> Hamlet in madness hath Polonius slain
> And from his mother's closet hath he dragged him,

which implies that the murder occurred in some other place than that in which the King is now speaking; further, it relates the scenes to one another as the closely-linked sequence which Shakespeare seems to have intended.

Imogen's bedchamber (*Cymbeline*, II ii), on the other hand, seems to require the inner stage on the lower level; Cloten's attendance at her chamber door in the scene following (II iii) demands a door which the upper stage could not provide.

The scene of Gloucester's blinding seems to have been acted in the chamber. The preceding scene (*King Lear*, III vi) took place in a farmhouse near Gloucester's castle, with the King asleep; it demanded the enclosure of an inner stage ("Here is better than the open air"), and therefore the rear stage on the lower level. The scene to follow is on the heath, the platform itself. Only the chamber is left for the intermediate scene; and it serves again, as four times before, as the lair from which Edmund projects his villainies. Besides, the scene itself, the most brutal in Shakespeare since *Titus Andronicus*, needs a relatively distant stage to make it bearable.

Dramatically speaking, the action of the Boar's Head Tavern scene (2

Henry IV, II iv) takes place in an upstairs room; Falstaff's carouse with Mistress Doll is a private affair, and calls for a room removed from the casual guests who frequent the inn's lower parlors. But theatrically to place the action in the upper stage would be a different matter altogether. In the course of the scene there are no fewer than eleven persons on the stage, seven of them concurrently from lines 253 to 382, and eight from 383 to 385, plus perhaps the Music. Besides, there is a table and at least one bench or stool, and the activity is boisterous, even including sword-play. The chamber, it would seem, could not contain all that; and therefore, to create the illusion that the tavern room was above while actually the stage was on the lower level, Shakespeare embodied upper-room indications in eight scattered lines of dialogue. The upstairs placement was a part of the fiction, just as it so often is on the modern stage; after all, it required no greater effort of imagination on the part of the Elizabethan audience to accept the lower stage as representing an upstairs room, than to accept it as serving for the Forest of Arden or a ship at sea.[12] When Falstaff moved from the inn in Eastcheap to that in Windsor, however, his room at the Garter was undoubtedly on the upper stage.

If this brief analysis is correct, therefore, it would seem that Shakespeare did not consistently use his second level for all those scenes which in real life would have taken place on the upper floor of a dwelling or palace or tavern.

Where so much is uncertain, it is dangerous to generalize, but a few things are clear. The chamber made it possible for the dramatist to have two or more inner-stage scenes in succession, without being forced to interpolate an outer-stage scene between them; as for example *King Lear*, III v, vi, and vii, in which Scene v takes place in a room in Gloucester's castle, vi in a farmhouse on the heath, and vii in the castle again. It enabled him to give separate localization to separate threads of the dramatic story, like the scenes in Orsino's palace in *Twelfth Night* as contrasted with those in the Countess Olivia's home, or those in Polonius' chambers as apart from those in the halls of Elsinore. Usually, it would seem, chamber scenes were domestic in nature, limited in the number of characters present, and relatively quiet in physical action. No rules can be given for spotting chamber scenes; they can be

[12] Cf. Granville-Barker, *Modern Language Review*, Vol. XXXIX No. 3 (July 1944), p. 298.

identified, if at all, only by their relationship to neighboring scenes and by other intimations with regard to which, as has already been seen, opinions may widely differ.

As to one group of chamber scenes, however, Shakespeare appears to have been reasonably consistent: he seems regularly to have used the upper stage for his prison scenes. Seldom, to be sure, is second-level placement explicitly stated; of the plays written in whole or in part by Shakespeare, only one, as a matter of fact, specifies the upper level by stage-direction. That one is *The Two Noble Kinsmen,* with its *"Enter Palamon and Arcite above"* at II i 58, and its *"Enter Palamon and Arcite in prison"* nine lines later at the beginning of II ii. But though the word "above" is lacking in the stage-directions of other prison scenes, their location in the chamber may be inferred from their relationship to scenes which immediately precede or follow, if, as would seem to be the case, all prison scenes needed the circumscription of an inner stage, as contrasted with the openness of the platform, to convey the idea of confinement. Act V Scene v of *Richard II,* the scene of Richard's imprisonment and murder in Pomfret Castle, is a case in point. It is preceded by a sequence of two consecutive scenes in Windsor Castle, of which the first manifestly calls for staging in the lower rear stage with its lockable door. That stage therefore cannot serve for the prison scene; and if Richard is to be incarcerated in any inner stage, it must be that on the upper level. Or take *1 Henry VI,* II v, the scene of Mortimer's imprisonment in the Tower of London: it is preceded by a scene which calls for red and white rose-bushes, surely in the lower inner stage, and is followed by one in the Parliament House. For like reasons, Clarence's death in the Tower in *Richard III,* I iv, and the last moments of Rivers, Grey and Vaughan at Pomfret in III iii, seem clearly to have been chamber scenes; and so consistently did Shakespeare and his fellow dramatists place their prison scenes on the upper level, that the practice may be accepted as one of the few recognizable rules of Elizabethan stagecraft. In placing their prison scenes on an upper level of the stage, the dramatists doubtless reflected the conditions which they knew to exist in the Tower of London. There prisoners of high rank were normally incarcerated in the upper floors of the White Tower, probably on the second or third floors, and distinguished prisoners of lower rank in one of the minor towers, again if possible not at ground level. The ground floor was used for the accommodation of soldiery and guards, and the dungeons for tortures and racking.[13] The prison scenes in *Measure for Measure* are an exception to the upper-stage rule, perhaps because the action takes place not in a cell as in the majority of prison scenes, but rather in a lobby or common-room to which prisoners are brought from their separate cells. Act V Scene iv of *Cymbeline* is however not an exception, because, in spite of the modern editorial locality-notes, it is not a prison scene at all. Posthumus is in the custody of a jailor, yes, but he is not in jail; he lies on the outer stage as in an open field, manacled perhaps to a stage post, and in his dream sees Jupiter descend from stage-cover to platform, riding on the back of an eagle.

THE WINDOW-STAGES

The existence of stage windows, and the fact of their being on the upper level, are attested by several of Shakespeare's plays. In *Henry VIII*, V ii, for instance, there is the stage-direction *"Enter the King, and Buts, at a Windowe above."* In *Othello*, I i 81, the 1622 Quarto has *"[Enter] Brabantio at a window,"* and the Folio at the same point has *"[Enter] Bra[bantio]. Above."* The First Quarto of *Romeo and Juliet* has *"Enter Romeo and Juliet at the window"* as the opening stage-direction of III v, where the Second Quarto has *"Enter Romeo and Juliet aloft."* In *The Taming of the Shrew*, V i, *Two Gentlemen of Verona*, IV ii, iii and iv, *Two Noble Kinsmen*, II i-ii, and *The Merchant of Venice*, II vi, windows are specified or implied, and always the dialogue makes it clear that they are in an upper story. Doubtless the windows were used also in many another scene which fails to mention them explicitly, as for instance *The Merry Wives of Windsor*, IV v, in which Falstaff sticks his head out of the window of his upstairs room at the Garter Inn, or *2 Henry IV*, I i, in which the Porter comes to the gatehouse window in response to Lord Bardolph's call. Perhaps it was at a window that the tortured Moor gloated over the attempted murder of Cassio, in *Othello*, V i. The most famous window scene in all dramatic literature is, of course, *Romeo and Juliet*, II ii; for it was not on a balcony, but in a window, that Juliet appeared—"But soft! What light through yonder

---

[13] From information in a letter to the author, dated 4th September 1954, from Colonel E. H. Carkeet-James, author of *Her Majesty's Tower of London,* and then Resident Governor and Major of the Tower.

window breaks?"—to talk with Romeo in the Capulet orchard on the outer stage below.

In Burbage's old Theater of 1576 the windows had been relatively small, probably nothing more than simple unglazed openings in the tiring-house wall. References to lattice and to hinged casements began to appear a few years later. The windows at the Globe differed from their forerunners in being bay windows which projected from the scenic wall, in being larger, and in being situated in the flanking bays, so that they were "opposite" each other. It is as bay windows that they are spoken of in several non-Shakespearean Globe plays, and perhaps obliquely hinted at in *Twelfth Night*, IV ii, in Feste's "Why, it hath bay windows transparent as barricadoes."

The normal Tudor bay window was a three-sided affair, with its forward surface parallel to the supporting wall. Its upper casements were fixed; its lower casements were hinged to swing outward. It was glazed with small pieces of glass called "quarries," held together by lead strips or "cames," which in turn were reinforced by iron bars let into the mullion or into the casement sash. The earlier cames were usually diamond-shaped, about 4 inches on a side, but Tudor ingenuity expressed itself in the devising of scores of complex patterns based on the diamond, the rectangle, and the circle. English window glass was still imperfect—irregular in thickness, not yet colorless, not yet wholly transparent.

No direct evidence can be cited to prove that the Globe's bay windows surmounted the outer-stage doors, but such indications as there are point toward that conclusion. For one thing, there was no space otherwise unused in the second level of the tiring-house wall; for another, the association of window with door was a logical one, and consistent with the convention under which the stage doors often served for the street doors of houses. Then, too, the over-door position is suggested by the later windowed or latticed boxes over the proscenium doors in Restoration theatres, which probably had a pre-Restoration ancestry. However inconclusive the indications may be, the assumption that the windows were located directly over the outer-stage doors has been generally accepted by scholars who have studied the Elizabethan drama with a view to the reconstruction of the Elizabethan stage. So placed, the bay windows would have needed to span the entire bay in which each door was centered, for anything less than a full bay in width would have left an awkward and illogical gap between window and tarras; and from the fact that actors climbed from tarras to window, we know that no large gap existed.

The apertures of the Globe's bay windows were no doubt made as large as possible to ensure good visibility and to permit varied stage business; one of them, it will be remembered, needed to be large enough to allow Romeo to clamber through it for his descent by rope ladder to the stage below. The capacity of the window-stages is indicated by the plays, produced at the Globe or elsewhere, in which as many as six or seven actors appeared in a window-stage at the same time.

Some questions remain which have yet to be satisfactorily answered. For one, were or were not the casements glazed? If they were fully glazed, then one would expect the casements to be thrown open at the beginning of every window-stage scene, for otherwise (Elizabethan glass being what it was) visibility and audibility would be greatly impaired. Some window-stage scenes do begin with a stage-direction for the opening of the window, or refer to its opening in the dialogue, and some point to its closing when the scene comes to an end. Others, on the contrary, seem to indicate that the windows remain closed during a part or all of several window-stage scenes, one of them perhaps being *Romeo and Juliet*, III v, in which Juliet's "Then, window, let day in, and let life out" comes after forty lines of dialogue, presumably at the window. Others are more explicit, and leave no room for doubt; as for instance *The Widow*, I i, which has the stage-direction "*Philippa and Violetta appear above at a window,*" followed several lines later by Philippa's "Open not the window, and you love me." One is forced to believe, therefore, that glass was used sparingly or not at all; it could have been used in the fixed casements at the top, but was hardly feasible in the hinged casements below. Possibly a grid of empty lead cames created the illusion of a glazed window without offering any impediment to sight or sound.

Again, certain plays refer to the presence of iron bars in the window-stage, as for instance the Globe play *The Picture,* in which Ubaldo speaks of "the windows grated with iron." Is it possible that one aperture, perhaps that facing the side spectator galleries, was fitted with a heavy grate or lattice of iron bars, in contrast with the hinged casements used elsewhere? Yet another difficulty arises in connection with the opening of the windows. If they swung outward, English fashion, the casements can hardly have failed to screen the window openings from spectators in the side galleries; and if they swung inward, French fashion, they would have inconvenienced actors and hampered the use of the window curtains.

Several plays illustrate the ease and rapidity with which an actor could pass from window-stage to chamber, as from a window to the interior of a room of which the window formed a part. Scale Drawing II shows this ease of access. An actor moving from one stage to the other need be out of sight of the audience for only a second or two.

In some playhouses regularly, and at the Globe occasionally, a window-stage served as a music room, and largely for this reason the windows were hung on the inside with sheer curtains designed to conceal the source of the music and to hide the musicians' coming and going. But because the curtains were hung at windows used frequently by actors who required the curtains to be open (unlike the musicians who needed them closed), they gave rise to not a few allusions in dialogue, such as that in *Henry VIII,* V ii, in the King's "Let 'em alone, and draw the curtains close."

CHAPTER XI

THE MUSIC GALLERY

ON the third level of the Globe's tiring-house there was a small inner stage which normally served as the domain of the playhouse orchestra, but which on rare occasions was used as an area of dramatic action to represent some place high above the other stages—a tower, a prison keep, or the mast-head of a ship.

The existence of this third-level stage has been doubted by some writers. They do not deny the existence of a third story in the tiring-house, but they do question whether any part of it was visible to the audience and included in the sphere of dramatic activity. The problem is related to the location of the superstructure—the "heavens"—the under side of which was pierced with trap doors through which gods and goddesses made their descents from heaven to earth. If the under side of the heavens was in the plane of the third-gallery *floor*, then obviously the scenic wall at third level was lost in the superstructure, and no third-level stage was possible. If, on the other hand, the under side of the heavens was on a plane with the third-level *ceiling*, then the scenic wall at third level was included in the visible scene and susceptible of development as a unit of the multiple stage. The majority of scholars incline to the former theory; and since their theory rules out the possibility of a third-level inner stage, they are forced to place the tower and mast-head scenes in the superstructure itself.

Of the extant drawings of playhouse interiors, only one—the DeWitt sketch—includes within its area a sufficient height to show any third level at all; only that one, therefore, can have any bearing upon the present discussion. Unfortunately, its evidence cannot be interpreted with any degree of assurance: the viewer's position is such that the under side of the "shadow" is concealed at the point where it makes contact with the scenic wall, and the drawing therefore fails to make it clear whether that contact is at third-gallery floor level or higher. This much is sure, however, as experiments with a ruler laid over the DeWitt drawing conclusively show: if the lower edge of the shadow meets the tiring-house wall at *floor* level, then no spectator in the third gallery would be able to see more than a small part of any second-level scene; worse than that, no spectator in a side bay of the top gallery would be able to see the lower stage door on the side opposite to his. But if the point of meeting is at third-gallery *ceiling* height, then not merely stage doors and balcony, but third-level stage as well, would be within the view of spectators in the top gallery. It is impossible to believe that the stage-cover, which could so easily be set at the higher level—and with added effectiveness in celestial descent scenes—should be set so low as to render the entire top gallery undesirable for spectators. The cross-sectional drawings of the Globe (Scale Drawings X and XII) lead to the same conclusions with respect to the Globe as the DeWitt sketch leads to with respect to the Swan; namely, that if the stage-cover were only two stories above the platform, it would interfere with the visibility of scenes not only on the second level, but even of some on the first, for many of the spectators in the topmost gallery.

Let us approach the question from another direction. It has already been stated, and will shortly be proved, that certain scenes call for dramatic action on a higher level than the second. If no third-level stage existed, then only the superstructure itself would be left for the staging of tower and mast-head scenes. But for spectators seated or standing at the rear of any of the galleries, a view of the superstructure would be blocked by the forward edge of the gallery immediately overhead (cf. Scale Drawing XII); and to this indication of the superstructure's unsuitability may be added the further fact that some of the tower scenes allow an insufficient time for an actor to climb the two-story distance from the tarras to the huts. The conclusions are inescapable, therefore, that the under side of the Globe's stage-cover was not lower than the ceiling of the third spectator gallery, that the third-story façade of the tiring-house was an integral and visible part of the scenic wall, and that it held an inner stage available for use in tower and mast-head scenes.

A stage-cover projecting from the scenic wall may be supposed to have served admirably as a sounding-board for speech and music originating in the stage just beneath it. Probably the actors and musicians of Shakespeare's day were well aware of the acoustical value of the stage-cover, but no contemporary references prove their awareness. Somewhat later, however, in 1675, artisans installed "a new Ceiling in the Theatre in Whitehall that ye Voyses may ye better be heard. . . ."

The earliest of the plays which require a third-level acting area is
1 Henry VI. In Act III Scene ii, the action takes place before the gates
of Rouen, which now is held by the English under Talbot's command. Joan
of Arc (la Pucelle) enters the outer stage with soldiers, and by stratagem
gains entrance to the town. As soon as the city gates have closed after her,
French nobles enter the platform by an outer-stage door, on the watch for
her beacon to guide them into the city. At line 25 the stage-direction reads:
"Enter Pucelle on the top, thrusting out a torch burning." The signal is
pointed out to the Dauphin:

> See, noble Charles, the beacon of our friend.
> The burning torch in yonder turret stands.

The French enter the town, and a few lines later Joan descends from the
turret and re-enters upon the tarras, while at the same time the English
enter the outer stage as below the walls of Rouen: *"Enter Talbot and Burgundy without* [*i.e., on the platform*]: *within, Pucelle, Charles, Bastard and
Reignier on the walls."* In this scene, "tower," "top," and "turret" all refer
to a position above the level of the tarras; and the fact that la Pucelle is
given an "enter" when she appears upon the walls indicates that she dis-
appears from the view of the audience in making her descent from the topmost stage to the tarras.

The word "turret" is used three times in *1 Henry VI*, and nowhere else
in all Shakespeare. In addition to the line just quoted, it occurs twice in I iv,
in the stage-direction *"Enter Salisbury and Talbot on the Turrets, with
others,"* and in the line "Discourse, I prithee, on this turret's top." The use
of so distinctive a word suggests that it refers to the same stage unit in both
scenes, and therefore that Salisbury and Talbot in the earlier scene, like
la Pucelle in the later, make their entrance to the music gallery.

In *Claudius Tiberius Nero*, Scene xiv, Germanicus and his Roman legions
are besieging the castle of Vonones, King of Armenia. They scale the walls
in spite of the Armenian defense, and Vonones flees. A moment later he
reappears *"on the Keepe,"* and demands a chance to meet Germanicus in
single combat. Germanicus, still on the tarras, accepts the challenge, and
tells Vonones to descend; and then *"Germanicus comes downe to the Stage"*
(the platform), and four lines later *"Vonones commeth downe,"* for the duel

in which Vonones is slain. Here, as in *1 Henry VI,* a stage higher than the tarras is plainly required.

The Double Marriage, a Globe and Blackfriars play, has a ship scene in which the platform serves as the main deck, the tarras as the raised quarter-deck, and the music gallery as the main-top or crow's-nest, with the Duke of Sesse *"above"* (on the tarras), and the Master and sailors *"below"* (on the platform). A boy is sent to the main-top, and after him a sailor. The sailor needs twelve lines of dialogue to reach the crow's-nest from the outer stage, just about twice the time normally allowed for an actor to mount from plat-form to tarras. In another ship scene, in *Fortune by Land and Sea,* the boy has just five lines to reach the main-top from the tarras. These ship scenes are two of five which Dr. Adams cites as making use of a mast-head or other similarly elevated point of observation.

The most arresting and important of the scenes which made dramatic use of the third-level stage was that in *The Tempest,* III iii, in which Prospero entered *"on the top (invisible)"*; and it is interesting to note that the phrase "on the top," here used by Shakespeare in one of the last of his plays, is the same as that which he used in *1 Henry VI,* one of the earliest, written twenty years before; it suggests the thought that "on the top" may have been a playhouse idiom, with a specific and well understood application. In *The Tempest,* Prospero's appearance on the top was dictated by the need that he should dominate the entire stage, theoretically invisible to the other actors but fully visible to the audience, and that, for purely practical reasons, he should be in a position to transmit music cues to the musicians in the gallery behind him and thunder cues to the stagehands in the superstructure a few feet overhead.

But the occasions on which the topmost stage was used as an area of dramatic action were few; normally it was the realm of the playhouse orches-tra. Play after play illustrates the fact that the musicians performed in a gallery high up in the tiring-house, in such stage-directions as these: *"Trumpets small above"; "Strange music is heard above"; "Still music from above";* or in such lines of dialogue as the following:

> As she ascends, the spheres do welcome her
> With their own music . . .
>
> Hover, you wing'd Musicians, in the air.
>
> I have sought him, my lord . . . in air, wheresoever I
> heard noise of fiddlers.

Strike music from the spheres.

What music's this?
Descends it from the spheres? Hangs it in the air?
Or issues it from hell?

and this from *1 Henry IV*, III i:

And those musicians that shall play to you
Hang in the air a thousand leagues from hence,
And straight they shall be here. Sit, and attend.

The stage-directions and dialogue quoted above imply not merely that the music came from a point aloft, but that the musicians were unseen. Their concealment by curtains seems to have been thought necessary both because a visible human source of celestial music would be disillusioning and inartistic, and because they were frequently called upon to descend singly or in groups to provide incidental music or an accompaniment for songs in one of the lower stages, as in *The Merchant of Venice*, V i, *Much Ado*, II iii, *Cymbeline*, II iii, *Othello*, III i, and *The Two Gentlemen of Verona*, IV ii. When a dance was to be given on the lower stage (as in *Romeo and Juliet*, I v, *Much Ado*, II i, or *Henry VIII*, I iv), the musicians usually moved down to a window-stage so that their music might be heard the more clearly both by actors and by audience; and when playing in a window-stage, they played, as we have seen, with the sash-curtains closed. If, for some reason or other, it was not desirable to bring the musicians down from their gallery aloft, signals were often provided to cue the music to the action or the song below. A number of dramatic texts give evidence of such signals as taking the form of gestures, "strikes" with a wand, etc.

Nothing has come to light which gives any clue as to the dimensions of the music gallery. In Shakespeare's day, however, orchestras were relatively small, and it seems reasonable to assume that the Globe's music gallery was perhaps half the width of the chamber below. Its curtains needed to be thin and translucent, both to avoid muffling the music and to admit light by which the musicians could play.

BACKSTAGE AREAS

The properties and costumes owned by the Globe's company needed storage space of some size and security, and it may be supposed that the great backstage lofts on the third level of the tiring-house, with their approximately 1,200 square feet of floor space, were primarily devoted to this purpose. From there the properties were brought down to first or second level for use in the day's play, and the necessary costumes were taken to the dressing rooms.

The backstage areas on the first level served primarily as lobbies where actors could assemble to await their cues. There triumphal processions lined up before going on, or funeral processions with their coffins and mourners, or armies that charged on in pursuit of an enemy. There, too, were held such properties as had been brought down from the third-level storage lofts in preparation for a lower-stage scene. Crowded as the lobbies were, they could afford no space for dressing rooms, and none for the permanent storage of large properties.

The dressing rooms were probably on the second level, in the two rooms at the sides behind the upper boxes. There they would be accessible and yet off the beaten track, and well lighted by casements in the outer wall. There the tire men could lay out costumes, beards, hats, and hand-props. The space behind the window-stages could accommodate such large properties as had been brought down from the storage lofts for use in chamber scenes.

PROPERTIES

More detailed information survives as to the properties used in Elizabethan plays than as to any other aspect of stage production, and it does so because Philip Henslowe made, and Dulwich College has preserved, an inventory of the properties owned by the Admiral's Men at the Rose in 1598. Henslowe's full inventory contains 182 entries, most of which itemize several articles. The following selection, given in modern spelling, is representative of the list as a whole:[1]

> i rock, i cage, i tomb, i Hell mouth.
> viii lances, i pair of stairs for Phaeton.
> ii steeples, & i chime of bells, & i beacon.
> i heifer for the play of Phaeton, the limbs dead.
> i globe, & i golden sceptre; iii clubs.
> ii marchpanes, & the City of Rome.
> i golden fleece; ii rackets; i bay tree.
> i wooden hatchet; i leather hatchet.

[1] From *Introducing Shakespeare*, by G. B. Harrison, copyright 1947 by Penguin Books, Inc.

i wooden canopy; old Mahomet's head.

i lion skin; i bear's skin; & Phaeton's limbs & Phaeton's chariot; & Argus' head.

Neptune's fork and garland.

i "croser's" staff; Kent's wooden leg.

Iris head, & rainbow; i little altar.

viii visards; Tamberlain's bridle; i wooden mattock.

Cupid's bow, & quiver; the cloth of the Sun & Moon.

i boar's head & Cerberus' iii heads.

i Caduceus; ii moss banks, & i snake.

ii fanes of feathers; Bellendon stable; i tree of golden apples; Tantalus' tree; ix iron targets.

i sign for Mother Redcap; i buckler.

Mercury's wings; Tasso's picture; i helmet with a dragon; i shield, with iii lions; i elm bowl.

i chain of dragons; i gilt spear.

ii coffins; i bull's head; and i "vylter."

iii timbrels; i dragon in Faustus.

i lion; ii lion heads; i great horse with his legs; i sackbut.

i wheel and frame in the Siege of London.

i Pope's mitre.

iii Imperial crowns; i plain crown.

i frame for the [be]heading in Black Joan.

i black dog.

i cauldron for the Jew.

The storage lofts at the Globe or Blackfriars held properties no less varied and colorful than those in Henslowe's list. Shakespeare's plays alone called for these items, among a host of others:

All the ordinary articles of household furniture: beds, tables, benches, chairs, etc.;

Musical instruments, such as drums, trumpets, oboes, recorders, and the like;

Trenchers and plates, cups and goblets;

Lanterns, candles, torches;

Military gear: swords, shields, halberds, pikes and partisans, flags, scaling-ladders, and so on, enough for small "armies";

A mole hill and a bank of flowers;

Red and white rose bushes, a box tree, a hedge, a pleached bower, and a dangling apricot;

A royal "state" or two, with dais and canopy; a judicial bench and bar;

Altars; a statue of Pompey; a cauldron; an ass's head;

"Heads" of Macbeth, Hastings, and others, and Yorick's skull;

Flying thrones, an eagle for Jupiter to ride on, and a pair of harpy's wings;

Stocks, and manacles, and an executioner's block;
A coffin, a catafalque or bier, a gravestone;
A box of tennis balls, and a chess set;
A rope ladder; caskets of gold, silver, and lead; and so on and on.

COSTUMES

Theatrical costumes were magnificent and expensive; the era of the play-houses coincided, as it happens, with the era of greatest extravagance in English dress. Fine raiment on the stage was of course necessary, partly because it was the current fashion, and partly because the actors' dress would be seen in daylight's bright glare and almost within arm's reach of spectators. Garments of silk and satin and velvet, trimmed with gold and silver lace, spangled with gold or faced with ermine, cut and slashed with all the fantasy of Elizabethan tailoring, were the ordinary wear of the Elizabethan actor. Such wardrobes were costly, and the outlay for costumes was, as a matter of fact, easily the largest item in the theatrical budget. The need to expend huge sums for stage apparel is perhaps hard to understand today; but Henslowe, who was nothing if not a shrewd businessman, spent more for some of his costumes than he received for an entire week's rent for the use of the Rose Playhouse in the same period, and paid £6 13s. for a woman's gown of black velvet for the play *A Woman Killed with Kindness*, as compared with the mere £3 which he paid to the dramatist, Thomas Heywood, for the play itself. His son-in-law, Edward Alleyn, once paid £20 10s. 6d. for "a black cloak with sleeves embroidered all with silver and gold," and that in an age when Shakespeare was able to buy New Place, the second-largest house in Stratford, for £60. It is not surprising that the actors' lavishness of dress should have been a principal target for contemporary satire and Puritan abuse. Nevertheless, it must have added not a little richness and color to Shakespeare's stage.

Whatever the supposed country or period of the play, the costume was still predominantly Elizabethan. There was little attempt at historical accuracy. Brutus wore a gown with a pocket, Caesar a doublet, the Athenian lovers in *A Midsummer Night's Dream* cloaks and hats and ribboned pumps, and Cleopatra undoubtedly a farthingale and ruff—"Cut my lace, Charmian, come!" And yet there seem to have been some vague leanings toward the classic or oriental if the play required. On this point we have the evidence of a drawing attributed to Henry Peacham and to the year 1595, which pictures a performance of *Titus Andronicus:* the only known contemporary drawing of a Shakespearean play (Plate 24). Titus himself wears a fair approximation of Roman attire, and Tamora a flowing robe conventionally classical. The man at the extreme left, with baggy trousers and scimitar and a chef's cap which might pass for a turban, is perhaps dressed in a costume accepted as being oriental. The rest of the characters, however, wear clothes which in whole or part are frankly Elizabethan. The anachronisms and incongruities seem to have troubled no one.

There is reason to think that distinctive dress sometimes marked the difference between separate groups in the same play: between Scotchman and Englishman in *Macbeth* (Malcolm seems to recognize Ross as his countryman by his dress at IV iii 160), between Volscian and Roman in *Coriolanus,* Egyptian and Roman in *Antony and Cleopatra,* Briton and Roman in *Cymbeline.* In *Troilus and Cressida,* Aeneas is immediately recognized as a Trojan when he enters the Greek camp at I iii 214, and knows Achilles to be a Greek at IV v 75, although he does not know his name. The theory that distinctive dress was used as an index of nationality is supported by two stage-directions in Heywood's *The Iron Age, Second Part* (c. 1613), which, like *Troilus and Cressida,* deals with the Trojan wars. The first stage-direction reads:

> *Enter Prince Chorebus with other Troians in Greekish habits.*

and the second, 27 lines later, reads:

> *Enter Aeneas with his father, who taking Chorebus for a Grecian by reason of his habite, fights with him and kils him.*

The distinction between Trojan and Greek was probably suggested by dressing one group in Elizabethan costume, and the other in costumes conventionally accepted as being classical or pagan.

CHAPTER XII

THE SUPERSTRUCTURE

M OST of the old maps or views of the Bankside, beginning with the Norden map of 1600, show a superstructure on the top of every playhouse.[1] The DeWitt drawing shows a comparable superstructure in the Swan. Visscher and his followers picture the Globe as being surmounted by a superstructure composed of two separate huts (or possibly three, of which the most distant is concealed by the nearer two), with two windows on each of the visible gable ends, and with a square tower rising above them. The tower also has two windows in its only visible side, and a four-sided sloping roof which rises to a peak topped by a flagpole and a large unpatterned flag. In Hollar, the second Globe (misnamed the bear-baiting house) has two massive huts and a tower capped with an onion-shaped dome, but no flag. DeWitt's Swan has a single hut of simpler design, no tower, and a stunted flagpole flying a flag which bears the device of a swan. In all of the more fully developed drawings, the huts are brought well forward toward the center of the amphitheatre so as to project over the platform below and allow space for traps in the overhanging portion of their floors.

THE SUPERSTRUCTURE TRAPS

The principal function of the superstructure was to provide the means by which celestial beings could descend to the outer stage and then rise again to their starry abode. Early dramatists were content to lower a single actor seated upon a chair, as in Greene's *Alphonsus of Aragon* (acted in 1589), which opens with the stage-direction *"After you have sounded thrise, let Venus be let downe, from the top of the Stage . . . ,"* and which ends with *"Exit Venus. Or if you can conveniently, let a chaire come downe from the top of the stage, and draw her up."* From such simple and tentative beginnings, overhead trapwork developed in the years that followed into something more complex, spectacular, and assured. The "chaire" became a "gilded throne," the "top of the Stage" became the "painted heavens" or a

---

[1] The exceptions are the round amphitheatre in Hondius and its derivatives, all of the amphitheatres in the *Civitas Londini* panorama, and one building in each of Inigo Jones's backdrop sketches.

146

"radiant roof," and several actors at a time were lowered in one or more Olympian conveyances. For instance, in *A Wife for a Month* (a Globe and Blackfriars play acted in 1624), there is a masque which opens with *"Cupid descends, the Graces sitting by him, Cupid being bound the Graces unbind him . . ."* and which has, twenty lines later, *"Cupid and the Graces ascend in the Chariot."* In *The Prophetess,* II iii, there is the stage-direction *"Enter [i.e., descend] Delphia and Drusilla, in a Throne drawn by Dragons"*; and in Shirley's Cockpit play, *The Ball,* there is the direction *"A golden Ball descends, enter [from it] Venus and Cupid."*

But well before the dates of the plays just mentioned, Shakespeare had already broken away from the conventional chair or car; in 1610 or there-abouts he had written *Cymbeline,* with this stage-direction in Act V Scene iv:

> *"Jupiter descends in Thunder and Lightning, sitting uppon an Eagle: hee throwes a Thunder-bolt. The Ghostes fall on their knees."*

After twenty lines in mid-air, Jupiter gives the order "Mount, eagle, to my palace crystalline," and his ascent is thus described by Sicillius:

> He came in thunder; his celestial breath
> Was sulphurous to smell; the holy eagle
> Stoop'd, as to foot us. His ascension is
> More sweet than our blest fields; his royal bird
> Prunes the immortal wing and cloys his beak,
> As when his god is pleas'd. . . .
> The marble pavement closes; he is enter'd
> His radiant roof.

The flight on an eagle's back seems to have caught the public imagination; Heywood promptly copied it in his Red Bull play, *The Golden Age,* performed the following year.

Some details are noteworthy in connection with Jupiter's descent. For one thing, he came only part-way down: the eagle's foot apparently came no lower than the heads of the apparitions on the stage. For another, his visit lasted for twenty lines, which seems to have been the average for a visit from above, and his return to heaven needed six, from his "Mount, eagle" to Sicillius's "The marble pavement closes." This latter fact suggests that some six lines were needed to cover the time required to raise an adult actor from a point perhaps seven feet above the outer stage into the heavens, and to close the trap door. In some other plays, therefore, where more time is allowed, one may suppose that the flight was deliberately retarded.

Shakespeare's only other use of the superstructure, for flights, was in *The Tempest* a year or two later. Ariel's descent *"like a Harpey"* used no chair or car or eagle's back; Ariel flew at the end of a wire attached to a harness concealed by his costume or by the harpy's wings. It was the first "free" flight in the history of the English public stage, and as such the direct ancestor of Peter Pan's flights today. Both a free flight and a celestial car are pictured in Plate 23, which shows flying apparatus used in an Italian theatre in the 17th century.

Normally, of course, the car descended straight down to the lower stage, without reference to any part of the scenic wall; a few scenes, however, prove that actors could be landed on the tarras. In *The Prophetess*, for example, the stage-direction previously quoted (*"Enter Delphia and Drusilla, in a Throne drawn by Dragons"*) is followed immediately by the following lines spoken by Delphia:

> Fix here, and rest awhile your sail-stretch'd wings
> That have out-stript the winds. . . .
> Look down, Drusilla, on these lofty towers,
> These spacious streets, where every private house
> Appears a palace to receive a king:
> The site, the wealth, the beauty of the place,
> Will soon inform thee 'tis imperious Rome,
> Rome, the great mistress of the conquer'd world,

and during the ensuing scene they remain somewhere aloft (but not in flight, since the dragons are resting their sail-stretch'd wings) while they watch the action unfold on the stage below. At the end Delphia gives the order "Mount up, my birds," and four lines later (only four, be it noted) they vanish into the heavens. In another play, *The Silver Age,* performed at the Red Bull in 1610, this passage occurs:

> *Thunder, lightnings, Jupiter descends in his majesty,*
> *his Thunderbolt burning.*

> *Jup.* Thus wrapt in storms and black tempestuous clouds,
> Lightning and showers, we sit upon the roofs
> And trembling tarrases of this high house
> That is not able to contain our power.

The subsequent action, as well as the use of the word "tarrases," strongly suggests that he has alighted upon the tarras, whence he goes to Semele's bed in the chamber; finally *"he ascends in his cloud."* These two scenes indicate that it was possible to divert a descending car from its direct path, perhaps by pulling it tarras-ward with a secondary rope in the hands of men in the chamber; they suggest further that the normal path of the car was near to the tarras, just far enough in front to clear its forward edge, for otherwise a landing on the tarras would be difficult or impossible.

Some scenes call for the separate lowering or raising of actors, as for instance Part IV of *Four Plays in One,* in which *"Jupiter and Mercury descend severally. Trumpets small above,"* or the concluding episode of *The Golden Age,* with *"Jupiter first ascends upon the Eagle, and after him Ganimed."*

Disguise sounds—trumpets, thunder, and the like—usually accompanied the operation of the heavens trap and its raising-and-lowering mechanism, just as it accompanied the operation of the floor-trap in the middle of the outer stage, and for the same reasons. Often the descending car or eagle was surrounded by "clouds" composed of billowing folds of light cloth, both to enhance the celestial effect and to hide the ropes by which the car was suspended. The clouds are referred to in many a descent scene, and are listed as an expense item in the Revels Accounts for 1575: "Pulleys for the clowdes and curteynes." Middleton, who presumably wrote the Hecate scenes in *Macbeth,* intimates that Hecate rises in a "foggy cloud" at the end of Act III Scene v.[2]

In two earth-bound scenes, the windlass in the huts seems to have been called upon to provide the actual power by which actors were raised from the lower stage, while ostensibly the raising was being done by other actors within view of the audience. The first such scene occurs in Haughton's *Englishmen for my Money,* written for the Rose in 1598 and played there and at the Fortune for several years thereafter. In this play a corpulent elderly Dutchman named Vandalle is paying unwelcome court to a girl named Laurentia. Hoping to cool his ardor, she persuades him to climb into a basket and be hauled up to her window in the expectation of being ad-

[2] Clouds and their operating mechanisms, together with other 17th-century theatrical effects, are pictured in a contemporary engraving reproduced in *The Globe Restored,* Plate 51.

mitted, by way of the window, to her chamber. He gets into the basket, and Laurentia and her two sisters hoist him up; but instead of permitting him to enter, they leave him dangling outside the window all night long, shivering with cold and fright, afraid to jump down. Nothing in the text unmistakably indicates that the lifting was in fact done by stagehands in the huts, but it seems to be probable for several reasons, and for one reason in particular which I take to be conclusive. That one is the fact that Vandalle's basket was free to spin: "Hoyda, hoyda, a basket: it turns, ho!" If the basket were actually suspended by a rope which passed over the window-sill, it would have been tied throughout the night snug against the lower wall of the window-stage, and its contact with the wall would have kept it from turning as the text says it did. Only a free-hanging basket could turn, and therefore the supposition must be that it was hoisted and suspended by means of a rope which descended from the huts. Possibly another rope came from the huts to the hands of the girls in the window, so that they might pull on it and seem to be exercising the force that lifted Vandalle into the air. The whole business perhaps reflected the age-old practice of raising objects by means of a block and tackle secured to an overhead projecting beam, as is done in the haylofts of thousands of barns to this day.

The farcical affair in *Englishmen for my Money* is a far cry from the tragic scene in which the dying Antony is heaved aloft, in *Antony and Cleopatra*, IV xv, but the mechanical procedures were probably much the same in both. Terrified by the recent turn of events, Cleopatra has fled with her retinue to her stronghold, the Monument; and as the scene opens, *"Enter Cleopatra, and her Maides aloft, with Charmian & Iras."* Antony, wounded and with his death upon him, is carried by his guard to the outer stage; fearing capture by Caesar, Cleopatra dare not go to him or permit the gates to be unbarred to let him in:

> I dare not, dear.
> Dear my lord, pardon! I dare not,
> Lest I be taken. . . .
> But come, come, Antony!
> Help me, my women. We must draw thee up.
> Assist, good friends.
> *Ant.* O, quick, or I am gone.
> *Cleo.* Here's sport indeed! How heavy weighs my lord!
> Our strength is all gone into heaviness:

That makes the weight. Had I great Juno's power,
The strong-wing'd Mercury should fetch thee up
And set thee by Jove's side. Yet come a little!
Wishers were ever fools. O come, come, come!
                    They heave Antony aloft to Cleopatra.
And welcome, welcome! Die where thou hast liv'd!
Quicken with kissing.

This is not the place to undertake a full study of the original staging of
this difficult scene. Together with the second scene in the Monument (V ii),
it has been the subject of more conjecture and argument than any other in
the canon, with the exception of the scenes in Juliet's bedchamber. It is
sufficient for the present purpose to point out that the raising of Antony,
like that of Vandalle, was probably managed by stagehands in the huts,
while seemingly it was done by Cleopatra and her maids. The raising of a
full-grown man to a height of 12 or 15 feet would take some strength; and
if the ropes originated at a point no higher than window-sill or balcony rail,
the last two or three feet would be an undignified scramble to get the dying
man over the edge and safely in. If, however, the ropes ran clear to the huts,
with free ends seemingly returned to the women on second level, the raising
could be done easily and securely by strong men, and the boys who played
the parts of the maids would need merely to draw him in after he had been
raised to a suitable height. Whether Antony was drawn in at a window or
at the tarras is an arguable point. The tarras, especially if it were rail-free,
would offer greater ease for the actors and visibility for the audience; the
window-stage, on the other hand, would better accord with Shakespeare's
source material in Plutarch, whose narrative Shakespeare followed with
extraordinary fidelity, and who relates that Antony was "trised up" to a
high window. In either case, it may be supposed, he was carried by Cleopatra
and her women to the balcony, and there laid on a couch.[3]

---

[3] Dr. Adams would have Antony hoisted to a window and remain there. "Had this part
of the scene," he says, "been played in a window-stage, and had Antony, lying upon his
shield, been drawn feet first through the window to the point where his head and
shoulders came within reach of Cleopatra's embrace, the audience's view of Antony's
death and of Cleopatra's lament over him would have been unexcelled" (*Globe Playhouse*,
p. 347 n. 17). True; but his precarious position, balanced on the window-sill, would
perhaps have distracted attention from the emotional content of the scene.

Both because of the difficulty involved in raising the dying man, and because of the
problem posed by the earlier line about "th' other side your monument" (line 8), Dover
Wilson (*Antony and Cleopatra*, New Shakespeare Edition, pp. 102 and 230) and

The trap scenes already cited, plus a few others like them and no more explicit as to mechanical details, provide the only data upon which one can base a reconstruction of the position and dimensions of the heavens trap. Since two or more flights were occasionally in the air at the same time, it may be supposed that the trap's long axis was parallel to the tiring-house façade, so that all flyers could be seen to the best advantage. Its rear edge would need to be far enough forward to ensure that descending cars would not strike the edge of the tarras, but no farther, for landings sometimes had to be made on the tarras itself. The trap cannot have been less than 4 feet wide, since a throne drawn by dragons could pass through it, and an eagle with spread wings and Jupiter on its back, and a ball large enough to hold two persons. The Vandalle episode would seem to indicate that an end of the trap extended far enough toward one side so that a rope dropped from it would pass close to a window-stage; and if, for reasons of symmetry or convenience, the other end of the trap extended equally far toward the opposite side, the trap cannot have been much less than 20 feet long. The safety of the heavens crew demanded that the trap should have a cover, and that it be kept closed except when a flight was actually in progress; for ease in handling, the huge cover was probably divided into sections, one or more of which could be opened as occasion might require.

There is reason to believe that the heavens held not only the great trap already discussed, but also a smaller trap some feet forward of it, and used primarily for pyrotechnic displays. Fireworks of various sorts were an almost daily event in one or another of the Elizabethan playhouses; and in view of the fact that wooden playhouses had existed for thirty-seven years before one of them was leveled by fire (and even then not by fireworks), it must be supposed that the stage-crews knew how to manage their pyrotechnic displays safely. They would probably not consider it safe to set their fireworks ablaze in the main-trap area, with its inflammable harpy's wings and eagles, its heavenly cars and clouds of billowing cloth. More probably they took the flashes of lightning, burning planets, flaming swords, and so on, to the relative safety of a separate wing, and displayed them through a trap of their

C. Walter Hodges (*The Globe Restored*, pp. 58 ff.) would have Antony raised to the top of a property monument erected on the outer stage. But this solution would seem to be unacceptable, if only because the monument would need to be erected, in full view of the audience, at a time when the tragedy is sweeping to its consummation. Such a break in tension and attention at such a time is unthinkable.

own, far enough forward of the scenic wall so that falling sparks would drop clear of the curtains. The existence of this secondary trap is confirmed (if not for the Globe, then at least for the Red Bull) by a bit of stage business in Heywood's *Brazen Age,* in the final scene of the play. Hercules, on the platform, is seated atop his funeral pyre. At the close of his dying oration, he says "Alcides dies by no hand but his own"; and then follows the stage-direction:

> *Jupiter above strikes him with a thunder-bolt, his body sinkes, and from the heavens discends a hand in a cloud, that from the place where Hercules was burnt, brings up a starre, and fixeth it in the firmament.*

Translating the direction into terms of the physical stage, it would appear that the pyre was built upon the large trap in the middle of the platform; that to an accompaniment of Jovian thunder, the trap dropped, and Hercules with it; that from the forward trap in the heavens a hand was let down by a cord or wire, and disappeared after Hercules; and that someone in the hell affixed a star to the hand, and sent it back to heaven again. It follows as a consequence that the forward trap in the heavens was directly over the main trap on the outer stage.[4]

THE STAGE-COVER

The heavens traps were cut through the under side of a stage-cover, "shadow," or "heavens," which overhung much of the outer stage. Its upper side was occupied in part by the huts, and the rest was covered with a roofing material. The Fortune contract calls for "a shadow or cover over the said stage . . . to be covered with tile and to have a sufficient gutter of lead to carry and convey the water from the covering of the said stage to fall backwards." The Hope contract stipulates that Katherens, the builder, "shall also

---

[4] It goes without saying that the windlasses shown in Scale Drawing XIV are wholly conjectural, for no drawing or verbal description of Elizabethan superstructure apparatus is known to exist.

A design by Inigo Jones for the staging of the masque *Salmacida Spolia* in 1640 has been reproduced by Reyher from Lansdowne Ms. 1171, and reprinted in Ashley H. Thorndike's *Shakespeare's Theater* (1916), p. 188. It postdates the first Globe by nearly a generation, and few of its details are applicable to the conditions of the Elizabethan public stage. Nevertheless, it shows an apparatus operated by ropes and winch, and the four-handled winch shown in Scale Drawing XIV has been copied from it directly, for lack of any more apposite material.

build the Heavens all over the said stage . . . and all gutters of lead needful for the carrying of all such rain-water as shall fall upon the same."

The stage-cover was primarily a structural unit; only secondarily was it a protecting roof. In all playhouses other than the Hope (which, it will be remembered, had a removable stage), posts rose from the platform or below

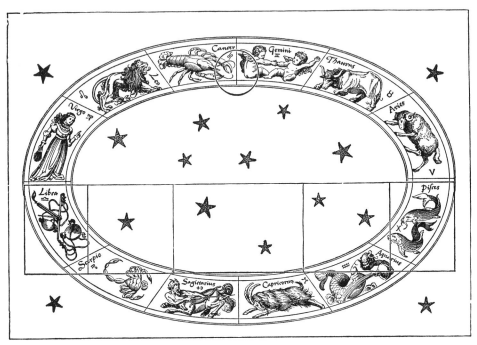

FIGURE 9.   A ZODIAC FOR THE GLOBE'S "HEAVENS"

A conjectural design adapted from zodiacs drawn by Hans Holbein and Albrecht Dürer.

it to support a fabric of beams which in turn supported the forward elements of the superstructure. In the Globe, a 24-foot beam may be supposed to have spanned the heads of the posts; other beams ran back at right angles to engage the corresponding vertical members of the playhouse frame, and yet others ran out diagonally to brace against the flanking wall sections and to assure rigidity for the whole assembly.

Over the structural beams was laid a flooring of wood, whose smooth under side was clearly visible to the audience. Malone, in 1821, was the first to suggest that it was painted or decorated: "The internal roof of the stage was anciently called 'the heavens.' ... It was probably painted of a sky-blue colour; or perhaps pieces of drapery tinged with blue were suspended across the stage, to represent the heavens"; and allusions in various plays and other writings of the Elizabethan and Jacobean periods create the further presumption that it was decorated with a zodiac and stars. For instance, in *Titus Andronicus*, IV iii, there is a scene in which Titus and his kinsmen are shooting arrows into the air, bearing messages for the gods. At line 63 the following dialogue ensues:

> *Tit.* Now, masters, draw. O, well said, Lucius!
> Good boy, in Virgo's lap! Give it Pallas.
> *Marc.* My lord, I aim a mile beyond the moon.
> Your letter is with Jupiter by this.
> *Tit.* Ha, ha!
> Publius, Publius, what hast thou done?
> See, see, thou hast shot off one of Taurus' horns!
> *Marc.* This was the sport, my lord. When Publius shot,
> The Bull, being gall'd, gave Aries such a knock
> That down fell both the Ram's horns in the court.

and a prefatory poem to Richard Brome's plays, collected and published in 1653, contains the lines:

> The Bull take courage from applauses given,
> To echo to the Taurus in the Heaven.

There are many allusions to stars in the playhouse heavens, of which the following are representative: "yonder roof, that's nail'd so fast with stars"; "stars / Stuck in yond' azure roof"; "the great star-chamber o'er our heads"; and "a million of glorious lights / That deck the heavenly canopy."[5]

It will be remembered that in *Cymbeline*, V iv, in the description of Jupiter's return to his palace crystalline, the heavens floor was referred to as "the marble pavement." Timon uses the same adjective in *Timon of Athens*, IV iii 191, when he speaks of "the marbled mansion all above." Since *Cymbeline* and *Timon* were presumably written at about the time

[5] The zodiac shown in Figure 9 and in Plate 31 was adapted from an engraving made by Hans Holbein during the reign of Henry VIII, of which a copy is preserved in the Boston Museum of Fine Arts. It may be compared with Dürer's zodiac, from Ptolemy's *Almagest*, as reproduced in *Shakespeare's England*, I 449. Both Holbein and Dürer depict Cancer as a lobster, rather than as a crab as in today's zodiacs.

when the King's Men began to play at the Blackfriars, the two references to marble have led C. Walter Hodges to ask whether the Blackfriars heaven may not have been painted in imitation of marble,[6] as we know the stage posts at the Swan to have been.

THE HUTS

Reconstruction of the size and position of the heavens traps has been a necessary preliminary to a reconstruction of the size and position of the huts themselves. It has been established that the floor of the huts held a trap some 20 feet long and so situated that an object descending from it would just clear the tarras 20 feet below, and that it probably also held a smaller trap directly over the trap in the middle of the platform. The floor-plan of the huts therefore presumably took the form of a fat T or of a cross (Scale Drawing IV), with the transverse arms holding the larger trap and the stem holding the smaller. Upon this floor-plan the huts were erected, but how they were arranged one cannot be sure. DeWitt shows one hut only, with its long axis parallel to the tiring-house wall. Hollar shows two, side by side, with their gable ends forward. Visscher shows two, or perhaps three, with an improbable roof pattern. Perhaps the Globe's huts took the form of a large transverse hut comparable to the single hut in the Swan, with another intersecting it and projecting forward to house the secondary trap; or perhaps, as in Dr. Adams's reconstruction, there were three huts side by side, with the middle one longer than the other two. Essentially, the doubt involves nothing more than the direction of the roofs' ridge-poles.

The raising and lowering of gods and goddesses constituted only one of the duties assigned to the stage-crew in the huts. At a hut window or door stood the trumpeter who "sounded" thrice before the play began. The "sounding" had originated in the parade by which strolling players gathered an audience for an inn-yard performance; in the permanent playhouses it survived as a means of giving final warning to stragglers. The DeWitt sketch shows a trumpeter sounding from a doorway in the Swan's superstructure.

The crew in the huts had the duty of rolling the heavy ball of stone or iron which, in combination with a battery of snare-drums and kettledrums in the music gallery, was used to make thunder. Shakespeare alludes to the thunder-balls in *Othello*, V ii, in the line

[6] *The Globe Restored*, p. 77, n. 2.

> Are there no stones in heaven
> But what serves for the thunder?

and Ben Jonson, in *Every Man in his Humour,* speaks of the

> roll'd bullet heard
> To say, it thunders.

The huts held the cannon or "chambers" which were shot off during battle scenes or as salutes. They were fired at least twice in *Henry V*, once during the Chorus describing the sailing of the English fleet toward France, and again at the close of III i, when the English troops charged the breach at Harfleur. Twice they were fired in *Othello*, II i, each time as a shot of courtesy to announce the arrival of a friendly ship. Twice in *Hamlet*, in I iv and V ii, the kettledrum and trumpet brayed out the triumph of a royal pledge,[7] and each time the salute was completed by the firing of the chambers. In V ii a cannon-shot heralded the arrival of young Fortinbras; and at the tragedy's end, when Hamlet's body was carried off on the shoulders of four captains, "*A Peale of Ordenance are shot off.*" In *Henry VIII*, I iv, drum and trumpet, and chambers discharged, preceded the arrival of the King at the Cardinal's palace; and it was this shot which resulted in the burning of the playhouse on the afternoon of June 29, 1613.[8]

In the tower above the huts hung the great bell which by its dreadful summons roused the citizens of Cyprus in *Othello*, II iii. In *Macbeth*, II iii, it called to parley the sleepers of the house, and in V v it rallied Macbeth's few remaining followers for a final sally. It sounded the hours in *Twelfth Night*, III i, *Julius Caesar*, II i, *Cymbeline*, II ii, and *Richard III*, V iii. Perhaps twelve strokes upon the bell preceded the entrance of Francisco upon the battlements at Elsinore; its doleful clangor would have made an appropriate opening for *Hamlet*, and seems called for by the line, " 'Tis now struck twelve." Perhaps too the dead Ophelia was carried to her grave to its slow tolling. In *A Midsummer Night's Dream*, V i, twelve strokes sounded

---

[7] Possibly the drum and trumpet served as cues for the cannoneers in the huts high overhead. Similar cues are intimated as preceding the firing of the cannons in the two other instances in which they were used in *Hamlet* (V ii), in "*March afar off*" in the first case, and "soldier's music" in the second.

[8] The cannon shown in the sectional drawing in Scale Drawing XIV was copied from an old woodcut printed in *Webbe his Travailes*, as reproduced in *Shakespeare's England*, Vol. I, 140.

again under very different circumstances, when the wedding festivities had been ended:

> The iron tongue of midnight hath told twelve.
> Lovers, to bed; 'tis almost fairy time.[9]

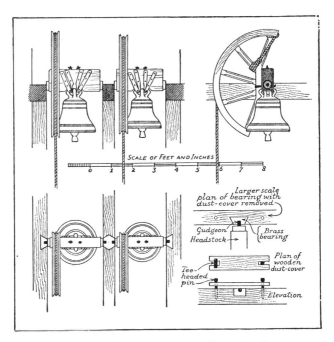

FIGURE 10.   BELLS FOR THE GLOBE'S BELFRY
A 24-inch and a 21-inch bell and their hangings.

THE PLAYHOUSE FLAG

In a period when the unroofed public playhouses might on any given day be prevented from opening by rainy skies, or by an official ban called forth

[9] The bell-hangings shown in Scale Drawing XIV and in Figure 10 were drawn from sketches and written instructions sent to me by an English authority on ancient bells, Frederick Sharpe, Esq., of Bicester, Oxon. Mr. Sharpe generously sent drawings and pamphlets of his own, and corrected the preliminary sketches that I mailed to him in return. The bell-ropes, shown in Scale Drawing XIV as ending vaguely somewhere in the huts, more probably ran down through the floor of the superstructure to the music gallery below, where cues could be more easily heard by the bell-ringers. They may on occasion even have run all the way down to the platform.

by the plague, a signal was needed to let would-be playgoers know that a play would be presented that afternoon. Flags served that purpose. Whenever a play was to be given, each Bankside playhouse flew at its mast-head a flag large enough to be seen on the far side of the Thames. Playhouse flags are pictured in all of the early engravings and drawings after the Norden map of 1593. The flag in the DeWitt sketch displays a swan on a white background; flags in Hondius, Delaram and Hollar bear the device of a St. George's cross; those in Visscher and its derivatives are unpatterned. Henslowe laid out 26s. 8d. to buy "a flage of sylke" for the Rose in 1602; and from this and other references it would appear that silk was the usual material for playhouse flags in the 17th century.

There are many contemporary allusions to playhouse flags. An angry Puritan, writing in 1583, protested that

> Those flagges of defiance against God, & trumpets that are blown to
> gather together such company, will sooner prevail to fil those places
> then the preaching of the holy worde of God . . . to fill Churches.[10]

and a later comment in *The Curtain-Drawer of the World*, 1612, is to the same effect:

> Each play-house advanceth his flagge in the aire, whither quickly at the
> waving thereof are summoned whole troops of men, women, and children.

Two allusions refer specifically to the Globe's flag. A contemporary ballad entitled "A Sonnet upon the Pitiful Burning of the Globe Playhouse in London" contains these lines:

> This fearfull fire beganne above,
>   A wonder strange and true,
> And to the stage-howse did remove,
>   As round as taylors clewe;
> And burnt downe both beame and snagg,
> And did not spare the silken flagg.

and from the "Elegy on the Death of Richard Burbadge" these lines are quoted:

> And you his sad Compannions, to whome Lent
> Becomes more Lenton by this Accident,
> Henceforth your waving flagg, no more hang out

[10] John Field, *A godly exhortation,* cited from Chambers, IV, 219.

Play now no more att all, when round aboute
Wee looke and miss the Atlas of your spheare.

The flag continued to fly until the play was done. Then, as the playhouse emptied and the audience left for home in the gathering dusk, the men in the huts unfastened the halyards and took the flag in.

CHAPTER XIII

SHAKESPEARE'S PLAYS

ON THE GLOBE'S STAGE

TODAY'S scholars maintain a tireless study of the original texts of Shakespeare's plays, in an effort to discover his precise intention with respect to every word that he wrote to be spoken on the stage. To their study they bring the aid of new tools, new techniques, new theories of editorial policy. Little attention, however, is given to those other words that have found their way into modern editions of the plays—the act- and scene-divisions, the locality-notes, the stage-directions, inserted by editors after Shakespeare's death. Few voices are raised in question or protest, in spite of the fact that the words are not Shakespeare's, that they reflect the conditions of the post-Restoration stage rather than the Elizabethan, and that they often do violence to the dramatist's purpose. Act- and scene-breaks sometimes imply a pause in the action or a relaxation of tension where Shakespeare wanted none. Locality-notes often suggest a place or a change of place that Shakespeare never contemplated. Stage-directions, designed to justify the interpolated breaks and localizations, lend a spurious plausibility to the whole faulty system. The search for Shakespeare's meaning should be broadened to include these intrusions as well as the spoken word; and in this search a knowledge of Shakespeare's stage, and a reconstruction of the staging of his plays in their original environment, are of the first importance.

As a means of indicating some of the ways in which a study of original staging may throw light upon the dramatist's intent, I shall attempt to reconstruct the presentation of two of his plays upon the stage of the Globe. My choice falls upon *Romeo and Juliet* and *King Henry IV, Part II,* because both plays utilize the resources of the multiple stage fully and with unusual freedom, because both contain scenes which are and deserve to be the subject of debate, and because both have sequences of scenes whose treatment in modern texts undoubtedly violates Shakespeare's design with respect to their staging.

In both plays there are stretches of continuous action, in an unchanged locality or in closely related localities, which extend over one or more present-day scenes. In all such instances, the unit of continuous action will be discussed as if it were a single scene.

ROMEO AND JULIET

ON THE STAGE OF THE GLOBE

Romeo and Juliet was probably written some four or five years before the first Globe was built; it is known, however, to have been acted on the Globe's stage, for the Fourth Quarto professes to print the text "as it hath beene sundrie times publikely Acted by the KINGS MAIESTIES SERUANTS at the GLOBE."

The text of *Romeo and Juliet* comes down to us in four Quartos and the Folios. The First Quarto (1597) is a pirated edition which prints the play in a shortened and corrupt form; the Second (1599) is an authorized edition. The Third Quarto (1609) is a reprint of the second, and served as printer's copy for the First Folio text. The Fourth is of unknown date and of no textual authority. None of the texts divides the play into acts or scenes; but in the First Quarto there are printer's ornaments, beginning after the end of Act III Scene iv, which for the most part fall at clearances of the stage and therefore seem to mark scene-breaks. The First Quarto is remarkable also for its graphic stage-directions, which proclaim their own authenticity even when the neighboring dialogue is manifestly at fault. Modern scholars believe that the text as a whole was reported from memory, probably by one or more actors who had previously performed in the play. Whether because they had acted a shortened version or because memory flagged, the text of the First Quarto is some 800 lines shorter than that of the Second. The presence of the illuminating notes on stage business is therefore the more arresting. There was no need for the reporter to add them; their absence would never have been noted. If his memory had failed him for a word or a line of dialogue, he might have needed to cudgel his brains lest mutilated rhythm or sense betray him; but this would not be true in the case of marginal notes on stage business. He put them in solely because he had seen the pieces of business in actual performance, and because they had made a vivid impression upon him.

Romeo and Juliet is perhaps the most difficult of Shakespeare's plays to reconstruct in terms of its original staging; it is safe to say that more scholars have spent more hours pondering the stagecraft of this play than of any other. It bristles with difficulties which seem not to be susceptible of any completely satisfying solution; for when various alternative stagings of a given scene have been considered and abandoned, and there remains only one seemingly defensible solution of the problem, even that one, as it often turns out, fails to account for all the conditions; there still remains some line, some phrase, some word, which refuses to be accommodated. One can hardly do more than to marshal the evidence and suggest which of the alternatives seems to be preferable, and at the same time to point out the considerations which stand in the way of its being accepted conclusively.

The Prologue (14 LINES)

Chorus enters the platform, presumably through the central break in the stage curtains, and departs the same way.

Act I, Scenes i and ii (350 LINES)

The action clearly calls for a street or public place, and therefore the platform. There is a ballet-like symmetry in the early entrances: first Sampson and Gregory of the house of Capulet, and Abram and Balthasar of the house of Montague; then Benvolio of the Montague faction, and Tybalt of the Capulet; then on each side citizens; then old Capulet with his Lady, and Montague with his; and finally the Prince. It seems probable that all the Capulets enter by one of the two outer-stage doors and all the Montagues by the other, if merely to associate them with their respective houses on their initial entrances. The equal balancing of part against part suggests that Prince Escalus, when he enters at line 87, may come through the central break in the curtains, both to preserve the studied symmetry and to symbolize his freedom from association with either part. Each person exits as he entered, except that Capulet goes out with the Prince through the center curtains at line 110. It will later appear that one of the stage doors, with the window above it, is probably identified with the Capulet house throughout much of the play, and that the identification has already begun, with the entrance of Sampson and Gregory in the opening stage-direction. The other door's brief association with the Montague faction has already faded.

In Scene ii the action continues on the platform, without change of place or lapse of time. Old Capulet, with the County Paris and a servant, enters from his own door. In the interval since he left with Prince Escalus at I i 110, he has gone to Freetown to hear the Prince's warning against further breaches of the peace, and Montague has gone there later on the same errand. These off-stage events might suggest the need for a change of stage to indicate the passage of time, were it not for the fact that Shakespeare's habitual fore-shortening of elapsed time would make the final 135 lines of Scene i seem sufficient to cover Capulet's interview with the Prince and his return home. He gives his servant a list of guests to be invited to a feast at his home that same night, and then he and Paris—"Come, go with me"—either turn back into the house or go off by the opposite door. The servant remains on the platform, there to be met by Romeo and Benvolio. First the servant, and then Romeo and Benvolio together, depart by the non-Capulet stage door.

Act I Scene iii (106 LINES)

This scene, which presents Juliet for the first time, is vaguely localized. Undoubtedly it takes place somewhere about the Capulet ménage, but whether upstairs or down, indoors or out, is not indicated. It is probably staged in the chamber on the second level, partly because Lady Capulet and her daughter are far enough removed from the entrance door to be unaware of the fact that guests are already arriving, but more particularly because the upper stage will later be the scene of Juliet's joy and agony, and Shakespeare has perhaps wished to associate her with the chamber thus early in the play. At the end of the scene the upper-stage curtains close.

Act I, Scenes iv and v (120 LINES)

Scene iv opens on the platform as on a street in Verona. Romeo, Mercutio and Benvolio, with five or six other maskers and with torch-bearers, enter by the non-Capulet door. Their masks tell that they are on their way to a masked ball; the torches show that it is now night. At the end of the scene *"They march about the Stage, and Servingmen come forth with their napkins."* Thus the stage-direction reads in the Folio: a single stage-direction, unmarred by scene-break.

The march of the maskers, symbolizing their journey to Capulet's house, is a relic of the mediaeval device deriving from the multiple scene in the Mysteries and Moralities, which permitted any distance within reason to be traversed in full sight of the audience. Modern texts have an *"Exeunt"* for the maskers after *"They march about the stage,"* and an *"Enter"* for them at I v 16. The original texts have neither of these. The maskers remain continuously on the platform, and while they march the curtains of the rear stage open to reveal the inner stage as the Capulet ballroom, with servants bustling across from side to side carrying trenchers or shifting furniture. Capulet, with others of his family and guests, perhaps enters the rear stage through its side curtains, and moves downstage to greet the maskers. Now that the curtains are open, the entire stage, platform as well as inner stage, becomes a hall in the Capulet house; the festivities of the masked ball continue on the combined stages, to music from the music gallery or a window-stage.

As the dance ends, the departing guests may be supposed to drift toward the inner stage. Romeo and Juliet are left together on the platform. The Nurse interrupts them with "Madam, your mother craves a word with you," and Juliet joins her mother in the inner stage. Romeo, on the forestage with the Nurse, asks "What is her mother?" and hears the answer; Benvolio drags him away. The last of the guests and maskers disappear, and Juliet and the Nurse are left alone in the rear stage for the final 17 lines of dialogue. They depart, and the stage curtains close.

Prologue (14 LINES)

The sonnet-Chorus is spoken on the platform, with entrance and exit by way of the center curtains.

Act II, Scenes i and ii (233 LINES)

This sequence brings up the knotty problem of the orchard wall: was it or was it not a property physically present on the Elizabethan stage? The question is one that has puzzled editors and commentators ever since Rowe, and opinions are about equally divided on the subject. These seem to be the basic facts:

Romeo enters the stage alone as II i opens. "Can I go forward when my heart is here?" he asks; "Turn back, dull earth, and find thy centre out." At this point nearly all modern editions print a stage-direction which reads substantially as follows: *"Romeo climbs the wall and leaps down within it"*; no corresponding stage-direction, however, is to be found in any of the original texts. Benvolio and Mercutio enter; they call Romeo, but he is nowhere to be found. "He is wise," says Mercutio, "And, on my life, hath stol'n him home to bed." Benvolio counters with "He ran this way, and leapt this orchard wall." These, however, are mere guesses; neither man saw Romeo leave, and one or both of them must be wrong. Later, at line 30, Benvolio ventures a second guess: "Come, he hath hid himself among these trees." Benvolio was right the first time, however. The proof of it comes in the next scene, with Juliet's question (II ii 62):

> How cam'st thou hither, tell me, and wherefore?
> The orchard walls are high and hard to climb.

and with Romeo's reply:

> With love's light wings did I o'erperch these walls;
> For stony limits cannot hold love out.

But although Romeo is later proved to have leaped an orchard wall, he seems to have remained within earshot of Mercutio and Benvolio throughout II i; for Mercutio's ribaldry about the chaste Rosaline would have little dramatic point unless Romeo heard it, and Benvolio's parting line needed Romeo's overhearing to elicit his reply in the second line of the rhymed couplet which editors have disrupted with a scene-break.

Let us suppose, for the sake of argument, that a property wall is actually thrust out upon the stage for Romeo to climb. A difficulty immediately arises in the fact that Romeo, Benvolio and Mercutio must be visible to the audience on one side of the wall, and Romeo again on the other side after his leap. Placed anywhere and at any angle, the wall would obstruct the view to one or the other of its sides for some part of the spectators, since they stood or sat on three sides of the stage; but perhaps it would offer the least obstruction for the greatest number if it were placed at a right-angle to the curtain line, with an end facing forward. In that position, however, the wall would enclose nothing, and therefore would merely symbolize a continuous wall surrounding an orchard; furthermore, since Romeo could walk around its forward end more easily than he could climb it, his leap too would be symbolic, and perhaps absurd. One hesitates to accept such a reconstruction of the action.

As has already been said, no original text carries any stage-direction indicating either a wall or a leap. The absence of such a notation is particularly significant in the case of the First Quarto, with its frequent and circumstantial stage-directions. It seems unlikely that the pivotal and unusual stage business of leaping the Capulet wall would have been overlooked by a reporter who was so observant as to record the Nurse's wringing of her hands and the strewing of Juliet's bed with rosemary. Most importantly, neither actual wall nor actual leap are necessary to a full understanding of the situation, especially in view of the fact that both Benvolio's guess and Juliet's confirmation of it are *post facto*. On the whole, one must agree with Snout in *A Midsummer Night's Dream,* III i 67, when he says categorically "You can never bring in a wall."

Romeo disappeared from view at II i 2, it will be remembered, not because he wanted to hide from his friends, but because he intended to return to the Capulet house. It may therefore be supposed that he turned back toward the stage door by which he had just entered, and that he hid behind a doorpost when he heard his friends approach. Wherever he is hidden—whether behind door-post or stage post or curtain-flap—he keeps the audience aware of his presence on the stage and of his hearing his friends' conversation. They leave, and he steps out of hiding; and then:

> But soft! What light through yonder window breaks?
> It is the East, and Juliet is the sun!

Juliet has appeared above at a window: at a window, be it noted, and not on a balcony. There is no stage-direction of any kind, not even an *"Enter"* for Juliet, in any of the original texts, but Romeo's "yonder window" appears in all five of them. The traditional designation of "Balcony Scene" is thus a misnomer.

The entire sequence probably takes place on the platform and at a window-stage. The curtains remain closed, holding the rear stage in readiness to serve as the Friar's cell in the scene to follow. As a consequence, it must be supposed that there are no properties onstage to create the illusion of an orchard, unless one assume that stagehands have walked out on the platform to set property trees in place as the spectators watched. It would seem more probable that "these trees" of II i 30, like "this orchard wall" of II i 5, "the orchard walls" of II ii 63, and "these walls" and "stony limits" of II ii 66-67, exist only in the words of the speakers and the ears of the listeners.

Act II Scene iii (94 LINES)

This is the first of four scenes in Friar Laurence's cell; it is followed by others at II vi, III iii, and IV i.[1] In each the localization is specific, by clear-cut reference in the closing lines of the scene which precedes each of them. The present scene is pre-localized by Romeo's lines at II ii 190-191:

> Hence will I to my ghostly father's cell,
> His help to crave and my dear hap to tell.

This first scene tells little about the cell itself, beyond the fact that it is in rural surroundings; the second tells even less. The third, however, shows that it has a door upon which a person can knock without being seen by those within or by the audience (III iii 70-80), and an adjoining room—a "study"—to which the Friar tells Romeo to run (III iii 76) and from which, presumably, he had called him forth as the scene began. The fourth cell scene shows further that Juliet's approach can be observed by a person within before she enters—"Look, sir, here comes the lady toward my cell" (IV i 17)—and that the cell has a door that can be shut (line 44). The rear stage on the lower level meets all the requirements, and is the only stage that does so and is at the same time suitable and available. It may safely be assumed therefore that it serves for the Friar's cell in all four scenes, with the door and window in its back wall opening to the outer world and one of its side curtains to the study.

The 247 lines of Prologue II and of Act II, Scenes i and ii, have given the stagehands more than adequate time to remove the properties of the Capulet ballroom and to replace them with properties appropriate to the Friar's cell. In this first cell scene, Friar Laurence enters or is discovered as the curtains open. Romeo enters by the rear door. The Friar agrees to perform the marriage ceremony, and he and Romeo go out together.

Act II Scene iv (231 LINES)

This is plainly a street scene, acted on the platform. Benvolio and Mercutio, and later Romeo, probably enter by the non-Capulet door. Perhaps the Nurse and Peter do so too, and they almost certainly depart that way, to avoid conflict with Juliet's entrance in the scene that follows.

---

[1] I exclude V ii, which, although placed in the Friar's cell in modern locality-notes, probably takes place on the street before the Friar's threshold.

Act II Scene v (80 LINES)

This scene and the second scene of Act III are twin scenes to a remarkable degree. Each has Juliet and the Nurse as the only characters present (except for a brief mute appearance of Peter in II v). Each begins with a soliloquy by Juliet, in which she speaks her impatience for the arrival of the Nurse with messages from Romeo. Each is preceded by a street scene and followed by a scene in the Friar's cell. Each is labelled "Capulet's orchard" in modern locality-notes, but in neither is there any clear indication of place. The extraordinary parallelism of the two scenes suggests that they were probably played upon the same stage. Together, they constitute one of the minor problems of staging.

Just what are the indications of place? At II v 19 Juliet says to the Nurse "Send thy man away," and the Nurse complies with "Peter, stay at the gate," which, in the use of the word "gate" rather than "door," carries a faint implication that the scene is outdoors. At II v 58-61 we find this exchange:

> *Nurse* . . . . . . Where is your mother?
> *Juliet*   Where is my mother? Why, she is within.
> Where should she be?

which again intimates, by no means conclusively, that the speakers themselves are without.[2] Finally, at III ii 138, we have the Nurse's "Hie to your chamber," which proves negatively that they are not in the chamber as they speak.

If they are not in the chamber, then the inner stage on the upper level is debarred. The rear stage on the lower level is debarred because both scenes are followed by others which utilize it to represent Friar Laurence's cell. The window-stages are excluded both because they are unsuitable to the action of the scenes—the dismissal of Peter, Juliet's rubbing of the Nurse's back at II v 51, the Nurse's arrival with the rope ladder at III ii 31, Juliet's lament over Tybalt's death and Romeo's banishment—and because they are not specified in the text.[3] Only the platform is left.

[2] The word "within," as used in a stage-direction, normally has the purely theatrical meaning of "within the tiring-house," and therefore off-stage, without conveying any implication of the dramatic placement of the off-stage action. As used in dialogue, however, the word normally means "indoors."
[3] Shakespeare has been explicit about the use of a window in the two undoubted window-

Use of the platform would accord with the outdoor intimations already noted, but would require that these scenes should immediately follow, on the same stage and without intermission, other scenes that take place on a Verona street. As mentioned on page 80, the scenes may thus be supposed to be examples of the use of the platform as if it were two stages in one, to represent different places in consecutive scenes. Probably also the twin scenes are threshold scenes, with Juliet entering to her doorway as the place to which she would naturally go in order to catch first sight of the Nurse on her return. In each instance the doorway itself would serve as a localizing factor for the second in each pair of consecutive platform scenes, and would be used for all entrances from and exits into the Capulet house.

In the first of the two twin scenes, Juliet learns from the Nurse (70-71, 79) that Romeo awaits her at Friar Laurence's cell:

> Then hie you hence to Friar Laurence' cell;
> There stays a husband to make you a wife. . . .
> Go; I'll to dinner; hie you to the cell.

and darts thither to meet him as the scene ends.

Act II Scene vi (37 LINES)

With this pre-localization, the action returns to the rear stage as to the Friar's cell. Romeo and the Friar are discovered by the opening of the curtains; Juliet enters by the door in the back wall. At the end they exeunt through the side curtains for the marriage ceremony, and the stage curtains close.

Act III Scene i (202 LINES)

This furious scene, in which Mercutio is slain and Romeo kills his bride's cousin Tybalt, is staged on the platform as representing a street or public place. Entrances are perhaps governed by the same rules as applied in I i, but the Capulet door is probably not used for final departures, lest they conflict with Juliet's solitary appearance at the threshold in the scene to follow. Since no dead bodies may be left upon the outer stage, Mercutio is helped

---

stage scenes. To be sure, there is no stage-direction specifying a window in the earlier of the two scenes (II ii), but the dialogue leaves no room for doubt. In the later scene (III v), stage-directions place the action *"at the window"* in Q1, and *"aloft"* in the other quartos and the Folio, and again the dialogue permits no shadow of doubt.

into a neighboring house before he dies, and Tybalt's body is carried away at the end.

Act III Scene ii (143 LINES)

After the tumult of the preceding scene has died down, a lyric mood succeeds as Juliet comes alone to the threshold of her home to await news of her husband's coming. The Nurse brings the news and a ladder of cords, but brings news also that Tybalt has been slain and Romeo banished. The closing lines again show that the next scene will be in the Friar's cell.

Act III Scene iii (175 LINES)

As the stage curtains open, the Friar enters hurriedly by the door in the back wall, bringing tidings to Romeo of the Prince's doom; he calls to him to "come forth," and Romeo enters through the side curtains as from the Friar's study. The Nurse knocks on the rear door[4] and is admitted by the Friar. At the scene's end Romeo and the Nurse depart by the rear door, and the Friar is concealed by closing curtains.

Act III, Scenes iv and v (280 LINES)

The first of these scenes is usually labelled "a room in Capulet's house" in modern texts, but it cannot be so. One of the inner stages, either below or above, would be needed to represent an interior at this juncture, but both are disqualified. The inner stage on the lower level is eliminated because it has just served as the Friar's cell, and that on the upper level because Capulet makes it clear that the action is taking place below, when, speaking of Juliet, he says "She'll not come down to-night" (III iv 5); and even if he did not make it clear, Juliet's bedchamber would be manifestly inappropriate to the action of the scene. The window-stages are unsuitable. Then, by elimination, it must be played on the platform; and if on the platform, it is presumably an exterior scene; and if an exterior, then probably a threshold scene at the door of Capulet's house, whither he and his Lady have come to bid farewell to their departing guest, the County Paris.

---

[4] Stage-directions in F1 and Q2 are confused at this point. Each has an *"Enter Nurse, and knockes,"* and then a second *"Enter Nurse"* a few lines later, after the knocking. It seems probable that the first stage-direction is less a direction for her to appear on the stage than a prompter's note for her to be ready off-stage to knock on the rear door. Both Q1 and Q4 support the supposition that she knocks first and enters afterwards.

It is late at night, going on toward dawn. Paris has been calling on Juliet's father and mother to urge his suit for her hand, and the marriage has been agreed upon for the following Thursday. He is about to leave: as early as line 9 he says "Madam, good night." Capulet bids him farewell:

> Farewell, my lord. — Light to my chamber, ho!
> Afore me, it is so very very late
> That we may call it early by-and-by.
> Good night.

Paris departs. Capulet and his wife turn back into their house; and within an instant of their going, and directly over the door through which they pass, Romeo and Juliet appear aloft, at the window.

Reconstruction of the original staging does more, in this instance, than merely correct a faulty locality-note: it restores to the play a situation fraught with suspense, a situation which Shakespeare clearly intended but which modern editors have obliterated with their scene-break and its accompanying change of place. One may be sure that its tenseness was not lost upon the audience at the Globe. By now the window over the Capulet door was associated in their minds with Juliet; they knew it to be the window of her bedchamber. They knew that Juliet and Romeo would spend their marriage night there together before Romeo left at break of day for exile. They knew that the lovers were together in the upper room at the very moment when Paris was pleading for an early wedding and Capulet was agreeing that it should take place on Thursday. They must have been in an agony of suspense lest Juliet and her husband appear in the window above while her parents and suitor were still below. All this is lost in the conventional "Scene iv. A room in Capulet's house. . . . Scene v. Capulet's orchard."

As has been said on pages 125 and 129, the original staging of the next scene has been the subject of controversy, centering largely about this question: does the action, which clearly begins aloft, remain aloft, or does it move from upper stage to lower in the middle of the scene? In examining the data, it is necessary to consider the Folio and First Quarto versions separately, for they differ materially not only in dialogue, but also in stage-directions and the order of episodes.

The texts of the Second Quarto and the Folio are substantially identical. After the departure of Capulet, Lady Capulet, and Paris, each has the stage-direction *"Enter Romeo and Iuliet aloft"*; the window is not mentioned until line 41, in Juliet's "Then window let day in, and let life out." The stage-direction *"Enter Madam and Nurse"* comes at line 36; but the entrance for Madam must be supposed to be an error: it cannot apply to Juliet, who is already onstage, and Lady Capulet clearly does not enter until line 68. The Nurse brings a warning:

> Your Lady Mother is comming to your chamber,
> The day is broke, be wary, looke about.

and thereafter the dialogue makes it clear that Romeo descends from the window, says his final farewells to Juliet from the ground below, and departs at 59. At 68 there is the stage-direction *"Enter Mother,"* followed by these lines of dialogue:

> *Lad.* Ho Daughter, are you vp?
> *Iul:* Who ist that calls? Is it my Lady Mother.
> Is she not downe so late, or vp so early?
> What vnaccustom'd cause procures her hither?
> *Lad.* Why how now *Iuliet*?
> *Iul.* Madam I am not well.

Lady Capulet mistakes Juliet's grief over Romeo's banishment for grief over Tybalt's death, and to comfort her she tells of the wedding planned for next Thursday morn. Juliet will none of it. At 126, *"Enter Capulet and Nurse."* Learning of Juliet's refusal to marry Paris, the infuriated Capulet disowns his daughter. He exits at 197 and Lady Capulet eight lines later. The Nurse counsels Juliet to marry Paris; Juliet seems to agree, and at 233 she says:

> Go in, and tell my Lady I am gone,
> Hauing displeas'd my Father, to *Lawrence* Cell,
> To make confession, and to be absolu'd.

The version in the unauthorized First Quarto begins with the stage-direction *"Enter Romeo and Iuliet at the window."* After 37 lines, *"He [Romeo] goeth downe"*; and not until 17 lines after Romeo's descent does the Nurse enter with her warning. These lines follow:

> *Enter Nurse hastely.*
> *Nur:* Madame beware, take heed the day is broke,
> Your Mother's comming to your Chamber, make all sure.
> *She goeth downe from the window.*

Enter Iuliets Mother, Nurse.

Moth: Where are you Daughter?
Nur: What Ladie, Lambe, what *Iuliet?*
Iul: How now, who calls?
Nur: It is your Mother.
Moth: Why how now *Juliet?*
Iul: Madam, I am not well.

Lady Capulet vows vengeance upon Romeo for Tybalt's death, and tells her daughter of the proposed wedding. *"Enter olde Capolet"* at about the present-day line 124. After his denunciation of Juliet he departs at 197 and Lady Capulet at 205. The Folio's "Go in" at 233 is lacking in Q1. Both versions end with Juliet's departure for Friar Laurence's cell.

Some writers, including Chambers and Granville-Barker, maintain that the last part of the scene, including Capulet's outburst, is staged on the lower level, and presumably on the platform; Hosley would put the transition even earlier, directly after Romeo's departure. Chambers bases his theory upon the fact that "Juliet bids the Nurse [line 233] 'Go in', and herself 'Exit' to visit Friar Laurence."[5] Granville-Barker, it will be remembered, bases his upon the contention that the last part of the scene "could have been effectively played nowhere but on the lower stage"; and Hosley bases his largely upon the First Quarto's *"She goeth downe from the window."* Granville-Barker and Hosley would have the bedchamber move from upper level to lower with Juliet; Chambers apparently would have the last part of the scene played on the lower stage as outside the Capulet house.

The fact remains, however, that it is difficult to imagine any means by which the action can be brought from upper level to lower in the middle of the scene. There can be no doubt whatsoever that the scene begins aloft; and as it progresses Juliet is continuously onstage and involved in the dialogue, with no break during which she can make a backstage descent by the tiring-house stairs. As I see it, the scene opens with the farewells of the star-crossed lovers in a window-stage. Perhaps at the moment of their appearance, and in any event before line 36, the upper-stage curtains open to reveal the chamber, and from then on it is as if the chamber and the window-stage were a single

[5] *Elizabethan Stage*, III, 94 n. 2. References to other authors have been cited on page 125, note 4, and on page 129, note 11, of the present volume.

room. The Nurse enters with her warning; Romeo descends the ladder and goes away. Juliet remains at the casement to draw up and hide the ladder, and for that reason her mother fails to see her—"Ho, daughter, are you up?"—when she enters the chamber four lines later. Having made all sure, Juliet joins her mother in the chamber, and thereafter the action continues in the chamber until the end. As for Capulet's outburst, there seems to be no compelling reason why it should not be delivered on the upper stage, for he would not be seated and therefore seen through a balustrade, but standing, and probably immediately behind the guard-rail if a guard-rail existed. Moreover, line 125, with its "Here comes your father" in both F and Q1, seems to imply that he approaches Juliet and Lady Capulet, rather than that they go down to him. As for *"She goeth downe,"* it exists only in a corrupt text, and may be construed as applying to the Nurse rather than to Juliet. But the "Go in" at line 233, with its implication of outdoor placement, remains a difficulty; and still another minor difficulty exists in Juliet's "Then, window, let day in, and let life out" at line 41. It seems to suggest an opening of the window, but the casement must already have been open to make her voice and Romeo's audible to the spectators.

Act IV Scene i (126 LINES)

The rear stage on the lower level again serves as the Friar's cell. Friar Laurence and the County Paris are discovered by the opening of the curtains. Juliet enters by the rear door, and after Paris's departure receives the sleeping potion from the Friar. She bids him farewell, and the curtains close.

Act IV, Scenes ii, iii, iv, and v (283 LINES)

This sequence of four scenes has no counterpart in any other of Shakespeare's plays. The action alternates between lower stage and upper, with the lower serving twice as the scene of gay preparations for the morrow's wedding, and the upper as the scene of Juliet's solitary agony and her supposed death. The rapid contrasts of mood with mood, and later the poignant comment of the silent empty room above, are completely lost to sight in the conventional texts. The episodes are closely linked in time and action. It seems clear that Shakespeare thought of them as one integral scene played upon two levels, and that its mutilation by scene-breaks and changes of place is a violation of his dramatic purpose.

Since the previous scene has occupied the inner stage on the lower level, the opening scene of the present sequence is played on the platform as at the Capulet threshold. Capulet and his Lady and the Nurse bustle out from the house, busy with plans for the marriage feast. Juliet, returning from her talk with the Friar, enters by the opposite door. She asks the Nurse to help her in choosing her wedding garments, and she and the Nurse enter the house, followed a few lines later by Lady Capulet. Capulet himself crosses the stage and goes off to visit the County Paris. The time is "near night" (IV ii 39).

The upper-stage curtains open (IV iii) to reveal Juliet's bedchamber; the wedding attires have already been selected. Lady Capulet enters briefly to bid her daughter good-night, and she and the Nurse go out. Left alone, Juliet plays the agonizing solitary scene in which she drinks the potion and *"fals upon her bed within the Curtaines"* (Q1).

The bed-curtains that conceal her inert body are barely still before the hurly-burly starts up again on the stage below (IV iv). Perhaps this scene takes place at the threshold, as did the first scene of the sequence; or perhaps the lower-level curtains are now open to reveal the rear stage as a room in the Capulet house. The rear stage is now available if it be needed, since the 106 lines of IV ii and IV iii have intervened to permit the removal of the few properties called for by the Friar's cell. In any event, the scene is full of gay disturbance, in contrast with the lone anguish of the preceding scene, now kept in memory by the motionless bed-curtains in the empty room overhead. The time is three o'clock in the morning at IV iv 4, and daylight by the scene's end (line 21). Off-stage music (IV iv 23) announces the approach of Paris and his Musicians. Capulet sends the Nurse to waken Juliet; she can be heard calling Juliet as she mounts the stairs.

A moment later she enters the chamber (IV v), draws aside the bed-curtains, and finds Juliet apparently dead. Her outcries summon Capulet and Lady Capulet. They are joined in their lamentations by the Friar and County Paris, who have come to escort Juliet to the church for the wedding ceremony.

So much seems to be clear; but from now on the problems are multiplied. First, there is the question of the Musicians: when do they enter, and upon what stage? Their entrance is not noted at all in F1 or Q2, and their presence onstage is not revealed until one of them speaks at about line 96; Q1 gives their entrance in a stage-direction, but not until 42 lines after the entrance of the Friar and Paris, and after all but the Nurse have departed. The undated Q4, on the other hand, has them enter with Paris and the Friar at IV v 32. To what stage do they enter? Do they go up to the chamber? Probably not, for their presence would put eight persons in a little stage already crowded with a canopied bedstead; besides, there is no suggestion, in their later conversation with Peter, that they are in the presence of death. It is more likely that they remain on the outer stage, having originally come, as the custom was, to wake the bride on her wedding day with music under her window. But if so, one wonders how they know, without being told, that all is amiss within the house, and what leads the First Musician to say "Faith, we may put up our pipes and be gone" (96).

Then there is the related question of the Nurse's whereabouts as she speaks to the Musicians in the two lines following. F1 has an *"Exeunt"* before the line just quoted; Q2 has *"Exeunt manet,"* with the *"manet"* seemingly applying to the Nurse. Q1 is more specific, as it so often is in its stage-directions: *"They all but the Nurse goe foorth, casting Rosemary on her and shutting the Curtens."* Q1 thus seems to have the Nurse remain in the chamber after the other mourners have left, and yet only one line later she is talking to the Musicians, who presumably are on the lower stage. Finally, there is the "go you in" in the Friar's advice to Capulet, lines 91-92:

> Sir, go you in; and, madam, go with him;
> And go, Sir Paris.

Does the "go in" imply an entry into the house from a point outside? Or is it merely a carry-over of the theatrical idiom so often found in the old stage-directions, in which the "in" means simply "in the tiring-house," and therefore "off-stage"?

Certainly no staging of this difficult scene can be proposed with any degree of assurance, but the following reconstruction would seem to accord with most of the known facts. As Scene v opens, the Nurse, having climbed the backstage stairs, enters the chamber by the door in its rear wall. Alarmed by her outcries, Lady Capulet enters through the side curtains as from another room on the upper floor. Capulet, who a moment before had been on his way to meet Paris, perhaps turns back into the house and mounts the stairs. Paris and the Friar, accompanied by the Musicians, enter the outer stage; they go into the house and ascend the stairs, leaving the Musicians behind them on the platform. The Musicians learn the dolorous news from the sounds of grief above. The mourners in the chamber scatter rosemary upon the supposedly dead Juliet, draw the curtains, and all but the Nurse depart. She goes to the window, sees the Musicians huddled below, and calls down to them

> Honest good fellows, ah, put up, put up!
> For well you know this is a pitiful case.

Peter joins the Musicians on the outer stage. At the end they enter the house and make toward the kitchen—"Come, we'll in here, tarry for the mourners, and stay dinner."

This staging has at least the negative merit of violating only two of the known premises: the Friar's "go you in," and the delayed entrance of the Musicians in the First Quarto.

Act V Scene i (86 LINES)

Romeo's banishment to Mantua has been mentioned seven times in recent scenes, and these references serve to pre-localize the present action. We know nothing beyond the fact that the place is Mantua until line 37, at which point we learn that Romeo is on a street before an apothecary's shop. The apothecary comes to his door in answer to Romeo's calls, but the interior of the shop is not revealed—"Being holiday, the beggar's shop is shut." The practical need for the beggar's holiday is, it may be supposed, the need to keep the rear stage closed so that it may be set with the appurtenances of the burial vault in preparation for Act V Scene iii. The entire action passes on the platform.

Act V Scene ii (29 LINES)

All modern texts agree in placing this scene in Friar Laurence's cell. In this they are probably mistaken. This scene alone, of all the supposed cell scenes, lacks definite localization or pre-localization. But the important consideration is the need to keep the rear stage closed; and therefore the scene is in all probability played not in the inner stage as within the cell, but on the platform as at the Friar's threshold. But to place this scene on the platform is to bring two exterior scenes—one on a street in Mantua and one in Verona—

into juxtaposition on the same stage: a juxtaposition which Shakespeare occasionally permitted (we have already seen it twice in this play, at II iv-v and III i-ii) but which he tended to avoid. It can be avoided in the present instance only by placing the cell scene in the rear stage, and as a result allowing only 85 lines—the time that would elapse between the close of this scene and the moment when the jaws of the vault swing open in the scene to follow—for a major change of inner-stage setting. Such a time-allowance would seem too short by half. It seems probable rather that the stagehands need not only the first 85 lines of V iii, but also the 86 lines of V i and the 29 lines of V ii, to set up the gates of the monument, the catafalque and candles, and to hang painted cloths around the walls.

Act V Scene iii (310 LINES)

The curtains of the inner stage open to reveal a pair of gates stretching across the aperture of the rear stage and concealing its interior. Paris and his Page enter the platform. Paris tells his boy to keep watch "under yond yew tree" (3), and the boy lies down by one of the stage posts on the forestage. Paris drops flowers through the gate's wicket as a symbolic strewing of Juliet's grave. The boy's whistle warns him of an intruder's approach, and he hides, perhaps behind a door-post. Romeo and Balthasar enter with a torch, a mattock, and a crow of iron. Balthasar is dismissed; but instead of leaving as he is bidden to do, he too goes to the forestage, lies down by the other stage post, and falls asleep "under this yew tree here" (137). Romeo addresses himself to the door of the sepulchre:

> Thou detestable maw, thou womb of death,
> Gorg'd with the dearest morsel of the earth —

He inserts the tongue of his crowbar in the central crack of the gates and puts all his strength against the shaft—

> Thus I enforce thy rotten jaws to open,
> And in despite I'll cram thee with more food.

The gates now stand ajar. Romeo would open them wider, but he is prevented by Paris, who comes from hiding and challenges him. They fight, and Paris is slain. With his dying breath he begs to be laid in the tomb with Juliet. Romeo agrees.

> I'll bury thee in a triumphant grave.

Swinging the leaves of the gate outward on their hinges, he stands for a moment in the opening, gazing upon Juliet lying on her bier:

> A grave? O, no, a lanthorn, slaught'red youth,
> For here lies Juliet, and her beauty makes
> This vault a feasting presence full of light.

He picks up the body of Paris and carries it within.

> Death, lie thou there, by a dead man interr'd.

Romeo drinks the poison at line 119, and falls dead within the curtain-line. Friar Laurence enters the platform by a stage door, unsure of his way in the dark. He stumbles downstage and meets Balthasar, returns upstage to find the masterless and gory swords lying at the entrance to the sepulchre, and then enters the tomb to find Romeo dead and Juliet just awakening. He hears the Watch coming, and hurries away in fear. As the Watch and Paris's boy approach, Juliet stabs herself and dies. Then, in quick succession, come others of the Watch with Balthasar, the Friar, the Prince, Capulet and his wife, and Montague, all entering by a stage door and to the platform.

G. B. Harrison has made the suggestion that at the Prince's "Seal up the mouth of outrage for a while" (216), the stage curtains are closed to conceal the interior of the vault.[6] The line is usually glossed as an appeal to old Montague, and perhaps to other mourners also, to end their outcries; but the word "outrage" seems extravagant as a description of Montague's heart-broken reproof:

> O thou untaught! what manners is in this,
> To press before thy father to a grave?

I agree with Professor Harrison's interpretation, merely substituting the closing of the gates for the closing of the stage curtains. It is noteworthy that after the line in question nothing is said by any speaker which seems to indicate that the tomb's interior is still in view; and the closing of the gates thus early would relieve Romeo, Juliet, Paris, and Tybalt of the need to lie motionless for five minutes more. Whether the gates close earlier or later, they conceal the four bodies in the inner stage and remove the

---

[6] *Shakespeare: Major Plays*, p. 58, and *Shakespeare's Tragedies*, p. 64.

necessity for them to be carried away at the end of the play, as bodies must be in so many of the tragedies.

One word refuses to be accommodated in the staging proposed for this final scene: the word "descend" in Romeo's line (28) "Why I descend into this bed of death . . . ." No literal descent seems to be possible, and it may be supposed that Shakespeare took the word over, perhaps unconsciously, from Brooke's poem, which at lines 2627-30 reads as follows:

> Now Peter, that knew not / the purpose of his hart
> Obediently a little way / withdrew himselfe apart;
> And then our Romeus / (the vault stone set vpright)
> Descended downe, and in his hand / he bare the candle-light.

In this reconstruction of the original staging of *Romeo and Juliet,* only three changes of setting—or possibly four—have needed to be made in the rear stage on the lower level. The stage served first as a hall in Capulet's house in I v, with a setting prepared before the play began. With the 247 lines of Prologue II and of II i and II ii to provide time for the change, it then served for the Friar's cell in II iii, II vi, III iii, and IV i. It may have served again for a room in Capulet's house in IV iv and at the end of IV v, in which case the 106 lines of IV ii and IV iii gave time for the change. It served finally for the interior of the burial vault, with 200 lines provided to cover the change of setting. The inner stage on the upper level has been used only as Juliet's bedchamber, and has needed no changes.

KING HENRY IV, PART II

ON THE GLOBE'S STAGE

There is no direct evidence that *King Henry IV, Part II,* was presented at the Globe, but a strong presumption may be based upon the fact that the play was probably only about a year old when the Globe was opened in 1599, and that the title-page of the 1600 Quarto carries the statement that the play was "sundrie times publikely acted by the right honourable, the Lord Chamberlaine his seruants."

The Folio divides the play into acts and scenes, generally in accordance with the rule of the cleared stage; but later editors have divided the text still further by splitting up the Folio's Act IV Scene i into three scenes, and its Act IV Scene ii into two, on the basis of supposed changes of place. The editorial scene-breaks are regrettable, because unwarranted under the conditions obtaining on the Elizabethan stage. The sub-division of Act IV Scene ii was made by the Cambridge Editors as recently as 1864; it is thus the latest (and one hopes the last) gratuitous break to be imposed upon the Shakespearean text.

Induction (40 LINES)

The Induction is spoken on the platform, with the inner-stage curtains closed. The speaker, Rumour, intimates in lines 35-37 that he is standing in or before

> ... this worm-eaten hold of ragged stone,
> Where Hotspur's father, old Northumberland,
> Lies crafty-sick.

The Induction thus serves to pre-localize Act I Scene i, which follows immediately upon the same stage.

Act I, Scenes i and ii (ABOUT 494 LINES)

The first six or seven lines of the play's first scene provide one of the minor problems in staging. They read thus in the Quarto:

> *Enter the Lord Bardolfe at one doore.*
> *Bard.*   Who keepes the gate here ho? where is the Earle?
> *Porter*   What shall I say you are?
> *Bard.*   Tell thou the Earle,
> That the Lord Bardolfe doth attend him heere.
> *Porter*   His Lordship is walkt forth into the orchard,
> Please it your honor knocke but at the gate,
> And he himselfe will answer.   *Enter the Earle Northumberland.*
> *Bard.*   Here comes the Earle.

The First Folio has *"Enter Lord Bardolfe, and the Porter"* as the opening stage-direction. For the rest it follows the Quarto, except for variations in spelling and punctuation.

It would appear at first glance that three points of entry are needed: one, the stage door or other means of access by which Lord Bardolph enters; two, the gate mentioned by his lordship in his opening line, which, as we soon learn, leads to the orchard and is a hard structure upon which a person can knock; and three, the point of access by which the Porter enters.

The Cambridge and many other modern editors have inserted the stage-direction *"The Porter opens the gate"* after line 1. This however is contradicted by the Porter's lines 5-6,

> Please it your honor knock but at the gate,
> And he himself will answer.

unless it be assumed that there are two gates, through one of which the Porter enters, and the other which remains closed until opened by the Earl from within. Nearly all of the writers who have commented upon the staging of the scene have assumed three separate points of entry; and if three, then one of them can only have been the stage curtains or the door at the back of the rear stage (since it seems improbable that the property gates would be put in place for so short and relatively unimportant an episode). But this solution is not entirely acceptable, for the use of either of those entrances by Lord Bardolph or the Porter so early in the scene, before the place of action has been established as at Northumberland's gate, might be misleading.

These and other difficulties are immediately removed if one supposes that the Porter appears *above*. It is surprising that this point of entrance has been so generally overlooked by commentators, more especially since it was first proposed by Singer as long ago as 1826. Collier, in his *Notes and Emendations* of 1853, appropriated Singer's suggestion without acknowledgment, and professed to find a note in his "corrected" copy of the Second Folio to the effect that "the old practice was . . . for the Warder (so called) to show himself *above* the castle-gate, and from thence to answer Lord Bardolph." More recently (but this time with suitable acknowledgments) the same staging has been adopted by John Dover Wilson as editor of *2 Henry IV* in the New Shakespeare Edition, in the stage-direction *"A Porter appears on the wall above the gate."* Still retaining the words "above the gate," I would however add "at a window, as the window of a gate-house."[7] Use of an upper window by the Porter immediately reduces the need for points of entry to two: the stage door by which Lord Bardolph enters, and the other

---

[7] The handsome two-volume *Domestic Architecture of England During the Tudor Period*, by Garner and Stratton, reproduces more than forty photographs and drawings of English gate-houses. In every instance the gate-house has one or more upper windows, and almost invariably the window is centered directly over the gate, just as the Globe's window-stages were centered over their respective doors.

stage door serving as the orchard gate. But it does more than that: it at once explains the Porter's "Please it your honor knock but at the gate . . . ." No commentator, so far as I am aware, has remarked the fact that this is an extraordinary request for the Porter to make. If he stands with Lord Bardolph on the stage, as most editors have assumed, why should he not himself knock at the gate? His office as Porter, the courtesy due to a guest, and the respect due to rank, should all have moved him to do the knocking. If, however, he is in an upstairs window, his request becomes understandable, since he could not himself reach the gate without causing his lordship to wait. Further, it explains the fact that Lord Bardolph is the one who says "Here comes the Earl," for the Earl's approach would naturally not be seen by the Porter overhead. Even the truncated stage-direction in the Quarto seems to bear out this theory. *"Enter the Lord Bardolfe at one doore"* is the way it reads; and obviously it should be followed, according to the pattern set by dozens of stage-directions throughout the canon, by *"and the Porter at another."* But the author of the stage-direction seems to have realized, after he started, that the Porter did not enter at a door; so he stopped where he was, and left the stage-direction incomplete. The direction in the Folio, *"Enter Lord Bardolfe, and the Porter"* does not contravene the theory, for an entrance to a window is still an entrance.

The rest of the scene presents no difficulties in the staging. Travers hurries in with news from the field of Shrewsbury, and later Morton on a similar errand; both of them enter by the stage door by which Lord Bardolph made his initial entrance. At the end, on the Earl's invitation to "Go in with me," they exeunt by the opposite stage door, through the orchard to Northumberland's castle. All the action has been on the platform.

Scene ii follows upon the same stage, with the entrance of *"sir Iohn alone, with his page bearing his sword and buckler"* (Q). For the first hundred-or-more lines the scene is unlocalized; the association with Northumberland's castle has merely faded away. At line 107 there is a vague intimation that the action is outdoors, and perhaps on a street, in Falstaff's "I am glad to see your lordship abroad. . . . I hope your lordship goes abroad by advice." Thereafter all sense of locality is lost again. On the Globe's stage Scenes i and ii were probably acted continuously and without any suggestion of change of place.

Act I Scene iii (110 LINES)

This scene is an example of what may be called "first-speaker localization." It contains no hint of its whereabouts; but the editors, searching desperately for clues to locality where Shakespeare intended none, have elected arbitrarily to place the scene in the home of the first speaker,[8] who in this instance happens to be the Archbishop of York. As a matter of fact, there is no need to quarrel with the conventional locality-note, for the rotation of scenes makes it seem probable that the scene is acted in an inner stage to set it apart from the outer-stage scenes which precede and follow it. Both of the inner stages are available, but the rear stage on the first level seems to be the more suitable of the two, since the action lacks the domesticity which usually characterizes a chamber scene.

Act II Scene i (209 LINES)

This is manifestly a street scene, and played on the platform. The coming and going of the Hostess and the Officers, of Sir John Falstaff with Bardolph and the Boy, the Lord Chief Justice and his men, and later a messenger, all suggest a public thoroughfare.

Act II Scene ii (196 LINES)

In virtually all modern editions of the play, this scene is marked as taking place on "another London street." The locality-note is sheer editorial guess-work. Nothing internal to the scene places the action on a street, or anywhere else for that matter. Textually, the scene contains no hint of place. It is not likely, however, that it was played upon the stage of the Globe as an unlocalized scene: it is too long, too active, too much concerned with the present, whereas the unlocalized scene is usually short, deals with explanations, reflections and recapitulations, and is played as if suspended in space.

Again, as in other instances, the stage-placement of neighboring scenes throws some light upon a doubtful dramatic localization. The current scene is followed by one which must be played upon the platform as before Northumberland's castle; and although, as we have seen, Shakespeare sometimes permitted scenes in different localities to follow one another upon the

[8] Cf. *1 Henry IV*, IV iv; *Julius Caesar*, IV i; *Antony and Cleopatra*, I iv; II i; II ii; etc.

outer stage, he tended to avoid it. In the absence of strong indications to the contrary, therefore, it may be supposed that the present scene is played upon an inner stage; and if in an inner stage, then perhaps in the Prince's lodgings. Further, the mood of the scene seems to be better suited to a private room than to a public street. Take, for instance, Prince Hal's opening line, "Before God, I am exceeding weary." If, as Shakespeare began to write the scene, he thought of it as on a street, is it likely that he would have introduced it in just this way? Is it not more likely that he thought of the Prince, newly arrived from the campaign in Wales, as entering his lodgings, unbuckling his sword, and flinging himself down in a chair? Then, too, Bardolph arrives with a letter for the Prince, and he has known where to find him. These indications are admittedly faint and inconclusive, but they fit in with the fact that an inner-stage scene is otherwise suggested. Perhaps it is played in the chamber. Only two persons are present during the early part of the scene, and four at the end. The chamber has not previously been used; the furnishings of the Prince's lodgings could therefore have been put in place before the play began.[9]

Act II Scene iii (68 LINES)

Again the action takes place before Northumberland's castle, as in the first scene of the play, and again on the platform.

Act II Scene iv (422 LINES)

The scene is an upstairs room in the Boar's Head Tavern in Eastcheap. The Boar's Head was a famous inn of Shakespeare's day, already known to playgoers as the favorite haunt of Sir John Falstaff from the well-remembered tavern scene in 1 Henry IV.

On page 131 I ventured the opinion that the scene is played on the lower stage in spite of the fact that its dramatic placement is an upstairs room. Shakespeare has been specific and insistent in placing the room on the upper level: "Sir, Ancient Pistol's below, and would speak with you" (75); "Call him up, drawer" (109); "Pray thee go down, good Ancient" (164, 168); and later "Thrust him down stairs" three or four times repeated, at 202,

[9] John Dover Wilson, alone among modern editors, places the scene in the Prince's lodgings. He does so on the grounds that "the privacy of the Prince's house seems more suitable to the dialogue" (op. cit., p. 150).

204, 209, and 218. These lines strongly suggest the use of an upper-level stage. On the other hand, the number of persons present, the necessary properties, and the nature of the action, all seem to call for space that only the lower stage can provide. As has already been said, no fewer than eleven persons are onstage during the course of the scene, seven of them concurrently for a stretch of 130 lines, and eight of them briefly. There is a table—"Why then, cover" (11)—and at least one bench or stool—"Sit on my knee, Doll" (246) —and much stage activity, including even a threatened duel with rapiers between Pistol and Sir John. In view of all the facts, it would seem that Shakespeare's very insistence upon the upper room tends to substantiate the idea that the scene is played upon the lower stage: because the scene is acted on the lower level as in an upper chamber, the illusion of upstairs placement needs to be created by the spoken word. This long scene, then, may be supposed to occupy the combined stages, with an appropriate setting in the inner stage. The 473 lines of Act II, Scenes i, ii, and iii, have

FIGURE 11. PRELIMINARY SKETCH FOR A MINIATURE FALSTAFF

The little figure of Sir John, which serves to give visual scale in some photographs of the Globe model, was whittled from soft pine and colored with casein paints. This drawing guided the whittling.

intervened since the last previous use of the rear stage, to permit properties to be set in place behind closed curtains.

Act III Scene i (108 LINES)

According to the stage-direction in the Quarto, the King enters "in his night-gowne" (i.e., his dressing-gown), and by his attire establishes the fact that the scene is indoors and therefore probably acted in an inner stage. Since the inner stage on the lower level has just been used, the chamber on the upper level seems the necessary and completely suitable choice. Not more than three persons are on the stage at any one time.

Act III Scene ii (ABOUT 359 LINES)

The scene is acted on the platform as before Justice Shallow's house in Gloucestershire, with one of the stage doors serving as the door of Shallow's house and the other as a mere unspecified point of entrance or departure. Justice Silence enters by the latter door, as do Bardolph and Sir John later, and crosses the stage to be vociferously greeted by his host at the threshold: "Come on, come on, come on, sir. Give me your hand, sir; give me your hand, sir" (1-2). There are seats on the stage—"Will you sit?" (104)— perhaps left over from the Boar's Head Tavern scene. After Falstaff's outrageous examination of the recruits, he and the Justices enter the house at line 234 in response to Shallow's urgent and repeated invitation: " . . . and so I pray you go in with me to dinner. . . . Come, let's to dinner; come, let's to dinner"—a dinner which, by the way, lasts for only 23 lines or about one minute. At the end, having bid the Justices farewell at Shallow's threshold, Falstaff leaves by the opposite stage door, as Bardolph and the recruits have done before him.

Act IV, Scenes i, ii, and iii (493 LINES)

The Gaultree Forest sequence forms a single scene in the First Folio, a scene which has been broken up by editors, following Capell, into three, with the insertion of "Another part of Gaultree Forest" at the head of Scene ii, and still "Another part of the forest" at iii. On the Elizabethan stage the action was continuous and the place unchanged.

The scene begins with one of Shakespeare's rare specifications of place in a stage-direction: *"Enter the Archbishop, Mowbray, Bardolfe, Hastings, within the forrest of Gaultree"* (Q). The dialogue opens with these lines:

> *Arch.*   What is this forest call'd?
> *Hast.*   'Tis Gaultree Forest, an't shall please your Grace.

Apparently the fact of its being a forest is already obvious to the Archbishop, and therefore presumably to the audience also; his question relates merely to its name. This, plus Shakespeare's particularity in the stage-direction, suggests that the stage is dressed with whatever properties the

playhouse affords to indicate a woodland setting. Presumably they are set up for the most part in the rear stage; the more than 350 lines of the scene before Shallow's house have provided ample time for the change of setting.

At the close of the modern Scene i there is an instance, rare in Shakespeare, of a simulated journey presented conventionally by having the actors march about the stage in view of the audience—a journey entirely comparable to the march of the maskers in *Romeo and Juliet*, I iv-v. The following events lead up to it:

The rebel leaders are in Gaultree Forest. They have sent out spies to learn the strength of the enemy, and one of them returns with the word that the royalist forces, led by Prince John, are scarce a mile away and thirty thousand strong. The Earl of Westmoreland arrives as emissary from Prince John to propose a parley; the rebel lords accept his offer, not without misgivings. He leaves to report their acquiescence to his commander, and then returns. At this point the modern texts distort the stage-directions so greatly, to accommodate them to the present-day subdivisions of the scene, that it becomes necessary to quote the relative passage in its original form. The Quarto has this:

> *Mow.* Be it so, here is returnd my lord of Westmerland.
> *Enter Westmerland.*
> *West.* The Prince is here at hand, pleaseth your Lordship
> To meet his grace iust distance tweene our armies.
> *Enter Prince Iohn and his armie.*
> *Mow.* Your grace of York, in Gods name then set forward.
> *Bishop.* Before, and greete his grace (my lord) we come.
> *Iohn* You are well incountred here, my cousen Mowbray.

The corresponding passage in the First Folio is substantially the same, but with these differences: the Folio has Prince John enter two lines later than does the Quarto, after "(my Lord) we come," and the Folio is silent as to the army that accompanies him. In neither text is there any suggestion of a clearance of the stage, as in today's texts. There is instead a simple entrance by Prince John, with or without an army.

It may be supposed that at the beginning of the sequence the rebel leaders have entered to the wooded rear stage to establish their presence in the forest, and that thereafter they move well down to the forestage. Westmoreland, entering by a stage door, meets them on the platform. He leaves after arrang-

ing the parley, and returns to announce the near approach of Prince John
and to propose a meeting "just distance 'tween our armies." To Mowbray's
"Your Grace of York, in God's name, then, set forward," the rebel lords
and their followers begin a march about the full perimeter of the platform
as representing a march of about half a mile, ending, as they began, well
downstage. As the march ends, Prince John enters at the rear of the inner
stage, some 36 or 37 feet distant, and the leaders of the two factions meet
in the center of the platform as midway between the armies. The rest of the
sequence, with Prince John's perfidy in IV ii and Falstaff's encounter with
Coleville in IV iii, follows without difficulty in the staging.

Act IV, Scenes iv and v (373 LINES)

Like its predecessor, this sequence forms a single unbroken scene in the
First Folio. Modern editors, following Clark and Wright, have split it into
two, again in spite of the fact that there is no clearance of the stage. Sir
Edmund K. Chambers calls it "a continuous scene divided, with unanimity
in ill-doing, by modern editors in the middle of a speech,"[10] and Sir Mark
Hunter laments that the editors "begin a new scene at line 133 in the middle
of a speech, though interrupted sense and mutilated rhythm cry out in
protest against them."[11] But whether divided into two scenes or not, the
sequence is one that presents real difficulties in terms of its original staging;
as mentioned in my Preface, discussion of the problem occupies one and a
half pages of small type in the New Variorum Shakespeare. There can be
no question that the dying King is moved from the Jerusalem Chamber to
a neighboring room, and presumably from one stage unit to another; the
question is whether the action begins on the outer stage and moves thence
to the inner, or whether it commences in the inner stage and is transferred
to the outer. As reported in the New Variorum, the first alternative seems
to be supported by Fleay, Miss Porter, Rhodes, Haines, and Ridley; the
contrary theory by Brodmeier, the Cambridge Editors, Neuendorff, and
Shaaber. Neither hypothesis avoids all the difficulties.

The events that have a bearing upon the staging of the sequence may be
summarized as follows:

The King, with two of his younger sons and other nobles, is in a palace

[10] *Elizabethan Stage*, III, 65 n. 3.
[11] *Review of English Studies*, Vol. II (1926), p. 297.

room which is later identified as the Jerusalem Chamber. Westmoreland, and a few minutes later Harcourt, arrive to report the crushing of the rebellion and the execution of the rebel leaders. Overcome by emotion, the King is suddenly ill, and the princes and nobles gather round him. At line 131 he says:

> I pray you take me up, and bear me hence
> Into some other chamber. Softly, pray.
> Let there no noise be made, my gentle friends,
> Unless some dull and favourable hand
> Will whisper music to my weary spirit.
> > *War.*   Call for the music in the other room.
> > *King*   Set me the crown upon my pillow here.

The King is now in the second room. At some point during his five-line speech, and presumably after his "Softly, pray," he has been taken up by his retainers and borne into another chamber, and placed upon a bed (IV v 182) that has a pillow on it (IV v 5). Prince Hal enters, but for several lines fails to see the bed on which his father lies dying. At IV v 20 all the lords, excepting only the Prince, "withdraw into the other room," and the Prince sits down to watch by the King. He sees the crown lying on the pillow, puts it on his head, and goes out with it at line 47, leaving the door open behind him (56), but without passing through the chamber where the nobles are waiting (57). Warwick and the younger princes return to find Prince Henry gone, but Warwick soon locates him "in the next room" (83). The Prince re-enters, and at the King's command is left alone with him for the touching scene between father and son. Some 130 lines later Prince John enters with Warwick. The King asks the name of the room in which he first did swound, and is told by Warwick that it is called Jerusalem. He recalls an old prophecy that he should die in Jerusalem, and, feeling his death close upon him, asks to be taken back to that chamber:

> Laud be to God! Even there my life must end.
> It hath been prophesied to me many years,
> I should not die but in Jerusalem;
> Which vainly I suppos'd the Holy Land.
> But bear me to that chamber; there I'll lie.
> In that Jerusalem shall Harry die.

And so the scene ends, with a conventional *"Exeunt"* in the Folio, but without even that in the Quarto. Neither of the original texts indicates that the act of carrying him back is completed.

So much for the dramatic requirements. How were they probably met on Shakespeare's stage? Clearly, the upper stage cannot be utilized either alone or in combination with the lower, in the first instance because it fails to provide two acting areas of adequate size, and in the second because the text allows no time for a backstage passage from one level to the other.

Let us first suppose that the action begins in the rear stage and moves thence to the platform. The first part of the sequence—that part which is now designated as Act IV Scene iv—goes smoothly enough in the inner stage, but a difficulty arises when the King becomes ill and is carried to the outer stage; for by what device does there happen to be a bed there awaiting his need? Has it been there all along, is it brought from the inner stage with the King, sent up on the trap, or dragged out onto the platform through one of the stage doors? None of the possible alternatives seems fully to escape artificiality and awkwardness, but none is impracticable. The King, then, is laid upon the bed, his crown on the pillow beside him. The Prince enters the rear stage and talks there with his brothers, slow to see the gravity of their faces; he leads them to the platform, still not aware that his father lies there dying. The younger brothers retire to the inner stage, leaving the Prince alone to watch by the King's bed and to speak his apostrophe to the crown. He departs by a stage door, leaving it ajar. The King wakes and calls for the Prince of Wales; Warwick, following the clue of the open door, finds him "in the next room" weeping. The Prince returns, and the ensuing 130-line scene between father and son is played on the outer stage. At the end, the King, still in his bed, is trundled to the rear stage as to the Jerusalem Chamber, and the curtains close behind him.

Let us now suppose, alternatively, that the action begins on the platform and moves thence to the rear stage when the King becomes ill. All difficulty in connection with the bed immediately vanishes; it has been set in place behind closed curtains, ready for the King when he enters the inner stage. Now one of the stage doors becomes that by which the Prince makes his first entrance, remote enough from the inner stage to explain his failure to see the dying King; later, with the crown on his head, he departs by the door in the back wall, leaving it open behind him. The subsequent 130-line dialogue between the King and his heir is spoken in the inner stage. But what then happens at the end of the sequence? Do the nobles merely leave the King where he is at the last, ignoring his request to be carried back to the Jerusalem Chamber? And if they do carry him back to the platform, what then? How does he leave the stage? An easy answer would be that the nobles begin the action which ostensibly would bring the King to the outer stage, but that the scene is cut short by the closing of the rear-stage curtains. That perhaps is the way a similar dilemma would be resolved on today's stage; but the closing of curtains to interrupt an action or to create a final tableau is foreign to the nature of Elizabethan staging.

Yet another alternative would have the inner stage divided into two compartments by a traverse running at a right-angle to the rear wall.[12] Such an arrangement would meet all the dramatic requirements, but the compartments would be narrow and deep and their visibility therefore poor, and the whole scene would lack the spaciousness appropriate to the death of a king.

With the two leading alternatives thus evenly balanced in the present analysis and in critical opinion, the external factor of scene-rotation is found to throw some light upon the problem. The preceding scene, it will be remembered, was in Gaultree Forest, and presumably a forest setting was suggested by woodland properties in the inner stage. Their removal would take some time. It therefore seems probable that the 132 lines of Scene iv are played on the platform before closed curtains, and that the inner stage is not revealed until the King is carried into the second room. For this reason, if for no other, one is thus forced to suppose that the action of the sequence begins on the platform, moves thence to the rear stage, and ends there. To be sure, the problem of the final *exeunt* still remains; the King's dying request to be carried back to the Jerusalem Chamber is not obeyed. But, as has already been noted, Shakespeare makes no provision for the King to be carried back: the King makes the request, and then—*"Exeunt."* And perhaps Shakespeare's very omission to have the King carried back arose from his knowledge that the scene must not end upon the outer stage. A more serious disadvantage lies in the fact that the Prince's long scene with his father must be played in the inner stage; but there is no reason why the King's bed should not be set immediately behind the curtain-line, and thus almost as far forward as if it were placed at the rear of the outer stage.

[12] As suggested by W. A. Wright, *Academy*, XVII (1880), p. 271.

Act V Scene i (98 LINES)

Again, as in Act III Scene ii, the scene is Justice Shallow's house in Gloucestershire. Nothing clearly indicates whether the action takes place without the house or within; but since the earlier Shallow scene was certainly outdoors, and since the inner stage has just been used to represent a room in Westminster Palace, it may be supposed that the present Gloucestershire scene, like its predecessor, is played upon the platform as before Shallow's door.

Act V Scene ii (145 LINES)

This scene introduces Prince Hal as the new King Henry V, against the background of a royal palace in mourning for a dead monarch. The occasion would seem to demand the space and pageantry of a combined-stage scene. For this reason, as well as to set it apart from the platform scenes by which it is preceded and followed, it utilizes the rear stage to provide a setting for the whole. The inner stage is still dressed as a room in the palace, and in preparation for the present scene it has needed no other changes than the removal of the late King's death-bed and the addition of tokens of mourning.

Act V Scene iii (147 LINES)

Shallow opens the scene with these delightful lines:

> Nay, you shall see my orchard, where, in an arbour, we will eat a last year's pippin of mine own graffing, with a dish of caraways and so forth. Come, cousin Silence. And then to bed.

The lines have led Sir Edmund Chambers[13] and some editors, beginning with Capell and including John Dover Wilson, to assume that they constitute a description of the current stage scene. Professor Wilson is especially explicit:

> Gloucestershire. The orchard behind Justice Shallow's house; tables and benches under an arbour; a fine summer's evening.[14]

There can be no doubt that there is a table on the stage—"Spread, Davy;

[13] *Elizabethan Stage*, III, 56 n. 4.
[14] *2 Henry IV*, New Shakespeare Edition, p. 103.

spread, Davy" (9-10)—and benches too—"Now sit down, now sit down" (16) . . . "Sweet sir, sit . . . Most sweet sir, sit. Master page, good master page, sit" (28-30); but whether they are in the orchard and under the arbour mentioned in the opening lines is open to question. This arbour could be no small affair like that in *Much Ado About Nothing* or *The Spanish Tragedy*, easily pushed through a stage door or sent up on the platform trap; it would need to be large enough to accommodate a table with five men seated around it, and a sixth to serve them. Probably, therefore, the arbour is not an actual stage property; and this supposition is borne out by the fact that Shallow's invitation is in the future tense, and that the visit to the orchard is to be made just before bed-time. In other words, it may be supposed that the present Shallow scene is set just where the previous two were, on the platform as before or behind Shallow's house; and just as no arbour was referred to in either of the earlier scenes, so none is intended now.

Shallow and his guests enter by a stage door as from within the house. Table and benches are carried on through the same door, probably by Davy with the page to help him. At line 75 there is a knocking off-stage, and Davy enters the house and supposedly passes through it to open a distant door and admit Pistol. At the end of the scene Silence is carried into the house to bed, and Falstaff and Shallow, with Bardolph, Pistol and the page, leave for London by the opposite door.

Act V, Scenes iv and v (150 LINES)

For the first time in the play, a platform scene is followed by another platform scene in a different place. The action shifts from a Gloucestershire garden to a London street when Hostess Quickly and Doll Tearsheet are dragged onstage in the custody of beadles. Three Grooms enter (V v), strewing rushes along the path to be trodden by the new King on his way to Westminster Abbey for his coronation. The Grooms call for more rushes, hurrying to finish their task before the royal procession arrives. *"Trumpets sound, and the King, and his traine passe ouer the stage"* (Q), and depart by the opposite door as to the interior of the Abbey. Falstaff and his fellow-travellers enter. Some 38 lines later, trumpets off-stage announce the completion of the coronation ceremony, and the King and his train re-appear. The King encounters Falstaff, pauses, rejects him. The procession passes on and leaves the stage, but the Lord Chief Justice returns a moment later to arrest Falstaff and his friends.

The Epilogue (37 LINES) is spoken on the platform.

In this conjectural reconstruction of the original staging of *2 Henry IV*, the rear stage on the lower level has served successively as a room in the palace of the Archbishop of York in I iii, as the Boar's Head Tavern in II iv, as Gaultree Forest in IV i-ii-iii, and as a room in Westminster Palace in IV v and V ii. Only three changes of setting have been necessary. The setting for I iii was already in place before the play began; and of the subsequent changes, 473 lines were allowed for the first, 469 for the second, and 132 for the third. The inner stage on the second level has been used twice: as the Prince's lodgings in II ii, and (with an allowance of 490 lines for change of setting) as a palace room in III i.

In these two plays, certainly two of the most difficult in the canon with respect to their original staging, the multiple stage of the Globe has met every demand that Shakespeare could make upon it. It has provided him with space enough for the feuds of hostile Veronese families, for a masked ball, for the marching of armies, for a coronation procession; it has given him intimacy enough for Juliet's invocation to night and for Prince Hal's apostrophe to the crown. In *Romeo and Juliet* it has given him perhaps twenty-two changes of place with only three or four changes of setting, and in *2 Henry IV* fourteen changes of place with four changes of setting. Localization has been specific when it has needed to be, vague when it has not. The half-timbered façade of the scenic wall has served admirably for the outside of Capulet's house in Verona and of Shallow's house in Gloucestershire; it has faded into oblivion in the graveyard and in Gaultree Forest. In providing suitable and variable backgrounds, the stage itself has done most of the work; it has asked few concessions from the dramatist beyond an occasional line of poetry to set the place and the time and the mood.

The stage of the Globe was not a sudden discovery, but a slow growth. It had its roots in the mediaeval Mysteries and Moralities, and beyond them in street pageantries, with their traditions and rituals and symbolisms centuries old. It was itself symbolic. With its "heaven" above and its "hell" beneath, it was the very globe itself; and just as all the world was a stage, so the stage was all the world. Scenes acted upon it took on a new and larger dimension, and acquired an applicability to all human experience. It was a structure upon which life itself could be exhibited with intimacy and freedom and beauty. It was the perfect instrument for the presentation of the poetic drama.

In a thousand facets Shakespeare's plays reflect the conditions of the Globe's stage, the stage which he inherited and which he helped to create. If Shakespeare's stage had been other than it was, Shakespeare's plays would be other than they are. Whatever the stage, they would still be works of towering genius, but they would not be the plays that we have today.

THE SCALE DRAWINGS

D R. ADAMS'S model of the Globe Playhouse was built to the scale of 1 to 24, or 1 inch equals 2 feet. The scale drawings based upon the model are reproduced in this book at the scale of 1 to 160 (1 inch equals 13 feet 4 inches, or ¾ inch equals 10 feet).

The scale drawings fall naturally into three groups: floor-plans (I to IV), exterior elevations (V to IX), and interior sectional views (X to XIII). Scale Drawing XIV shows the acting areas in elevation and cross-section, and XV gives the principal dimensions of the Globe.

Since the Globe is known to have faced toward the north, the words North, North-West, West, etc., have been adopted as a convenient means of designating the aspects of the building. The floor-plans are shown with their northern sides down, so that a person looking at them faces the entrance door and the stage. East is thus at the left, and west at the right.

In each of the exterior elevations, there is a central area which lies parallel to the picture plane and at a right-angle to the line of vision; on each side of it there are walls which retreat at an angle of 45 degrees. These retreating walls are necessarily foreshortened in the drawings. In the more usual sort of building, one whose floor-plan is made up of rectangles or combinations of rectangles with walls running in two directions only, the problem of foreshortening does not exist; in conventional architectural rendering, such a building presents only one side at a time, and that one side is parallel to the picture plane. But the octagonal four-directional plan of the Globe presents three sides at a time in elevation or section, and thus unavoidably involves oblique planes. The central area can always be measured with a rule calibrated to the appropriate scale; the foreshortened side walls cannot however be read with any scale normally available. The side walls are nevertheless included in the drawings in order to give a complete and understandable picture of the structure as a whole; and if a wall be foreshortened and therefore unscalable in one drawing, it is shown as parallel to the picture plane, and therefore scalable, in the drawing immediately preceding or following.

A precisely similar situation exists with respect to the sectional views, the

FIFTEEN SCALE DRAWINGS
OF
THE GLOBE PLAYHOUSE

AS RECONSTRUCTED
BY JOHN CRANFORD ADAMS

THE following scale drawings are based upon the Adams model of the Globe. They include, however, some details that the model does not show, in interior arrangements, and in the sub-stage and superstructure machinery, etc.

The drawings are here reproduced at the scale of 1 to 160. At this scale, three-quarters of an inch equals 10 feet, or 1 inch equals 13 feet 4 inches.

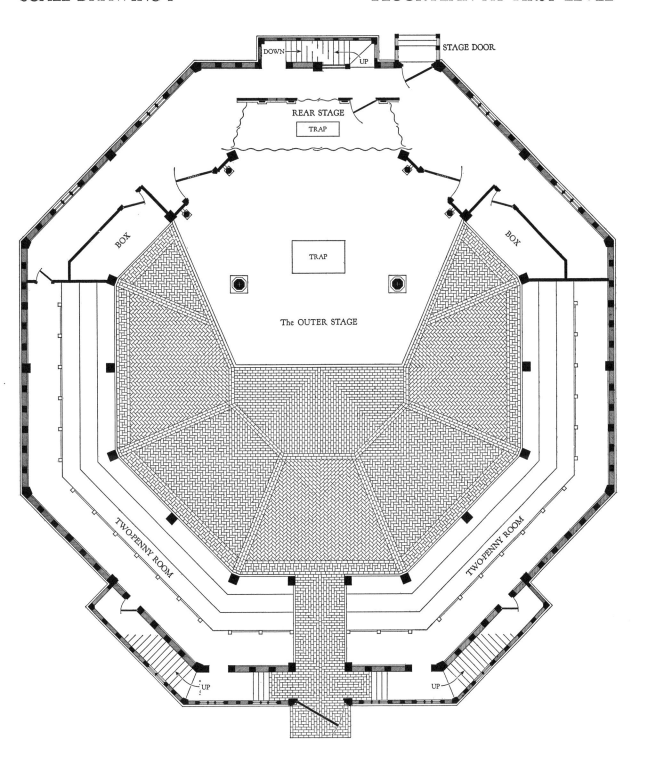

DOWN

UP

STAGE DOOR

REAR STAGE

TRAP

BOX

TRAP

BOX

The OUTER STAGE

TWO-PENNY ROOM

TWO-PENNY ROOM

UP

UP

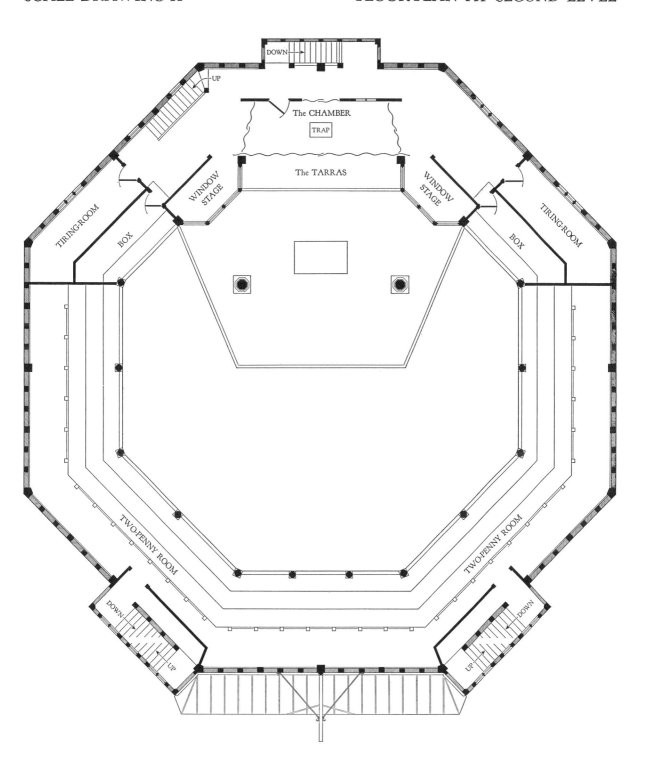

The CHAMBER

TRAP

The TARRAS

WINDOW STAGE

WINDOW STAGE

TIRING-ROOM

TIRING-ROOM

BOX

BOX

DOWN

UP

TWO-PENNY ROOM

TWO-PENNY ROOM

DOWN

UP

DOWN

UP

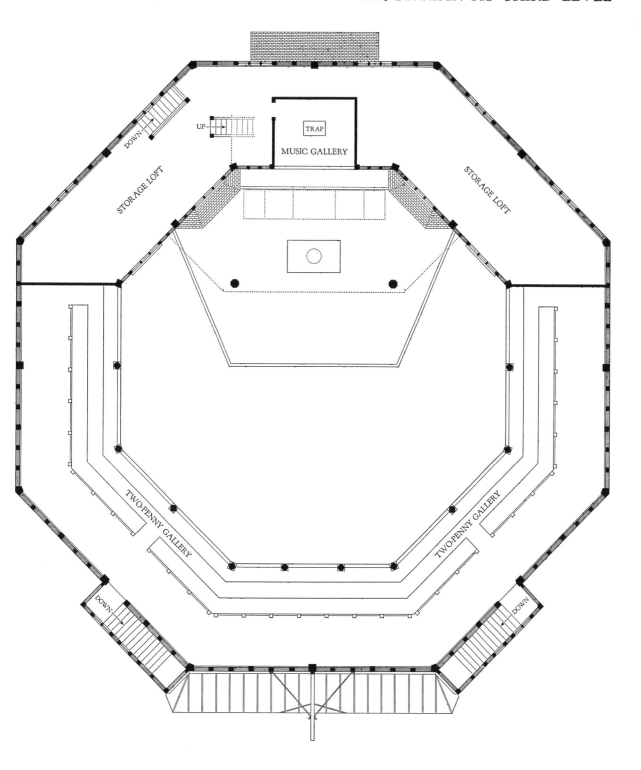

TRAP

MUSIC GALLERY

STORAGE LOFT

STORAGE LOFT

DOWN

UP

TWO-PENNY GALLERY

TWO-PENNY GALLERY

DOWN

DOWN

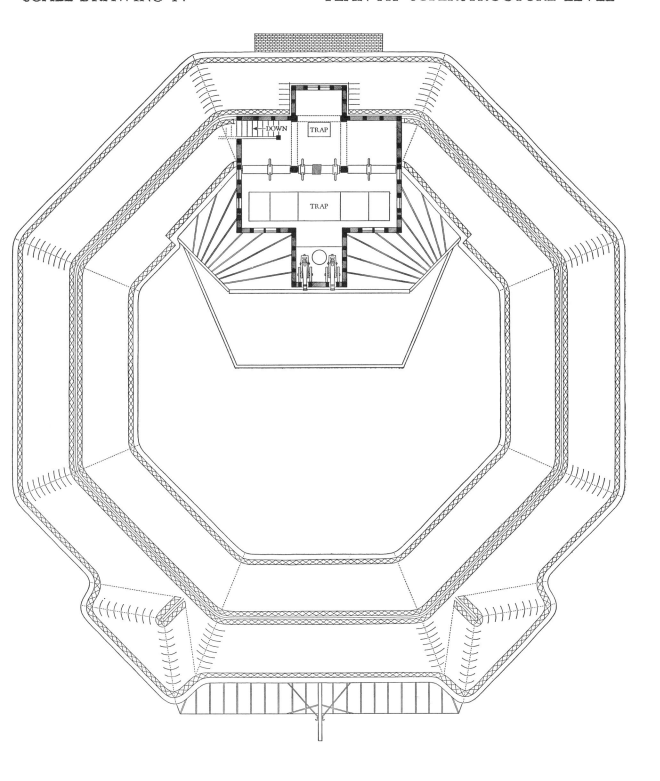

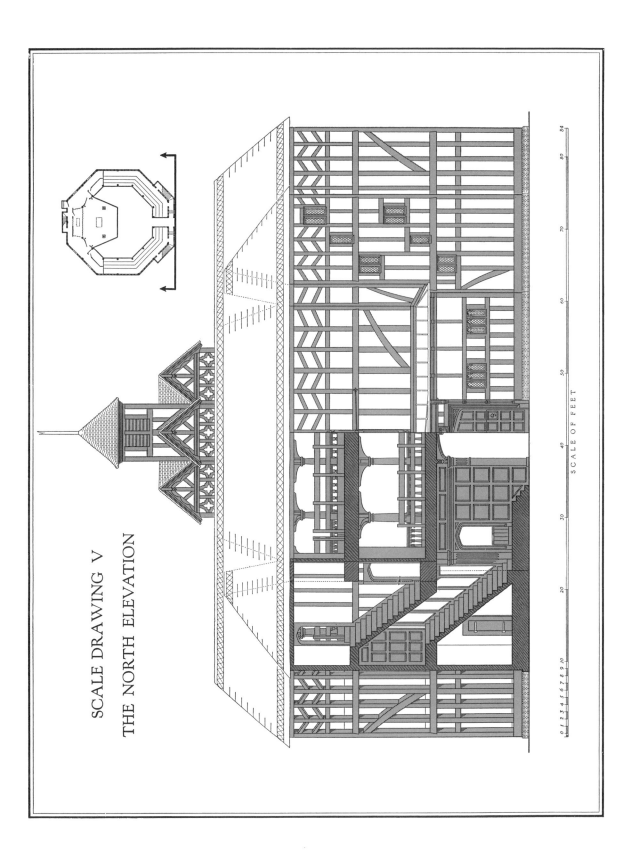

SCALE DRAWING V
THE NORTH ELEVATION

SCALE OF FEET

0 1 2 3 4 5 6 7 8 9 10   20   30   40   50   60   70   80 84

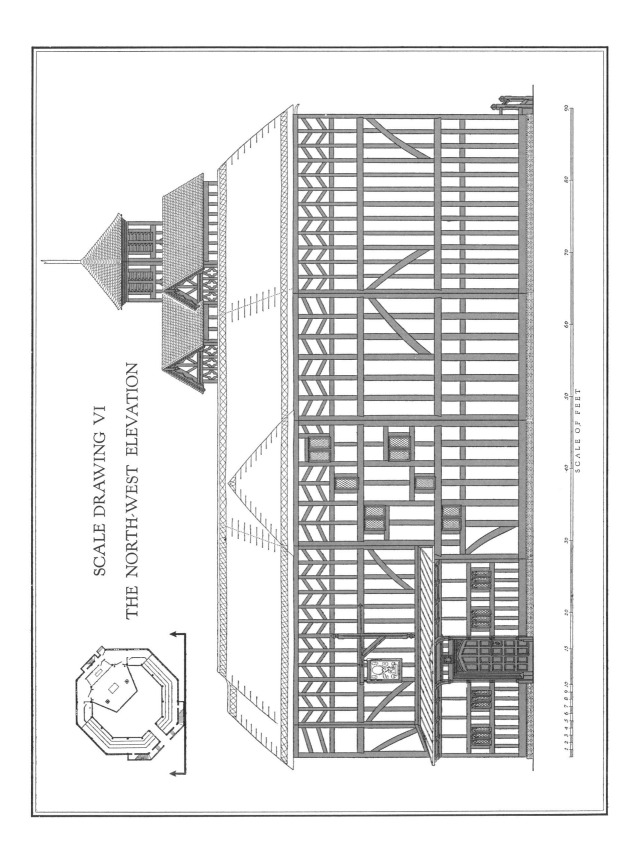

SCALE DRAWING VI

THE NORTH-WEST ELEVATION

SCALE OF FEET

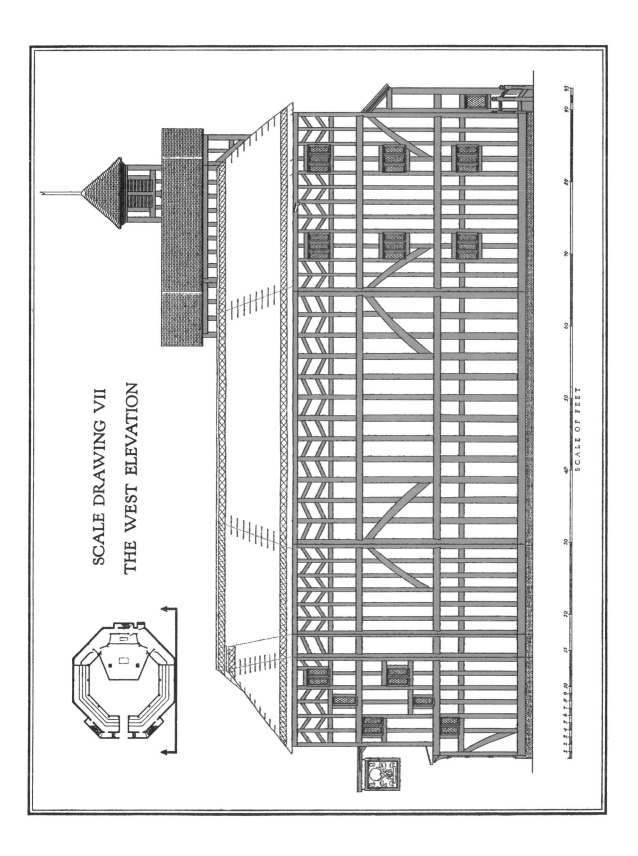

SCALE DRAWING VII
THE WEST ELEVATION

SCALE OF FEET

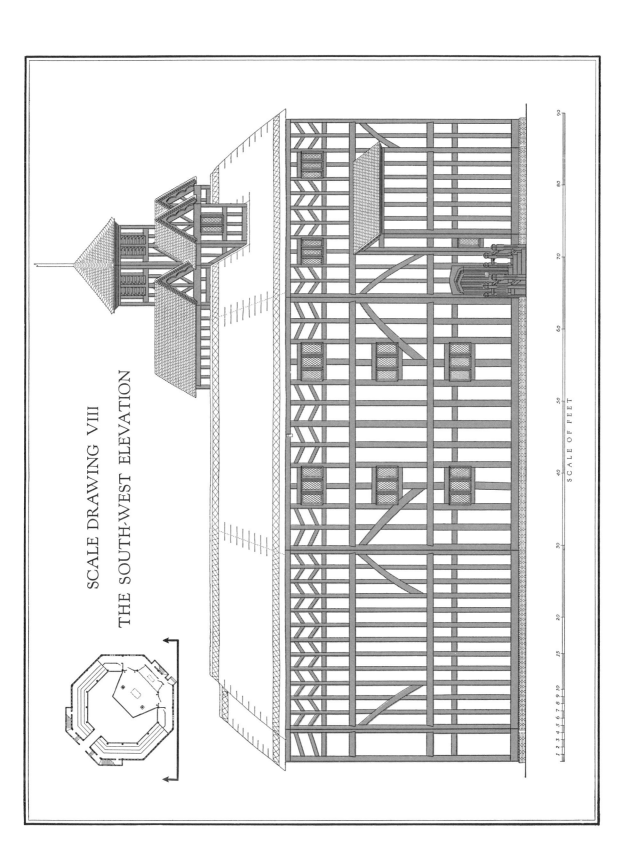

SCALE DRAWING VIII

THE SOUTH·WEST ELEVATION

SCALE OF FEET

SCALE DRAWING IX
THE SOUTH ELEVATION

SCALE OF FEET

0 1 2 3 4 5 6 7 8 9 10   15   20   30   40   50   60   70   80   64

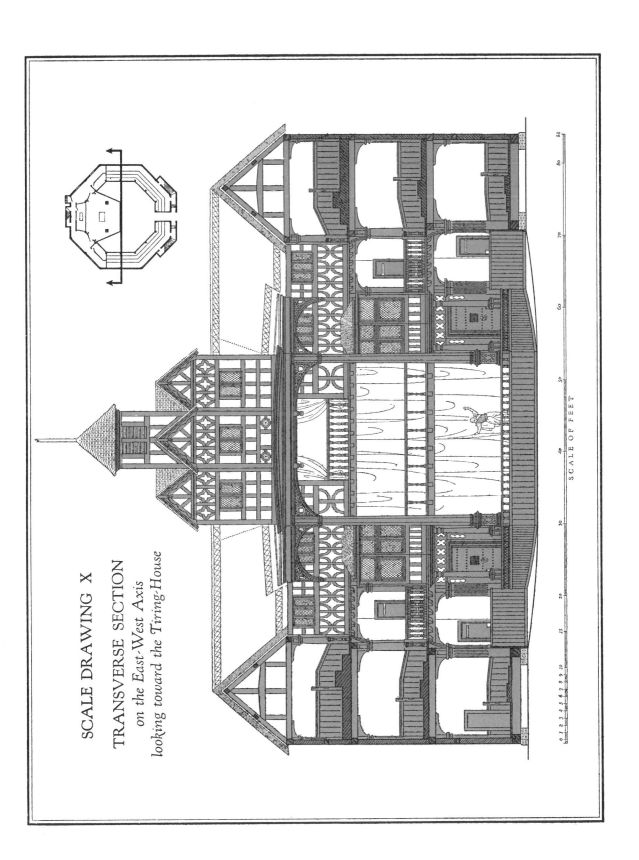

SCALE DRAWING X

TRANSVERSE SECTION
on the *East-West Axis*
looking toward the Tiring-House

SCALE OF FEET

0 1 2 3 5 6 7 8 9 10   15   20   30   40   50   60   70   80   84

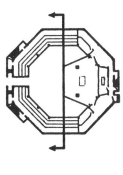

SCALE DRAWING XI

TRANSVERSE SECTION
on the East-West Axis
looking toward the Entrance Door

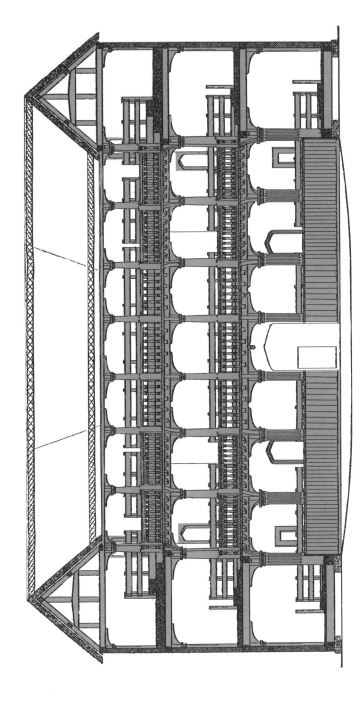

SCALE OF FEET

0 1 2 3 4 5 6 7 8 9 10   15   20   30   40   50   60   70   80   84

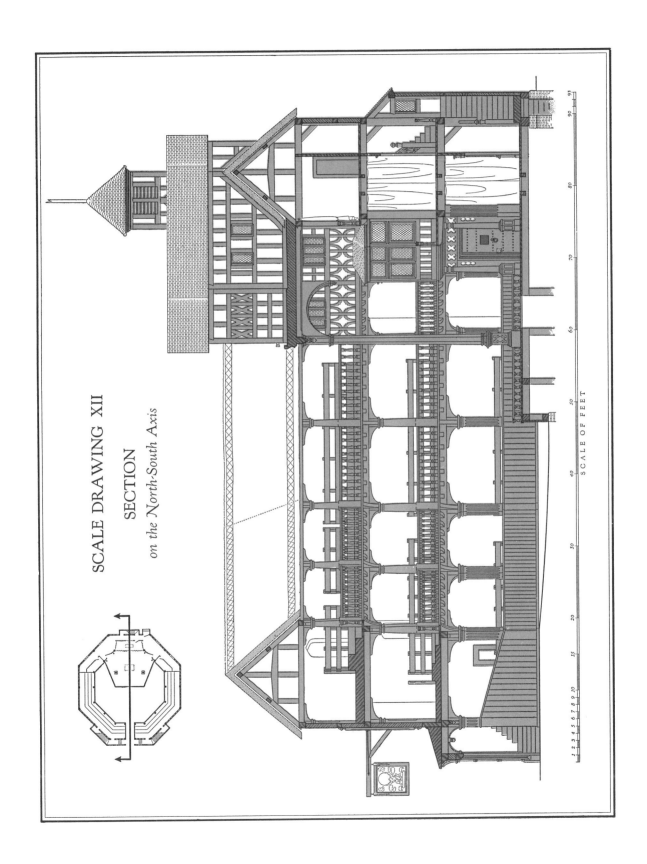

SCALE DRAWING XII

SECTION

on the North-South Axis

SCALE OF FEET

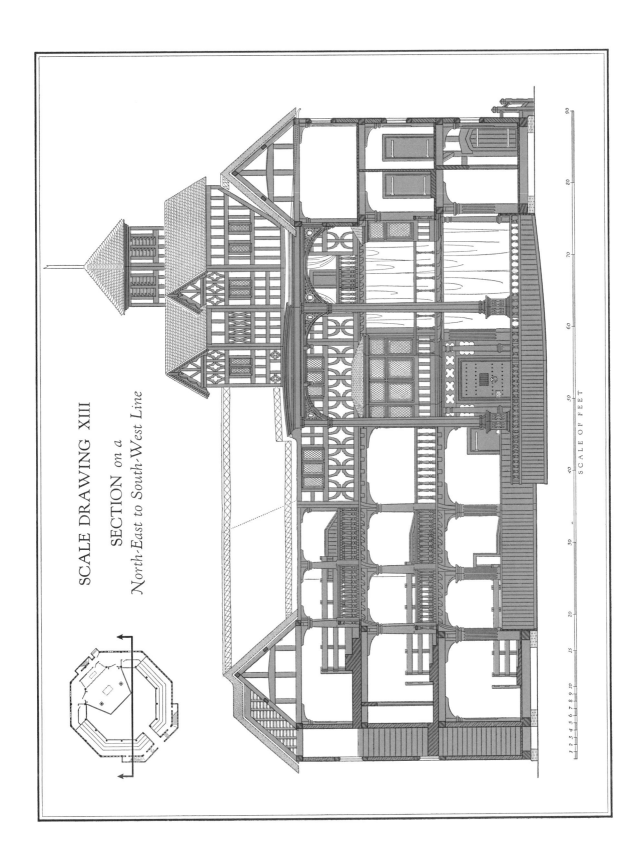

SCALE DRAWING XIII

SECTION *on a*
North-East to South-West Line

SCALE OF FEET

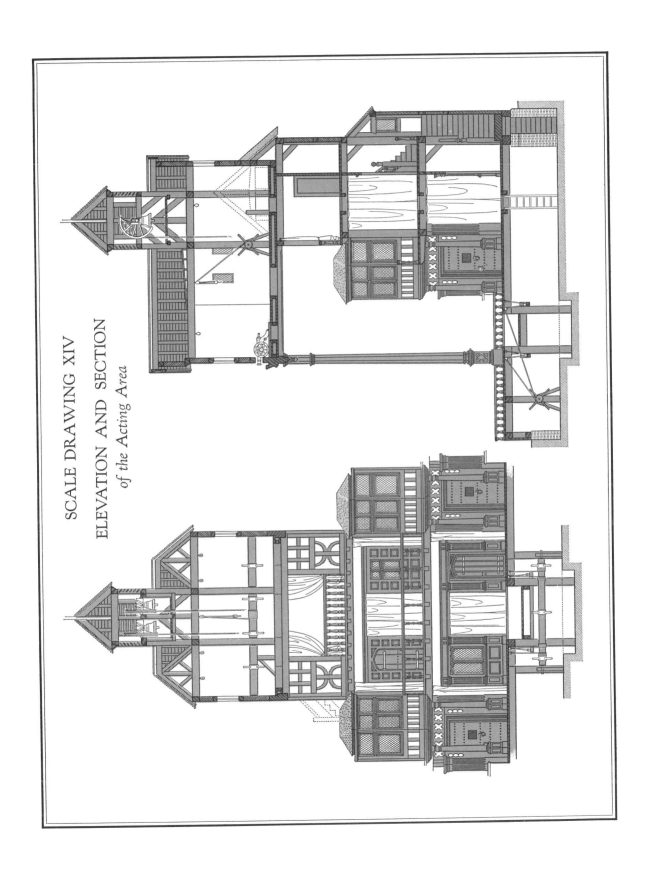

SCALE DRAWING XIV

ELEVATION AND SECTION

of the Acting Area

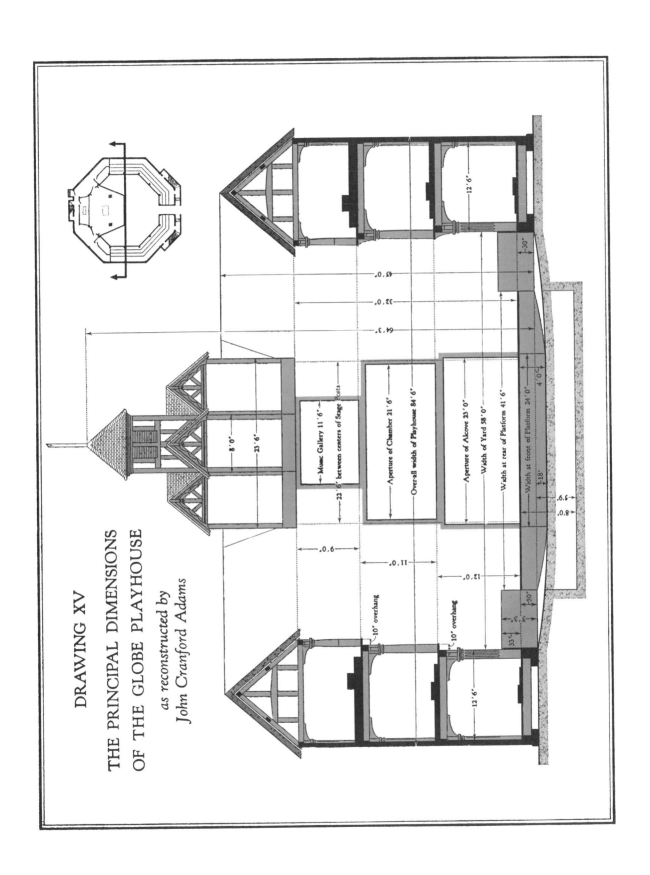

DRAWING XV

THE PRINCIPAL DIMENSIONS
OF THE GLOBE PLAYHOUSE

as reconstructed by
John Cranford Adams

Music Gallery 11′6″

22′6″ between centers of Stage Posts

Aperture of Chamber 21′6″

Overall width of Playhouse 84′6″

Aperture of Alcove 23′0″

Width of Yard 58′0″

Width at rear of Platform 41′6″

Width at front of Platform 24′0″

8′0′

23′6′

12′6″

12′6″

10′ overhang

10′ overhang

33″

30″

30″

45′0″

32′0″

64′3″

4′0″

18″

6′9″

8′0″

6′0″

11′0″

12′0″

3′3″

only difference being that in them the flanking walls approach toward the picture plane at a 45-degree angle, whereas in the elevations they retreat from it.

A small simplified version of the ground-floor plan is printed in the sky-area above each of the elevations and sectional drawings, for the purpose of indicating the orientation of the drawing and the directions of its planes. In each case, the little floor-plan is presented at an angle which corresponds to that of the main drawing, its horizontal lines representing the areas which in the large drawing are parallel to the picture plane. In the sectional views, a heavy line is drawn across the floor-plan to indicate the axis or other line upon which the playhouse is sectioned, and arrow-heads indicate the direction of view.

Measurements have not been indicated, for fear of over-complicating drawings that are already complicated enough. In the elevations and sectional views, however, a scale of feet is printed at the base of the drawing, and Drawing XV is devoted exclusively to giving the principal dimensions of the playhouse.

TUDOR PROTOTYPES

In the scale drawings (and of course in the model upon which the drawings are based), structural and decorative details have whenever possible been copied from specific Tudor prototypes. In general, preference has been given to exemplars which were representative and usual, as against those which, authentic though they might be, were less characteristic of Tudor design in its everyday conventions. The following books served as sources for most of the details reproduced in the model:

S. E. CASTLE, *Domestic Gothic of the Tudor Period* (1927);

SAMUEL CHAMBERLAIN, *Tudor Homes of England* (1929);

JOHN CLAYTON, *A Collection of the Ancient Timber Edifices of England* (1846);

FRED H. CROSSLEY, *Timber Building in England* (1951);

GARNER AND STRATTON, *The Domestic Architecture of England During the Tudor Period*, 2 volumes (1910);

NATHANIEL LLOYD, *A History of English Brickwork* (1925);

PARKINSON AND OULD, *Old Cottages, Farm-Houses and Other Half-Timber Buildings* (1904);

SMALL AND WOODBRIDGE, *Mouldings of the Tudor Period* and *Turnings of the Tudor Period* (both undated).

The course of double chevrons at the upper edge of the outer walls has its prototypes in Turton Tower in Lancashire,[1] a house near Eardisley in Herefordshire,[2] Speke Hall in Lancashire,[3] Ledbury Market in Herefordshire,[4] and in other buildings of the period.

Across the inner façade of the tiring-house on the third level, and across the fronts of the huts, there is an ornamental pattern made up of fretted corner braces which combine to form diamonds within squares. In identical or similar form, the pattern is found on the walls of Moreton Old Hall in Cheshire,[5] Chorley Old Hall in Cheshire,[6] Stokesay Castle Gatehouse in Shropshire,[7] The Ley in Weobley,[8] the Town Hall in Hereford,[9] the Court House in Shrewsbury,[10] and in many other Tudor buildings, including one or more in Stratford-on-Avon.

Over the heads of the two stage doors, the model has quatrefoils in white plaster, copied from Speke Hall in Lancashire,[11] Moreton Old Hall in Cheshire,[12] Hall i' the Woods in Lancashire,[13] Park Hall near Oswestry,[14] and other buildings.

Bargeboards, those decorative boards which cover the ends of projecting gable rafters, were often exceedingly ornate, with pierced, fretted and carved designs of which examples can be found in any book on Tudor architecture. A simpler pattern was chosen for the bargeboards on the huts, a mere repetition of shallow arcs, as in the cottages at Stoke-by-Nayland in Suffolk.[15]

The great columns which rise from the outer stage to support the heavens have, of course, no exact counterpart in Tudor domestic architecture; perhaps their closest counterparts are to be found in the arcadings

[1] Chamberlain, p. 183.   [2] Chamberlain, p. 141.   [3] Crossley, fig. 155.
[4] Crossley, fig. 197; Parkinson and Ould, Plate LXXII.
[5] Chamberlain, p. 169; Garner and Stratton, II, Plates CXXVII and CXXVIII; Crossley, fig. 149.
[6] Chamberlain, p. 170.
[7] Chamberlain, p. 148; Crossley, fig. 198.
[8] Garner and Stratton, II, Plate CXXIV; Clayton, not paginated.
[9] Clayton, Plate 8.
[10] Parkinson and Ould, Plate IV.
[11] Garner and Stratton, II, p. 169; Crossley, fig. 155.
[12] Garner and Stratton, II, Plates CXXVI and CXXVIII; Castle, Plate 38; Clayton, not paginated.
[13] Chamberlain, p. 184.   [14] Clayton, Plate 23.
[15] Castle, Plate 12.

which support church roofs in many English parishes, or which supported the upper stories of the now-demolished Town Hall at Hereford and of the former Market Hall at Leominster. Both of these latter buildings are pictured in measured drawings in Clayton's century-old book. The stage posts in the model were as a matter of fact taken entirely from Clayton, the bases from one page of his book and the pierheads from another. The bases were reproduced, line for line, from the drawing on Clayton's title-page, which shows the richly decorated porch of a building which is unidentified except for the date 1600, just one year later than the date of the Globe. The bases of the octagonal pillars are square in cross-section, and ornamented with the familiar pattern of a hollow diamond enclosed within a rectangular frame. They are headed with moulded caps, above which rise the long reaches of the eight-sided shafts. The heads of the stage posts are patterned upon those of the Hereford Town Hall as pictured by Clayton in Plate 8, their spandrels decorated with armorial shields within circles and with carved foliage designs. In the model, the octagonal shafts were painted with a harlequin pattern of diamonds in alternating colors, a pattern that has been associated with the theatre for many centuries and in many lands.

The frame of the entrance door was adapted from the photograph of a house at Ipswich in Suffolk,[16] but with the design in the spandrels borrowed from the doorway of Ford's Hospital in Coventry.[17] The door itself came from Chantmarle in Dorset.[18]

Mouldings in the model, except when they were parts of a larger assembly which was being reproduced in detail, were taken from Small and Woodbridge's *Mouldings of the Tudor Period.* Balusters and other turnings were for the most part taken from the companion portfolio entitled *Turnings of the Tudor Period.*

SCALE DRAWING I

FLOOR-PLAN AT FIRST LEVEL

Solid black polygons imbedded in the outer walls represent structural oak timbers, heavier at the corners and at the midpoints of the sides. Shaded

[16] Castle, Plate 48.
[17] Garner and Stratton, II, Plates CXIV and CXVI.
[18] Garner and Stratton, Plate CLXIII.

areas between them represent the plaster filling. Everywhere in this and the other plans, solid black forms or heavy black lines indicate timber pieces or structures standing vertically.

The entrance door is centered in the north wall (at the bottom of the drawing). Just inside it is a shallow vestibule, from which a brick-paved corridor leads forward to the yard. At either end of the vestibule there are steps rising to first-gallery level, and, beyond the first bend in the frame, longer flights of stairs mounting to the second gallery and eventually to the third. The spectators' means of access to each of the galleries is shown and explained in Scale Drawing V.

The tiring-house occupies approximately one-quarter of the octagonal frame; spectator galleries make up the remaining three-quarters. From the forward wall of the tiring-house the platform projects to the center of the yard. Two stage posts (their positions indicated by small black octagons set within square frames) rise from the platform to support the heavens and the superstructure 32 feet overhead. A trap, operated by a winch mechanism (see Scale Drawing XIV), descends from the center of the platform to the hell beneath. At each upstage corner of the platform is a stage door, flanked by door-posts which support the overhanging window-stages on the level above. In back of the platform lies the rear stage, here shown as enclosed by hangings (represented by serpentine lines) at its front, its sides, and at the aperture in its back wall. The "grave trap" is in the middle of the rear stage's floor.

The tiring-house is closed off from the spectator galleries by walls on all three levels; and, although no contemporary evidence supports the conjecture, it is reasonable to suppose that, as a mere matter of convenience, there was a door through the wall at some point to permit playhouse personnel to reach the front of the house if need should arise. Such a door is shown as piercing the dividing wall on the east side.

A twelve-penny box for lords and fashionable gentlemen lies just beyond the dividing wall on either side. Behind the lords' rooms and the scenic wall, and out of sight of the audience, are lobbies where actors may await their cues, and where soon-to-be-needed properties and costumes may be stored temporarily. A narrow passageway behind the rear stage connects the back-stage areas, and gives access to the outer door used by actors, stagehands, and occupants of the lords' rooms, and to the stairs which lead eastwardly up to the second level, or those which lead westwardly down to the sub-stage hell.

Along the forward edge of the spectator galleries, a series of stout oak posts (indicated on the plan by black squares scaling at 15″ x 15″ in cross-section) helps to support the second and third galleries with their close-to-a-thousand spectators. The gallery floors rise in three shallow steps or "degrees" to permit a better view of the stage for those seated or standing in the rear. Behind the last and highest degree is a guard-rail, mounted on upright posts, which separates seated spectators from the standees behind them and prevents their toppling over backward to the lower floor-level in back. The galleries are broken on the north side, on the first level only, by the corridor which runs from entrance door to yard.

Under the stairs on the north-east and north-west sides are closets, where perhaps were stored the boxes used in the collection of admission fees, or brooms for sweeping out the galleries.

The brick pattern in the pavement of the yard is discussed on page 54, footnote 8.

SCALE DRAWING II

FLOOR-PLAN AT SECOND LEVEL

Two window-stages project symmetrically from the scenic wall at the second level, directly over the stage doors on the level below. Between them stretches the long narrow expanse of the balcony or tarras. Behind the tarras lies the chamber, here shown as being enclosed by hangings represented by serpentine lines. The trap in the chamber floor is centered over that in the rear stage on the first level. The plan shows the ease with which an actor can pass from a window-stage to the interior of the chamber, by way of the break in the chamber's side curtains.

A narrow passageway behind the chamber connects the backstage areas; beyond it, in the exterior stairwell, is the stairway leading up from first-floor level. Just as the first-level approach to the stairs is opposite the door in the back wall of the inner stage, that on the second level is opposite the door in the chamber's back wall. Other backstage stairs, against the oblique south-east wall, lead up from second level to third. Dressing rooms, off the beaten track and yet easily accessible, are located behind the boxes on each side. The boxes correspond in position to those on the level below.

The spectator galleries on the second level are ten inches wider than those on the first, a difference accounted for by the "juttey forwardes" specified in the Fortune contract and undoubtedly applying to the Globe as well. The floors have the same sort of degrees as those in the first-level galleries, but steeper, to accord with the steeper angle of vision to the outer stage. Round posts, turned out of balks scaling at well over a foot square, rise from the forward edge of the gallery to support the third level and the roof.

Exterior stairs for the use of spectators are shown against the north-east and north-west walls. Outside the north wall, the roof of the entrance vestibule stretches from stairwell to stairwell, with parallel lines representing the welted seams in its lead sheathing.

SCALE DRAWING III

FLOOR-PLAN AT THIRD LEVEL

The music gallery occupies the center of the scenic wall at third level, flanked by backstage storage lofts. In its floor is a small trap, centered over and under corresponding traps in the two floors below and in the floor of the huts above. The stairs to the east of the music gallery give access to the superstructure.

Again the spectator galleries are ten inches wider, and again the degrees are steeper, than in the galleries just below. The tiled roofs are those of the window-stages and of the backstage stairwell.

Dotted lines in this plan indicate certain features which actually exist not at third *floor* level, but at *ceiling* level nine feet overhead; they are indicated here in order to show their positions with reference to other structures below. The huge five-part trap in the heavens, it will be noted, has its rear edge almost directly over the tarras railing; and the small round forward trap is centered over the trap in the middle of the platform floor. Still other dotted lines, skirting the stage posts and running from them to the neighboring walls of the octagonal frame, show the position of the leading edges of the stage-cover or heavens.

SCALE DRAWING IV

PLAN AT SUPERSTRUCTURE LEVEL

The plan of the huts is shown at floor level. Dotted lines forming a hollow square indicate the position of the tower or belfry, and a smaller plan at belfry level is printed on this page. The big five-part trap and the small circular trap, indicated in the last drawing in dotted lines, are shown again, this time in continuous line, as openings in the superstructure floor.

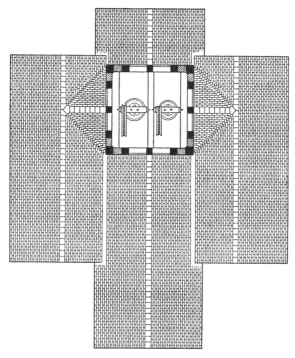

FIGURE 12.   TILED ROOFS OF THE "HUTS" AND
PLAN OF THE BELFRY

A series of winches, pictured in more understandable form in Scale Drawing XIV, stretches across the whole width of the huts, and provides the mechanism by which objects can be raised or lowered through any one of the three superstructure traps. Two small cannons point outwards through gunports in the forward limb of the huts. From within the huts a narrow stair, for the use of actors and stagehands and sound-effects men, descends to third-gallery level. Outside, a flattish roof covers the heavens, with the welts in its lead sheathing suggested by radiating lines.

For the rest, this drawing is little more than a conventional indication of thatched roof covering the galleries and the tiring-house. At eaves and ridge there is a decorative pattern of exposed "ledgers" (see page 46); and the pattern here suggested is actually a simplification of more elaborate patterns sketched at Stratford-on-Avon and Shottery. On outbending turns there are ledgers in parallel sequence, to prevent the thatch's being torn away by high winds.

It is not easy to suggest the forms of a thatched roof in a measured drawing, since all of its modulations are so subtle as to defy measurement and limitation. Lines which seek to define its planes are misleading, and yet without them the roof-plan is formless. With many misgivings, therefore, I have put dotted lines on the thatch to indicate the principal planes of the thatch in this and succeeding drawings. The reader is asked to remember that the roof surfaces would not be bounded by sharp edges, as the dotted lines seem to indicate, but by soft gentle curves flowing into one another imperceptibly.

SCALE DRAWING V

THE NORTH ELEVATION

Except for a single detail of the entrance door, the north elevation of the playhouse is thought of as being symmetrical, both externally and internally; and therefore, to avoid an unprofitable repetition of identical forms, the outside of the building is shown only on the right side of the center-line, and on the other side are shown the structures that would be revealed if the outer shell of the building should be removed. At the extreme left are structural timbers before they receive their filling of wattle and daub.

The cut-away area on the left of the center-line shows, at ground level, its half of the corridor leading to the yard, and the panelled vestibule; a little farther left, and four steps up, the arched door which gives admittance to the first gallery. Just beyond the first turn in the frame is the stairway to the second level, with a storage-closet beneath it. The spectator galleries on second and third levels are visible from the rear. On the right side of the center-line, in a position corresponding to the exposed stairwell on the left, are shown the windows, in rising sequence, which light the stairs.

The outer wall has been removed primarily to show the playgoers' means of access to each of the galleries. As a matter of convenience, the applicable sections of Chapter V are here repeated in condensed form:

The playgoer entered the building by the door in the middle of the north wall, and dropped his general-admission fee of one penny into a box watched over by the gatherer at the door. Once inside, he might, if he chose, go straight forward to the yard without payment of any further fee, there to stand, along with some 600 others, throughout the performance. If he preferred to sit or stand in one of the galleries, he turned left or right in the vestibule just within the entrance door, and paid a second penny to a gatherer stationed at the foot of the stairs. He could enter the first gallery, if he wished, upon payment of twopence more at the gallery door; or he could climb the flight of stairs to the second level and there find a seat or a standing, again upon payment of twopence to the gatherer posted at the door. On the second level an inward extension of the stairwell (see Scale Drawing II) permitted spectators bound for the third gallery to continue upwards without being compelled to pass the second-gallery gatherers. No further payment was demanded for admission to the third gallery; the two pennies previously paid, one at the entrance door and one at the foot of the stairs in the vestibule, were enough.

The entrance door, of which only one-half is shown in this drawing, is pictured in Plate 29.

SCALE DRAWING VI

THE NORTH-WEST ELEVATION

SCALE DRAWING VII

THE WEST ELEVATION

SCALE DRAWING VIII

THE SOUTH-WEST ELEVATION

These drawings call for no comments. The north-east, east, and southeast elevations have been omitted, because in each instance they would be simple mirror-views of the corresponding elevations on the other side of the playhouse.

SCALE DRAWING IX

THE SOUTH ELEVATION

This drawing, like the north elevation, shows the outside of the building only on one side of the center-line, and on the other side shows structures that would be revealed if the outer wall of the playhouse should be removed. Unlike the north, however, neither the outside nor the inside of the building is precisely symmetrical as viewed from the south. The rear entrance door exists only at the left, with no counterpart on the right-hand side of the center-line; and the stairs from first level to second, from second to third, and from third to the huts, exist only as they are here shown, without corresponding flights on the opposite side. The rear walls of the inner stages are asymmetrical, too; on the first level the window falls to the east of center and the door to the west, whereas on the second level their relative positions are reversed. These, however, are the only deviations from symmetry; and removal of the outer wall east of the center-line makes it possible, as it happens, to show most of the important features of the tiring-house as seen from the rear.

At the right of center on the first level, the backstage stairs rise to second level in their external stairwell. Under and beyond them can be seen a part of the curtain in the middle of the back wall of the inner stage, and near it the window. The right edge of the wall barely cuts the view of the fluted pillar which stands at the forward corner of the rear stage. To the right of the pillar is one of the two stage doors, and still farther to the right the door to one of the lords' rooms. Most of these details, as seen from the front, are shown in Scale Drawing XIV.

On the second level, just to right of the center-line, is a short section of the hand-rail which guards the stairwell, and beyond it a part of the curtain in the chamber's rear wall; near it and opposite the head of the stairs, the door in the back wall of the chamber. Farther to the right, a part of the window casement can be seen through the actors' entrance to the window-stage. The two doors beyond the upper stairs lead in the first instance to a lords' room, and in the second to a backstage dressing room.

No stage structures are visible on the third level except the outer edge of the music gallery and the stairs leading up to the huts.

On the right-hand side the thatch on the roof has been omitted, to reveal the roof construction and the preparation for the thatch covering.[19]

SCALE DRAWING X

TRANSVERSE SECTION ON THE EAST-WEST AXIS, LOOKING TOWARD THE TIRING-HOUSE

The section-line in this drawing passes through the midpoints in the east and west walls, and therefore along the front edge of the platform. The floor of the yard is indicated by a bowed line held to ground-level at its edges, and excavated to a depth of about 18 inches at its center. The spectator galleries are shown at their dead ends, close to the walls which at each level divide the galleries from the tiring-house. The ten-inch overhangs of the galleries and the degrees in their floors, already mentioned in connection with Scale Drawings I to III, are shown here in more intelligible form.

Both the rear stage on the first level, and the chamber on the second, have their interiors concealed by closed curtains in this drawing and in XIII; in XIV the curtains are removed and the interiors exposed. The stage-door and window-stage assemblies, here shown obliquely at a 45-degree angle, are shown as parallel to the picture plane in Scale Drawing XIII. Beyond the stage doors and windows are parts of the lords' rooms, two on each side, with doors leading to the tiring-house.

Along the oblique inner walls on the third level there are windows which give light to the interior of the storage lofts. The music gallery, with its curtains looped back, is in the center.

The eight-sided shafts of the great stage posts rise from squared bases to support the heavens and the huts. Their painted harlequin pattern has been omitted in the scale drawings, but is shown in the photographs and in the frame of the title-page.

An actor stands on the stage to give visual scale. He is 5 feet 8 inches tall, and therefore perhaps a tall man by Elizabethan standards.

[19] Cf. Crossley, Plate 122; Dollman and Jobbins, I, Plate 24; Davie and Green, *Old Cottages and Farm-Houses in Surrey*, pp. 18-21; Garner and Stratton, II, 159.

SCALE DRAWING XI

TRANSVERSE SECTION ON THE EAST-WEST AXIS,
LOOKING TOWARD THE ENTRANCE DOOR

The section-line in this drawing is precisely the same as in the preceding one, but the direction of view is the opposite: it faces away from the stage toward the auditorium and the entrance door.

The far walls of the galleries have been left largely undeveloped, to avoid confusion; only the doors have been indicated. On the first level, the arched doors are those that would be used by spectators entering the first gallery from the vestibule; the lower square-headed doors open upon closets under the stairs. Entrance doors are again indicated on the second and third levels; on the third, however, they are all but concealed by intervening posts.

SCALE DRAWING XII

SECTION ON THE NORTH-SOUTH AXIS

The section-line in this drawing is slightly erratic. Everywhere except in the huts, it follows the center-line of the building from north to south. In the huts, however, the center-line is ignored so that the huts can be shown in side elevation. They are shown as sectioned on the center-line in Scale Drawing XIV.[20]

At the extreme left, on the first level, is the entrance vestibule, with four steps rising to first-gallery level, and beyond them the stairway rising against an oblique wall just beyond the first turn in the frame. Over the vestibule hangs the sign-board, shown in larger size and more detail on page 50.

At the opposite end of the building, the inner stage on the first level is shown in section, closed off at its far end by overlapping curtains; behind its rear wall a narrow corridor, and in back of that the stairs rising to second level or descending to the hell. The ceiling beams of the inner stage project

[20] Consistency would have demanded that the huts be shown as sectioned on the center-line both in this drawing and in Scale Drawing XIV. Nowhere, then, would it have been possible to show the huts in side elevation; and to section them in both drawings would thus involve both an omission and a repetition. I have elected to section them in XIV, so that their traps and apparatus might be shown in relationship to other units of the acting area; and therefore, at the expense of consistency, I have chosen to show them in side-elevation in the present drawing.

well forward to support the tarras, with their ends tapered so as to interfere as little as possible with the view into the rear stage. The chamber also is shown with its far end closed off by curtains, and beyond them the stairs from second level to third. The music gallery, on the third level, is indicated by its rear wall and its entrance door.

The dividing walls which on each level separate the spectator galleries from the tiring-house, fall directly behind the stage posts, and therefore cannot be indicated.

SCALE DRAWING XIII

SECTION ON A NORTH-EAST TO SOUTH-WEST LINE

An axis running from midpoint to midpoint of the north-east and south-west sides would amputate the near corner of the platform and of the heavens. For this and other reasons, the present drawing is sectioned not on the axis itself, but on a line running parallel to the axis and about $8\frac{1}{2}$ feet to the near side of it. At the extreme left it cuts through the stairwell, and at the far right through the lords' rooms on first and second levels.

Alone among the drawings, this shows the stage door and overhanging window-stage as parallel to the picture plane.

SCALE DRAWING XIV

ELEVATION AND SECTION OF THE ACTING AREAS

These two drawings seek to give as much information as possible about the acting areas, without being too greatly hampered by strict consistency with respect to point of view or section-line. The drawing on the left shows the scenic wall as seen from some point behind the stage posts. Huts and belfry are shown with their forward walls removed. Sub-stage machinery is shown as if from a position near the front wall of the hell. The right-hand drawing shows all the structures as sectioned substantially on the center-line, but with slight deviations in the case of sub-stage and superstructure machinery.

For the first time in the series of measured drawings, the curtains on first and second levels are removed to show the rear walls of the inner stages. The back wall on the lower level is intended to suggest a richly-decorated wall appropriate to the rooms of state and palace halls for which the lower rear stage so often served as background. In scenes for which the ornate treatment of the back wall was inappropriate, such as a tomb's interior or a forest setting, the wall could be concealed by painted cloths: it would be easier to conceal a handsome wall in scenes to which it was inappropriate, than to create it as occasion might require. The chamber's rear wall is more modest architecturally, as befits the bedrooms and other domestic apartments which the chamber characteristically represented.

APPENDICES

THE CONTRACT FOR BUILDING

THE FORTUNE PLAYHOUSE

[Contract by Peter Streete with Philip Henslowe and Edward Alleyn for the erection of the Fortune at a cost of £440. Reprinted from the type-facsimile text given by W. W. Greg in *Henslowe Papers*, pp. 4-7, by permission of Sidgwick & Jackson, Ltd.]

THIS INDENTURE MADE the Eighte daie of Januarye 1599 And in the Twoe and ffortyth yeare of the Reigne of our sovereigne Ladie Elizabeth by the grace of god Queene of Englande ffraunce and Jrelande defender of the ffaythe &ce Betwene Phillipp Henslowe and Edwarde Allen of the pishe of Ste Savio^{rs} in Southwark in the Countie of Surrey gentlemen on thone pte And Peeter Streete Cittizen and Carpenter of London on thother parte WITNESSETH That whereas the saide Phillipp Henslowe & Edward Allen the daie of the date hereof Haue bargayned compounded & agreed wth the saide Peter Streete ffor the erectinge buildinge & settinge upp of a newe howse and Stadge for a Plaiehouse in and vppon a certeine plott or pcell of grounde appoynted oute for that purpose Scytuate and beinge nere Goldinge lane in the pishe of Ste Giles wthoute Cripplegate of London To be by him the saide Peeter Streete or some other sufficyent woorkmen of his provideinge and appoyntem^{te} and att his propper Costes & Chardges for the consideracōn hereafter in theis pn̄tes expressed / Made erected, builded and sett upp Jn manner & forme followinge (that is to saie) The frame of the saide howse to be sett square and to conteine ffowerscore foote of lawfull assize everye waie square wthoutt and fiftie fiue foote of like assize square everye waie w$^{th.}$in wth a good suer and stronge foundacōn of pyles brick lyme and sand bothe wthout & w$^{th.}$in to be wroughte one foote of assize att the leiste aboue the grounde And the saide fframe to conteine Three Stories in heighth The first or lower Storie to Conteine Twelue foote of lawfull assize in heighth The second Storie Eleauen foote of lawfull assize in heigth And the Third or vpper Storie to conteine Nyne foote of lawfull assize in height / ALL WHICH Stories shall conteine Twelue foote and a halfe of lawfull assize in breadth througheoute besides a Juttey forwardes in either of the saide Twoe vpper Stories of Tenne ynches of lawfull assize with ffower convenient divisions for gentlemens roomes and other sufficient and convenient divisions for Twoe pennie roomes wth necessarie Seates to be placed and sett Aswell in those roomes as througheoute all the rest of the galleries of the saide howse and wth suchelike steares Conveyances & divisions w^thoute & w^th:in as are made & Contryved in and to the late erected Plaiehowse On the Banck in the saide pishe of Ste Savio^rs Called the Globe W^th a Stadge and Tyreinge howse to be made erected & settupp w^thin the saide fframe wth a shadowe or cover over the saide Stadge wch Stadge shalbe placed & sett As alsoe the stearecases of the saide fframe in suche sorte as is p^rfigured in a Plott thereof drawen And wch Stadge shall conteine in length ffortie and Three foote of lawfull assize and in breadth to extende to the middle of the yarde of the saide howse The same Stadge to be paled in belowe wth good stronge and sufficyent newe oken bourdes And likewise the lower Storie of the saide fframe w^th:inside, and the same lower storie to be alsoe laide over and fenced wth stronge yron pykes And the saide Stadge to be in all other proporcōns Contryved and fashioned like vnto the Stadge of the saide Plaie howse Called the Globe W^th convenient windowes and lightes glazed to the saide Tyreinge howse And the saide fframe Stadge and Stearecases to be covered wth Tyle and to haue a sufficient gutter of lead to Carrie & convey the water frome the Coveringe of the saide Stadge to fall backwardes And also all the saide fframe and the Stairecases thereof to be sufficyently enclosed w^thoute wth lathe lyme & haire and the gentlemens roomes and Twoe pennie roomes to be seeled wth lathe lyme & haire and all the fflowers of the saide Galleries Stories and Stadge to be bourded wth good & sufficyent newe deale bourdes of the whole thicknes wheare need shalbe And the saide howse and other thinges beforemencōed to be made & doen To be in all other Contrivitions Conveyances fashions thinge and thinges effected finished and doen accordinge to the manner and fashion of the saide howse Called the Globe Saveinge only that all the princypall and maine postes of the saide fframe and Stadge forwarde shalbe square and wroughte palasterwise wth carved proporcōns Called Satiers to be placed & sett on the Topp of every of the same postes And saveinge alsoe that the said Peeter Streete shall not be chardged wth anie manner of pay[ntin]ge in or aboute the saide fframe howse or Stadge or anie pte thereof nor Rendringe the walls w^th:in Nor seeling anie more or other roomes then the gentlemens roomes Twoe pennie roomes and Stadge before remembred / NOWE THEIRUPPON the saide Peeter Streete dothe coveñnt promise and graunte ffor himself his executo^{rs} and admīstrato^{rs} to and wth the saide Phillipp Henslowe and Edward Allen and either of them and thexecuto^{rs} and admīstrato^{rs} of them and either of them by theis pñtes Jn manner & forme followeinge (that is to saie) That he the saide Peeter Streete his executo^{rs} or assignes shall & will att his or their owne propper costes & Chardges Well woorkmanlike & substancyallie make erect, sett upp and fully finishe Jn and by all thinges accordinge to the true meaninge of theis pñtes wth good stronge and substancyall newe Tymber and other necessarie stuff All the saide fframe and other woorkes whatsoever Jn and vppon the saide plott or pcell of grounde (beinge not by anie aucthoretie Restrayned, and haveinge ingres egres & regres to doe the same) before the ffyue & twentith daie of Julie next Comeinge after the date hereof AND SHALL ALSOE at his or theire like costes and Chardges Provide and finde All manner of woorkmen Tymber Joystes Rafters boordes dores boltes hinges brick Tyle lathe lyme haire sande nailes lade Jron Glasse woorkmanshipp and other thinges whatsoever wch shalbe needefull Convenyent & necessarie for the saide fframe & woorkes & eu^{r}ie pte thereof AND shall alsoe make all the saide fframe in every poynte for Scantlinges lardger and bigger in assize Then the Scantlinges of the Timber of the saide newe erected howse Called the Globe / AND ALSO that he the saide Peeter Streete shall furthwth aswell by himself As by suche other and soemanie woorkmen as shalbe Convenient & necessarie enter into and vppon the saide buildinges and woorkes And shall in reasonable manner proceede therein wthoute anie wilfull detraccōn vntill the same shalbe fully effected and finished / IN CONSIDERACŌN of all wch buildinges and of all stuff & woorkemanshipp thereto belonginge The saide Phillipp Henslowe & Edward Allen and either of them ffor themselues theire and either of theire executo^{rs} & admīstrato^{r}s doe Joynctlie & seu^{r}allie Coveñnte & graunte to & wth the saide Peeter Streete his executo^{r}s & admīstrato^{r}s by theis pñtes That they the saide Phillipp Henslowe & Edward Allen or one of them Or the executo^{r}s admīs-trato^{r}s or assignes of them or one of them Shall & will well & truelie paie or Cawse to be paide vnto the saide Peeter Streete his executo^{rs} or assignes Att the place aforesaid appoynted for the erectinge of the saide fframe The full some of ffower hundred & ffortie Poundes of lawfull money of Englande in manner & forme followeinge (that is to saie) Att suche tyme

And when as the Tymberwoork of the saide fframe shalbe rayzed & sett upp by the saide Peeter Streete his executo^{r}s or assignes Or wthin Seaven daies then next followeinge Twoe hundred & Twentie poundes And att suche time and when as the saide fframe & woorkes shalbe fullie effected & ffynished as is aforesaide Or wthin Seaven daies then next followeinge, thother Twoe hundred and Twentie poundes wthoute fraude or Coven PROUIDED ALLWAIES and it is agreed betwene the saide parties That whatsoever some or somes of money the saide Phillipp Henslowe & Edward Allen or either of them or thexecuto^{r}s or assignes of them or either of them shall lend or deliver vnto the saide Peter Streete his executo^{r}s or assignes or anie other by his appoyntem^{te} or consent ffor or concerninge the saide Woorkes or anie pte thereof or anie stuff thereto belonginge before the raizeinge & settinge upp of the saide fframe, shalbe reputed accepted taken & accoumpted in pte of the firste paym^{te} aforesaid of the saide some of ffower hundred & ffortie poundes And all suche some & somes of money as they or anie of them shall as aforesaid lend or deliver betwene the razeinge of the saide fframe & finishinge thereof and of all the rest of the saide woorkes Shalbe reputed accepted taken & accoumpted in pte of the laste pam^{te} aforesaid of the same some of ffower hundred & ffortie poundes Anie thinge abouesaid to the contrary notwthstandinge / IN WITNES WHEREOF the pties abouesaid to theis pñte Jndentures Jnterchaungeably haue sett theire handes and seales / Yeoven the daie and yeare ffirste abouewritten.

P S

Sealed and deliu^{r}ed by the saide Peter Streete in the p^{r}sence of me william Harris Pub Scr And me Frauncis Smyth appr to the said Scr /

[seal wanting; endorsed:]

Peater Streat ffor The Building of the ffortune

THE CONTRACT FOR BUILDING
THE HOPE PLAYHOUSE

[Contract by Gilbert Katherens with Philip Henslowe and Jacob Meade for the replacement of the Bear Garden at a cost of £360. Reprinted from the type-facsimile text given by W. W. Greg in *Henslowe Papers*, pp. 19-22, by permission of Sidgwick & Jackson, Ltd.]

ARTICLES Covenauntes grauntes and agreementes Concluded and agreed vppon this Nyne and Twenteithe daie of Auguste Anno Dñi 1613 / Betwene Phillipe Henslowe of the p̄ishe of St Savio^r in sowthworke wthin the coūtye of Surr˙ Esquire, and Jacobe Maide of the p̄ishe of St Olaves in sowthworke aforesaide waterman of thone p̄tie, And Gilbert Katherens of the saide p̄ishe of St Saviour in sowthworke Carpenter on thother p̄tie, As followeth That is to saie

INPRIMIS the saide Gilbert Katherens for him, his executo^{r}s administrato^{rs} and assignes dothe convenaunt p[ro]mise and graunt to and wth the saide Phillipe Henslowe and Jacobe Maide and either of them, thexecutors administrato^{rs} & assigns of them and either of them by theise p̄ntes in manner and forme followinge That he the saied Gilbert Katherens his executo^{rs} administrato^{rs} or assignes shall and will at his or theire owne proper costes and charges vppon or before the last daie of November next ensuinge the daie of the date of the date of theise p̄ntes above written, not onlie take downe or pull downe all that Same place or house wherin Beares and Bulls haue been heretofore vsuallie bayted, And also one other house or staple wherin Bulls and horsses did vsuallie stande, Sett lyinge and beinge vppon or neere the Banksyde in the saide p̄ishe of St Saviour in sowthworke Comonlie Called or knowne by the name of the Beare garden / But shall also at his or theire owne proper costes and Charges vppon or before the saide laste daie of November newly erect, builde and sett vpp one other Same place or Plaiehouse fitt & convenient in all thinges, bothe for players to playe Jn, And for the game of Beares and Bulls to be bayted in the same, And also A fitt and convenient Tyre house and a stage to be carryed or taken awaie, and to stande vppon tressells good substanciall and sufficient for the carryinge and bearinge of suche a stage, And shall new builde erect and sett vp againe the saide plaie house or game place neere or vppon the saide place, where the saide game place did heretofore stande, And to builde the same of suche large compasse, fforme, widenes, and height as the Plaie house Called the Swan in the libertie of Parris garden in the saide p̱ishe of St Saviour, now is / And shall also builde two stearecasses wthout and adioyninge to the saide Playe house in suche convenient places as shalbe moste fitt and convenient for the same to stande vppon, and of such largnes and height as the stearecasses of the saide playehouse called the Swan, nowe are or bee / And shall also builde the Heavens all over the saide stage to be borne or carryed wthout any postes or supporters to be fixed or sett vppon the saide stage, And all gutters of leade needfull for the carryage of all suche Raine water as shall fall vppon the same, And shall also make Two Boxes in the lowermost storie fitt and decent for gentlemen to sitt in / And shall make the p̄ticōns betwne the Rommes as they are at the saide Plaie house called the Swan / And to make Turned Cullumes vppon and over the stage / And shall make the Principalls and fore fronte of the saide Plaie house of good and sufficient oken Tymber, And no furr tymber to be putt or vsed in the lower most, or midell stories, excepte the vpright postes on the backparte of the saide stories (All the Byndinge Joystes to be of oken tymber) The Jnner principall postes of the first storie to be Twelve footes in height and Tenn ynches square, the Jnner principall postes in the midell storie to be Eight ynches square The Jnner most postes in the vpper storie to be seaven ynches square / The Prick postes in the first storie to be eight ynches square, in the seconde storie seaven ynches square, and in the vpper most storie six ynches square / Also the Brest sommers in the lower moste storie to be nyne ynches depe, and seaven ynches in thicknes and in the midell storie to be eight ynches depe and six ynches in thicknes / The Byndinge Jostes of the firste storie to be nyne and Eight ynches in depthe and thicknes and in the midell storie to be viij and vij ynches in depthe and thicknes / Item to make a good, sure, and sufficient foundacōn of Brickes for the saide Play house or game place and to make it xiij^{teene} ynches at the leaste above the grounde Item to new builde, erect, and sett vpp the saide Bull house and stable wth good and sufficient scantlinge tymber plankes and bordes and p̄ticōns of that largnes and fittnes as shalbe sufficient to kepe and holde six bulls and Three horsses or geldinges, wth Rackes and mangers to the same, And also a lofte or storie

over the saide house as nowe it is / AND shall also at his & theire owne prop[er]
costes and charges new tyle wth Englishe tyles all the vpper Rooffe of the
saide Plaie house game place and Bull house or stable, And shall fynde
and paie for at his like proper costes and charges for all the lyme, heare,
sande, Brickes, tyles, lathes nayles, workemanshipe and all other thinges
needfull and necessarie for the full finishinge of the saide Plaie house Bull
house and stable / And the saide Plaiehouse or game place to be made in
althinges and in suche forme and fashion, as the saide plaie house called the
swan (the scantling of the tymbers, tyles, and foundacōn as ys aforesaide
w^thout fraude or coven) AND THE SAIDE Phillipe Henslow and Jacobe maide
and either of them for them, thexecutors administrato^rs and assignes of
them and either of them doe covenant and graunt to and wth the saide
Gilbert Katherens his executo^rs administrato^rs and assignes in mann^r and
forme followinge (That is to saie) That he the saide Gilbert or his assignes
shall or maie haue, and take to his or theire vse and behoofe not onlie all
the tymber benches seates, slates, tyles Brickes and all other thinges belonginge to the saide Game place & Bull house or stable, And also all suche
olde tymber whiche the saide Phillipe Henslow hathe latelie bought beinge
of an old house in Thames street, London, whereof moste parte is now
lyinge in the Yarde or Backsyde of the saide Bearegarden AND also to satisfie
and paie vnto the saide Gilbert Katherens his executors administrato^rs or
assignes for the doinge and finishinges of the Workes and buildinges
aforesaid the somme of Three Hundered and three score poundes of good
and lawffull monie of England in mann^r and forme followinge (That
is to saie) Jn hande at thensealinge and deliuery hereof Three score pounds
wch the saide Gilbert acknowlegeth him selfe by theise pñtes to haue Receaued,
And more over to paie every Weeke weeklie duringe the firste Six weekes
vnto the saide Gilbert or his assignes when he shall sett workemen to
worke vppon or about the buildinge of the p^rmisses the somme of Tenne-
poundes of lawffull monie of Englande to paie them there Wages (yf theire
wages dothe amount vnto somuche monie,) And when the saide plaie house
Bull house and stable are Reared then to make vpp the saide Wages one
hundered poundes of lawffull monie of England, and to be paide to the
saide Gilbert or his assignes, And when the saide Plaie house Bull house
and stable are Reared tyled walled, then to paie vnto the saide Gilbert
Katherens or his assignes, One other hundered poundes of lawffull monie

of England / And when the saide Plaie house, Bull house and stable are fullie finished builded and done in mann^r and forme aforesaide, Then to paie vnto the saide Gilbert Katherens or his assignes, One other hundred Poundes of lawffull monie of England in full satisfacōn and payment of the saide somme of CCClx^{ll} And to all and singuler the Covenantes grauntes Articles and agreementes above in theise pn̄tes Contayned whiche on the parte and behalfe of the saide Gilbert Katherens his executo^{rs} administrators or assignes are ought to be observed p[er]formed fulfilled and done, the saide Gilbert Katherens byndeth himselfe his executo^{rs} administrators and as- signes, vnto the saide Phillipe Henslowe and Jacob Maide and to either of them, thexecuto^{rs} administrato^{rs} and assignes of them or either of them by theise p̄ntes   In witnes whereof the saide Gilbert Katherens hath herevnto sett his hande and seale the daie and yere firste above written

the mark G K of Gilbert Katherens

[no trace of seal; witnessed on back:]

Sealed and Deliuered in the p^{r}sence of
witnes Moyses Bowler
        Edwarde Griffin

[endorsed, last three words added by Alleyn:]

Gilbert Katherens articles & bond

BIBLIOGRAPHY

BIBLIOGRAPHY

ADAMS, JOHN CRANFORD, *The Globe Playhouse: Its Design and Equipment*, 1942.

———"The Original Staging of *King Lear*," *Joseph Quincy Adams: Memorial Studies*, 1948.

ADAMS, JOSEPH QUINCY, *Shakespearean Playhouses*, 1917.

ALBRIGHT, VICTOR E., *The Shaksperian Stage*, 1912.

BAKER, GEORGE PIERCE, *The Development of Shakespeare as a Dramatist*, 1907.

BALD, R. C., "The Entrance to the Elizabethan Theater," *Shakespeare Quarterly*, Vol. III No. 1 (January 1952), pp. 17-20.

BALDWIN, THOMAS W., *The Organization and Personnel of the Shakespearean Company*, 1927.

BRADBROOK, MURIEL C., *Elizabethan Stage Conditions*, 1932.

[BRAINES, W. W.], *The Site of the Globe Playhouse, Southwark*, 1924.

CAMPBELL, LILY B., *Scenes and Machines on the English Stage during the Renaissance*, 1923.

CHAMBERS, EDMUND K., *The Elizabethan Stage*, 4 vols., 1923.

COWLING, GEORGE H., *Music on the Shakespearian Stage*, 1913.

DE BANKE, CÉCILE, *Shakespearean Stage Production: Then and Now*, 1953.

GRANVILLE-BARKER, HARLEY, *Prefaces to Shakespeare*, 1927-1937.

———"The Stagecraft of Shakespeare," *Fortnightly Review*, CXXVI (1926), pp. 1-17.

GRAVES, THORNTON SHIRLEY, *The Court and the London Theatres during the Reign of Queen Elizabeth*, 1913.

GREG, W. W., *The Editorial Problem in Shakespeare*, 1942.

———Ed. *Henslowe's Diary*, 2 vols., 1904-08.

———Ed. *Henslowe Papers*, 1907.

———Ed. *Dramatic Documents from the Elizabethan Playhouses*, 2 vols., 1931.

HAINES, C. M., "The 'Law of Re-Entry' in Shakespeare," *Review of English Studies*, Vol. I No. 4 (October 1925), pp. 449-451.

HALE, EDWARD EVERETT, JR., "The Influence of Theatrical Conditions on Shakespeare," *Modern Philology*, June 1903.

HARBAGE, ALFRED, *Shakespeare's Audience*, 1941.

HARRISON, G. B., *Introducing Shakespeare*, 1947.

HART, A., "The Length of Elizabethan and Jacobean Plays," *Review of English Studies*, Vol. VIII No. 30 (April 1932), pp. 139-154.

————"The Time Allotted for Representation of Elizabethan and Jacobean Plays," *Review of English Studies*, Vol. VIII No. 32 (October 1932).

HODGES, C. WALTER, *The Globe Restored*, 1953.

————*Shakespeare and the Players*, 1948.

HOLZKNECHT, KARL J., *The Backgrounds of Shakespeare's Plays*, 1950.

HOSLEY, RICHARD, "The Use of the Upper Stage in *Romeo and Juliet*," *Shakespeare Quarterly*, Vol. V No. 4 (Autumn 1954), pp. 371-379.

HOTSON, LESLIE, *The Commonwealth and Restoration Stage*, 1928.

————*The First Night of "Twelfth Night,"* 1954.

HUBBARD, GEORGE, *On the Site of the Globe Playhouse of Shakespeare*, 1923.

JENKIN, BERNARD, "*Antony and Cleopatra*: Some Suggestions on the Monument Scenes," *Review of English Studies*, Vol. XXI No. 81 (January 1945).

JOSEPH, B. L., *Elizabethan Acting*, 1951.

KERNODLE, GEORGE R., *From Art to Theatre*, 1944.

KITTREDGE, GEORGE LYMAN, ed. *The Complete Works of Shakespeare*, 1936.

KNIGHT, G. WILSON, *Principles of Shakespearean Production*, 1936; new ed., 1949.

LAWRENCE, W. J., *The Elizabethan Playhouse and Other Studies*, Series I, 1912; Series II, 1913.

————*The Physical Conditions of the Elizabethan Public Playhouse*, 1927.

————*Pre-Restoration Stage Studies*, 1927.

————*Shakespeare's Workshop*, 1928.

————*Speeding Up Shakespeare*, 1937.

————*Those Nut-Cracking Elizabethans*, 1935.

LONDON COUNTY COUNCIL, *Survey of London, Vol. XXII (Bankside)*, 1950.

NICOLL, ALLARDYCE, "Studies in the Elizabethan Stage since 1900," *Shakespeare Survey 1*, 1948.

POEL, WILLIAM, *Shakespeare in the Theatre*, 1915.

PURDOM, C. B., *Producing Shakespeare*, 1950.

REYNOLDS, GEORGE F., "Some Principles of Elizabethan Staging," *Modern Philology*, April and June, 1905.

————*The Staging of Elizabethan Plays at the Red Bull Theatre, 1605-1625*, 1940.

————"*Troilus and Cressida* on the Elizabethan Stage," *Joseph Quincy Adams: Memorial Studies*, 1948.

——— "Was There a 'Tarras' in Shakespeare's Globe?," *Shakespeare Survey 4*, 1951.

RHODES, R. CROMPTON, *The Stagery of Shakespeare*, 1922.

SAUNDERS, J. W., "Vaulting the Rails," *Shakespeare Survey 7*, 1954.

SEWELL, ARTHUR, "Place and Time in Shakespeare's Plays," *Studies in Philology*, Vol. XLII No. 2 (April 1945).

SHAKESPEARE ASSOCIATION, *A Series of Papers on Shakespeare and the Theatre*, 1927. Among the papers are the following:
    F. S. Boas, "The Play within the Play";
    M. St. Clare Byrne, "Shakespeare's Audience";
    G. H. Cowling, "Shakespeare and the Elizabethan Stage";
    C. M. Haines, "The Development of Shakespeare's Stagecraft";
    G. B. Harrison, "Shakespeare's Actors";
    J. Isaacs, "Shakespeare as Man of the Theatre";
    Richmond Noble, "Shakespeare's Songs and Stage."

SHAPIRO, I. A., "The Bankside Theatres: Early Engravings," *Shakespeare Survey 1*, 1948.

——— "An Original Drawing of the Globe Theatre," *Shakespeare Survey 2*, 1949.

SMITH, IRWIN, "Theatre Into Globe," *Shakespeare Quarterly*, Vol. III No. 2 (April 1952).

SPRAGUE, ARTHUR COLBY, *Shakespeare and the Actors*, 1948.

——— *Shakespeare and the Audience*, 1935.

——— *Shakespearian Players and Performances*, 1953.

THORNDIKE, ASHLEY H., *Shakespeare's Theater*, 1916, 1949.

VENEZKY, ALICE S., *Pageantry on the Shakespearean Stage*, 1951.

WATKINS, RONALD, *Moonlight at the Globe*, 1946.

——— *On Producing Shakespeare*, 1950.

ON TUDOR BUILDING CONSTRUCTION

CASTLE, SYDNEY E., *Domestic Gothic of the Tudor Period*, 1927.

CHAMBERLAIN, SAMUEL, *Tudor Homes of England*, 1929.

CHARLES, C. J., *Elizabethan Interiors* (undated).

CLAYTON, JOHN, *A Collection of the Ancient Timber Edifices of England*, 1846.

CROSSLEY, FRED H., *Timber Building in England*, 1951.

DAVIE, W. GALSWORTHY, and E. GUY DAWBER, *Old Cottages and Farm-Houses in Kent and Sussex*, 1900.

DAVIE, W. GALSWORTHY, and W. CURTIS GREEN, *Old Cottages & Farm-Houses in Surrey*, 1908.

DOLLMAN, F. T., and J. R. JOBBINS, *An Analysis of Ancient Domestic Architecture*, 2 vols., 1861.

GARNER, THOMAS, and ARTHUR STRATTON, *The Domestic Architecture of England During the Tudor Period*, 2 vols., 1910.

HABERSHON, MATTHEW, *The Ancient Half-Timbered Houses of England*, 1836.

INNOCENT, C. F., *The Development of English Building Construction*, 1916.

LLOYD, NATHANIEL, *Building Craftsmanship in Brick and Tile*, 1929.

—— *A History of English Brickwork*, 1925.

—— *A History of the English House*, 1931.

NEVILL, RALPH, *Old Cottage and Domestic Architecture in South-West Surrey*, 1889.

PARKINSON, JAMES, and E. A. OULD, *Old Cottages, Farm Houses and Other Half-Timber Buildings in Shropshire, Herefordshire, and Cheshire*, 1904.

RICHARDSON, CHARLES JAMES, *Architectural Remains of the Reigns of Elizabeth and James I*, 1838.

SANDERS, WILLIAM BLISS, *Half-Timbered Houses and Carved Oak Furniture of the 16th and 17th Centuries*, 1894.

INDEX

INDEX